Gays on Broadway

Gays on Broadway

ETHAN MORDDEN

Oxford University Press is a department of the University of Oxford. It furthers
the University's objective of excellence in research, scholarship, and education
by publishing worldwide. Oxford is a registered trade mark of Oxford University
Press in the UK and certain other countries.

Published in the United States of America by Oxford University Press
198 Madison Avenue, New York, NY 10016, United States of America.

Library of Congress Cataloging-in-Publication Data
Names: Mordden, Ethan, 1947- author.
Title: Gays on Broadway / Ethan Mordden.
Description: New York : Oxford University Press, 2023. |
Includes bibliographical references and index.
Identifiers: LCCN 2022040741 (print) | LCCN 2022040742 (ebook) |
ISBN 9780190063108 (hardback) | ISBN 9780190063115 |
ISBN 9780190063122 (epub) | ISBN 9780190063139
Subjects: LCSH: Gay theater—United States—History. | American drama—20th
century—History and criticism. | Gay men in literature. |
Theater—New York (State)—New York—History—20th century.
Classification: LCC PN2270.G39 M67 2023 (print) | LCC PN2270.G39 (ebook) |
DDC 792.086/640973—dc23/eng/20221121
LC record available at https://lccn.loc.gov/2022040741
LC ebook record available at https://lccn.loc.gov/2022040742

DOI: 10.1093/oso/9780190063108.001.0001

Printed by Sheridan Books, Inc., United States of America

Portions of the section on *Company* in Chapter Seven first appeared in the author's blog,
Cultural Advantages, on August 22, 2015.

Illustrations courtesy of the Billy Rose Theatre Collection, the New York Public Library For
the Performing Arts, Astor, Lennox, and Tilden Foundations; and private collections.

Contents

Introduction

You *Mussst* Come Over!

This is a chronological review of both the plays and the people that brought the world of homosexuals, bisexuals, transsexuals, metrosexuals, and the sexually fluid to the American stage.

The plays—which take in a few foreign imports—treat strong gay content (e.g., *The Boys In the Band* or *The Killing Of Sister George*), or minor gay content (*Season In the Sun, The Nervous Set*), or even a phrase in passing (as in *New Faces Of 1956*'s joke about Rome's Piazza Di Spagna, so niche that perhaps fifty people got it during the show's six-month run).

I have included as well plays that portray gay through dog whistles (such as *Bell, Book and Candle*, in which the witches are really gay people) and even plays whose sense of parody or outright camp (such as *Little Mary Sunshine* or *Johnny Guitar*) are at least gay-adjacent.

As for the people in the book—writers, actors, creatives—I have included profiles of some who, though gay, had little interest in portraying gay lives—Edward Albee, for example, even as his influence not as a writer about gay but rather as a *writer who is gay* was extremely broad, so conclusive that he takes pride of place at the end of this volume. These so-to-say pre-Stonewall eminences—actor-manager Eva Le Gallienne is another one—are as much a part of the chronicle as such overtly gay-in-content writers as Terrence McNally.

Consider the case of lyricist-librettist John Latouche, whose work ranged from black folklore (in *Cabin In the Sky*) to Greek myth (in *The Golden Apple*) to silent-era Hollywood (in *The Vamp*), all "sexy" topics that never even glance at gay culture yet resound with the colorful doings that gays in particular respond to. One could argue that Latouche's chromosomes enabled his very agile imagination and love of the picturesque.

I make no attempt to include every relevant reference. Rather, I have tried to cover every type of gay activity, even if with but one or two examples. There isn't room for it all. Readers who feel important titles or people have been slighted should consider writing their own books, as the field is still wide open and could use some company. Live and let live.

1

The 1910s and 1920s

Shadowland

Like many great events, it all starts with drag queens. This may seem an implausible concept for early in the twentieth century, given the antagonism that gay men and women* have faced in their fight for visibility and civil rights. However, the many single-gender private schools of the day and their robust dramatic societies habituated Americans to men playing women and women playing men. Further, there was a popular genre of plays specifically calling for a male character forced against his will to disguise himself as a woman. There was even a classic in this line, a British comedy constantly performed here especially by amateur groups, Brandon Thomas' *Charley's Aunt* (first seen on Broadway in 1893), which proved hardy enough to turn into a hit musical, Frank Loesser's *Where's Charley?* (1948), starring Ray Bolger and running for two years.

No, it isn't quite Drag Queen Planet. Still, that same "man pretends to be a woman despite himself" premise was the standard plot for America's most prominent (of several) drag actor—or, as they were styled then, "female impersonator": Julian Eltinge. His form was musical comedy (or plays with a handful of songs, a common format around 1900), and his approach to drag delineated the impersonation so deftly in both grooming and behavior that some in the audience took him for a biological woman and were startled when, in his curtain call in drag, he would tear off his wig with a grin.

Eltinge was equally persuasive when playing male characters as well, which is what made him so successful: his shtick, really, was how totally he transformed from man to woman and back and forth thus all evening, because his men were virile and his women tender. In *Charley's Aunt*, the joke

---

* "Gay," when the word exploded nationally in its current meaning (as opposed to its older denotation of "chic and carefree") after the Stonewall Rebellion of 1969, referred to men and women alike. Over time, popular usage broke the category into gay men and lesbians, perhaps in recognizing differences in the two subcultures. I'm using "gay" in its 1969 sense, denoting males and females generally.

is that the female impersonation is deliberately grotesque yet fools the other characters completely.

But Julian Eltinge emphasized the illusion, even when he sang. Starting in vaudeville, he reached Broadway in 1904, in a British import, *Mr. Wix Of Wickham*. This was a major production, put on by Edward E. Rice, one of the founding fathers of the American musical, as composer and impresario. In fact, Rice cowrote and produced the first American show with a full-scale and largely integrated score, *Evangeline* (1874).[†]

Eltinge always moved in grand company. He was close with George M. Cohan and other Broadway bigwigs, and A. H. Woods, Eltinge's manager (the old term for "producer," though "agent" was sometimes part of the job as well), was one of the powers of the theatre industry. The original of the brash hondler who calls everyone "sweetheart," Woods actually built a playhouse in his star's honor, the Eltinge Forty-Second Street Theatre, in 1912.[‡] And after his years as a boldface stage name, Eltinge moved to California to go Hollywood, starring in silent films in his usual gender-bending approach and building as Villa Capistrano a mad showplace on Baxter Street in Silver Lake. A cross between Spanish Mission and a fortress, it was four stories high and perched on a hill with a CinemaScope view of the lake. Here was a very tower of fame, though the surrounding greenery made the structure nearly invisible from the street.

So Eltinge was big, supposedly the highest-paid actor of his generation—yes, a drag queen. True, his public profile accented cigars, boxing, and such. And his offstage photos revealed a chunky, amiable, middle-class guy, perhaps an insurance broker: nothing like the slithery, sarcastic performers famed in drag today. Open Daniel Blum's *Great Stars Of the American Stage* (1952), devoting two pages to each subject, with a kind of yearbook precis and stills in and out of costume, and there's Eltinge rowing a canoe, flanked on either side by beauties of the day in elaborate costume—belle epoque, schoolgirl, pour le sport, matronly . . . and they're all Eltinge, too! (The shot was made through double exposure, the CGI of its time.)

Ironically, none of Eltinge's four Broadway shows ran very long on The Street, though they did fine business on the road, making Eltinge a truly

---

[†] *Mr. Wix* also gave the then unknown Jerome Kern his first substantial credit, for Rice heavily revised the British score and Kern composed about half of the new music.

[‡] Seating nine hundred with a small orchestra and two balconies, the house still stands today, albeit at a different address: the entire two-hundred-thousand-ton structure was moved down the block and turned into a cineplex.

national celebrity. After *Mr. Wix Of Wickham* came *The Fascinating Widow* (1911), *The Crinoline Girl* (1914), and *Cousin Lucy* (1915). The major title in the set, the *Widow,* found Eltinge as two-fisted Hal Blake, forced to masquerade as a certain Mrs. Monte in order to expose a Society Cad and win the heroine. The score favored Eltinge's drag ID, complete with entrance number ("The Fascinating Widow"), a beach ditty with the chorus girls in swimming togs ("Don't Take Your Beau To the Seashore"), and the de rigueur rhythm piece ("The Rag Time College Girl"), among other numbers. Note, again, a collaboration with a theatre hot shot: though the music was by the unimportant Frederick W. Mills, the book and lyrics were the work of Otto Hauerbach (later Harbach), mentor of Oscar Hammerstein II and a major writing partner of Jerome Kern.

Now for the $64,000 question: was Eltinge gay? Of course, there were rumors, based for all we know on nothing—but Eltinge was a lifelong bachelor, then as now a curiosity. Straight men tend to marry.

Meanwhile, there was an openly gay drag artist, one who—unlike Eltinge—reveled in the campy rebellion of the male who is a queen and wants the world to know: Bert Savoy. Also unlike Eltinge, Savoy did not fit easily into story shows, having too much distracting gay baggage for the boy-meets-girl tales of the day. Rather, Savoy specialized in the "sophisticated" Broadway revue—the spectacular *Miss 1917* (coproduced by Florenz Ziegfeld) and the modest but chichi *Greenwich Village Follies*, in 1918, 1920, and 1922.

These variety shows allowed Savoy to work within a self-contained act. Using a "feeder"—in this case "straight man" Jay Brennan—Savoy would flounce about in fifi getups, so *drag* in the modern "flaming" sense that if gay hadn't already existed, Bert Savoy would have had to invent it.

Savoy had two catchphrases that gained a national presence, quoted even by folks who had no idea who Bert Savoy was or why anyone would address someone as "Dearie." One was "You don't know the half of it, dearie, you don't know the half of it." The words moved into popular song in George and Ira Gershwin's *Lady, Be Good!*, in "The 'Half Of It, Dearie' Blues," conjured up for Fred Astaire with rampageous tap breaks between the lines.

Savoy's other catchphrase achieved even larger circulation, as it offered Mae West the matrix for her famous "Come up and see me." The original version, Bert Savoy's, was "You must come over!," pronounced with a louche lilt of delight, hand on hip and eyes afire with mischief: "You *mussst* come over!" This line, too, found its way into song, as Lewis E. Gensler, B. G. De Sylva, and

Ira Gershwin again seized on the fad in a semi-hit musical of 1925, *Captain Jinks*, with "You Must Come Over Blues."

Central to Savoy's act was his recounting of the adventures of his forever unseen gal pal Margie. A typical episode might take off with a blatant double entendre, thus:

SAVOY: I've a new recipe for homemade candy. Oh, it's all the rage—*all-day suckers*! You *mussst* come over!
BRENNAN: You were telling me about your friend Margie.
SAVOY: Oh, that Margie! *Always* some new calamity! Why, just last week she and her beau went to the movies to spark in the balcony. All the kids do now, you know. Oh, they all go sparking—the peppy ones. Yes, but even before Margie and her cavalier take their seats, *he* gets into a conversation with a *handsome usher*, and my dear he simply *cannot* tear himself away! Oh, he's so *unusual*!

As the public laughs, Savoy moves downstage, Surveys the House, and sasses out, "You *mussst* come over!"

People who were around back then always said, in recalling men and women who were obviously gay, "You never spoke about it." Really *never*? Even with all the information coming from the popular arts? The bohemian life in Greenwich Village—a mixture of artists, political agitators, gays, prostitutes, and nonconformists of all kinds, not to mention a conservative Italian-American community—was a standing joke among New Yorkers. Once again, there was a song about it, in Jerome Kern's *Oh, Lady! Lady!!* (1918), to lyrics by P. G. Wodehouse, "[For there's something in the air of little] Greenwich Village." The second verse tells of "my favorite aunt Matilda," who left Oshkosh at the age of eighty-three to try life among the Village savages:

> She learned the ukalele [*sic*],
> She breakfasted at Polly's,
> And what is worse,
> She wrote free verse,
> And now she's in the Follies!

Note that Polly's, on MacDougal Street, was under police surveillance for its lawless habitués, both sex workers and gays. Wodehouse might have been referencing the restaurant simply as a Village landmark—but it had a Reputation. Just to mention it was to disseminate information about the thing You Never Spoke About.

Cole Porter, too, flirted with taboo, one year later, in *Hitchy Koo 1919*, in "My Cozy Little Corner In the Ritz," "'cause I like to watch the kings and let the queens see me,"—and he didn't mean the royal kind, as he was always sneaking Allusions into his lyrics. Ironically, one of the most potent such Porterisms is by Noël Coward, who wrote his own wicked verses to Porter's "Let's Do It (Let's Fall In Love)." There we learn that "Belgians and Greeks do it" and then "Nice young men who sell antiques do it." And Porter sang his version in his very successful Las Vegas cabaret turn, at the Desert Inn in 1955, before a mass audience, not a niche of sophisticates.

Not everyone clued into gay style was of the clan or clan-friendly, though. A New York tabloid of the 1920s and 1930s, *Broadway Brevities*, devoted to the doings of the famed and reckless, covered as well "pansies" and "dykes," emphasizing the popular stereotypes. Sample headline: FAG BALLS EXPOSED. Sample cartoon: a haughty, lipsticked gentleman enters the ladies' room as an aghast woman asks, "Oh, isn't there some mistake?" "Sez you," the man retorts. Sample newsbreak: Noël Coward supposedly has "discovered" a "lad" dancing "in a Bombay honky tonk" and "has kept him ever since."

Broadway Brevities was available on newsstands, its flashy covers right next to New York's dailies. Even more widely known was Anita Loos' *Gentlemen Prefer Blondes*, a satirical novella on the lovely blond gold digger Lorelei Lee and her worldly sidekick, Dorothy. When Lorelei encounters a French father and son who are always kissing each other (in the Gallic manner, *bien sûr*), Dorothy says "people would think that [they] painted batiks." Further, one of the heroine's wealthy boy friends has a sister who "always likes to spend every evening in the garage taking their Ford farm truck apart and putting it back together again."

At the same time, gay characters were cropping up in serious drama in the late 1920s, so they were not only speaking about it but portraying it. In *Machinal* (1928), expressionism based loosely on the decade's infamous Ruth Snyder–Judd Gray murder case that ended with their execution, playwright Sophie Treadwell doesn't tiptoe about: in a scene in a bar, she describes two minor players, billed as "a Man" and "a Boy," as, respectively, "a middle-aged fairy" and "young, untouched." The Man invites the Boy to his home to show him "a first edition of Verlaine that will simply make your mouth water."

More prominently, Eugene O'Neill's nine-act *Strange Interlude* (1928), which took so long to play because characters interspersed into their dialogue the content of their thoughts, included a closeted man in its storyline, one Charles Marsden. He's a major principal, with both the play's opening and closing lines, and while he neither does nor says (nor even "thinks" aloud) anything overtly gay, O'Neill tells us he has "an indefinable feminine quality about him," with "long, fragile hands" and "a quiet charm."

Well, that's a step up from a middle-aged fairy. But the key title in this era is *The Captive* (1926). A French play, Édouard Bourdet's *La Prisonnière*, it tells of a young woman who defies convention in her liaison with another woman. But is she truly a captive or a willing partner?

The American production, staged by Gilbert Miller in the translation of Arthur Hornblow Jr., respected the original rather than adapt it, though the Parisian setting and the French names were a tad exotic and though Bourdet's form was the old-fashioned "well-made" work in three acts, with exposition, complication, and disposition. To wit:

ACT ONE: Irène is evasive in her reluctance to marry her sweetheart.

ACT TWO: That sweetheart's old friend reveals that Irène is intimately involved with his wife in "the kingdom of shadows," from which there is no escape. "One can never overtake them!" he cries. And this wife is the ultimate femme fatale, with charm that turns the world upside down in a prison of love. "[I] hate her," he says. "I worship her."

Now, the well-made play habitually climaxes with the so-called *scène à faire*, the "obligatory scene" in which the play confronts its devils. The prodigal son shows up when his lover is marrying his brother. The villain unknowingly sips from the poisoned chalice. The treasure map is found: X marks the spot.

So, Bourdet has to produce Irène's amour, so we can see for ourselves this fascinating jailer of souls:

ACT THREE: The lesbian captor appears. She is insolent, sly, sure of herself. She is the Queen of Shadows!

No, wait. That's too obvious. Instead:

ACT THREE: She will be modest, attractive, pleasant, and she will give Irène up.

But Bourdet cleverly omits the *scène à faire* altogether. The captor never appears! And really, could any actress encompass the allure and terror that Bourdet had built up—Jezebel, Circe, and Mata Hari in one vessel? "She dominates three acts," John Mason Brown wrote in *Theatre Arts* magazine, "a hundred times more vividly than if she had ever appeared."

And who knows if this phantom really is a captor? Because just as matters seem to smooth themselves out, Irène ditches her fiancé after all and leaves to rejoin her lesbian lover. Is Irène truly the prisoner . . . or a willing participant in the imprisonment? Even . . . a captor herself?

The Captive was a classy production, not an indie affair but Big Broadway. Gilbert Miller was the son of Henry Miller, a major actor-manager who erected his own playhouse, rebuilt as the Stephen Sondheim Theatre. And Junior opened *The Captive* at the Empire, Broadway's most prestigious house, built by Broadway's most prestigious producer, Charles Frohman.[§] Further, *The Captive*'s cast was very presentable, led by Helen Menken as Irène and Basil Rathbone as her fiancé. In all, this was an imposing attraction, not to be mistaken for an exploitation piece like the "sex comedies" that had become popular since the late 1910s such as *The Woman In Room Thirteen*, *Up In Mabel's Room*, *She Walked In Her Sleep*, even the salacious-sounding *Twin Beds*.

Nevertheless, an openly lesbian character was dangerous stuff in 1926, for the authorities had an extra irritation to deal with in the person of Mae West, actress, playwright, director, and arguably one of the most influential figures in opening the culture to information that fascists of all kinds want kept secret. Remember, as Auntie Mame says, "Knowledge is power."

West was promulgating the avatar of the New Woman: independent, entrepreneurial, and sexual. West's characters—all versions of West herself—were living autonomously rather than within traditional social constructions. In other words, she was no man's woman. She knew this would outrage the authorities; she meant to, in fact.

Moreover, she habitually concocted stories that combined the outlaw world with Society, showing grandees getting involved with crooks. This threatened to destabilize Americans' respect for the elite, especially those whores the professional politicians.

[§] Frohman became a common noun like Kleenex or Frigidaire. When actor met actor and one reported that he was up for the new Fitch or O'Neill, his colleague would ask, "Yeah, but who's the Frohman?"

No wonder West insisted on writing her own lines when she got to Hollywood, in 1932: she couldn't trust anyone else to endow the West Woman with the appropriate worldview. Try this snippet of Paramount's *Goin' To Town* (1935), in which West tries to crash High Socì:

MAE: For a long time, I was ashamed of the way I lived.
MAN: You mean to say you reformed?
MAE: No, I got over bein' ashamed.

But we're here to discuss West's Broadway work; oddly, her twenties plays, credited to "Jane Mast," are just this side of barfulous, because she hasn't yet developed the persona she was to immortalize in her talkies, somewhat modeled on Bert Savoy—again, his "You mussst come over!" turned into West's "Come up and see me." Still, these Mast concoctions are historical, for West placed the gay male, his campy lines, and even a drag ball right on stage for the first time.

Sex (1926), which West appeared in as well as wrote, dealt with a more or less goodhearted prostitute mixed up with fancy folk, one Margie LaMont (another reference to Bert Savoy's routine). *Sex* ran a year despite the critics' irritation ("a nasty red-light district show" should have been a pull quote), partly because of the title's promise of sinful doings but mainly because the public was fascinated with West's unique performing style, with the cockeyed strut, the hand on hip, and the murmured umms and oohs, the pillow talk of the Magdalene.

West didn't appear in her more controversial shows, *The Drag* (1927) and *The Pleasure Man* (1928), but there the show-off parts were gay men, indulging in minty repartee. One of the parish met "a handsome brute of a taxi driver" and "he's been following me ever since." It was the *Broadway Brevities* come to life, the real thing.

The Drag folded on its tryout, as West was strongly discouraged from bringing it in. The District Attorney for New York County, a transplanted Texan named Joab H. Banton, was a crusader, against real crime but also against tolerance of what the *Brevities* liked to call "the Third Sex." With the sympathy of many city fathers behind him, Banton decided to close some "offending" Broadway shows and prosecute those involved, including the actors. Interestingly, he waited till the Mayor, James J. Walker, was out of town.

Banton didn't have to wait long, as Walker was notorious for his countless vacations. Nevertheless, for all the corruption of his administration, Walker was a live-and-let-live kind of guy, and he had many friends in what was then called "the show business." So Banton was not only a bigot, but a sneak.

And with Walker off at the beach somewhere during a cold February in 1927, Banton struck. It was not unprecedented, be it said, for city officials to persecute the stage. Earlier in the 1920s, they closed and indicted participants in the production of Sholem Asch's *The God Of Vengeance* (1922), an off-Broadway show that had moved to The Street. Written in Yiddish, the play had swept the Western world because of its melodramatic blending of sex and religion, personified in its high-strung protagonist[**] who is both Jewish zealot and bordello keeper.

Shocking for the day, the action is set for two of its three acts in the brothel, and Asch even includes a lesbian scene, quite delicately written, in which one of the prostitutes befriends the brothel keeper's daughter. It was perhaps this notion that sex workers might have tender and even spiritual instincts that offended the professional Grievance Committee that is always with us in one form or another. Those aggrieved even counted a conservative Jewish influencer, a prominent rabbi who was enraged by the depiction of his co-religionists working in a whorehouse.

So *The God Of Vengeance* was shuttered by force, right in the middle of a successful run. Yet this example of how the state can decide what theatregoers can and cannot see did not startle the theatregoing community as much as one might think, for the play was an exotic—European in origin, composed (though translated, by Isaac Goldberg) in a language spoken only by obscure immigrants, and played by actors no one had ever heard of. This even though Rudolph Schildkraut, the show's protagonist and director, was the father of Joseph Schildkraut, who had just broken into fame in the title role of Ferenc Molnar's *Liliom* (the source of the musical *Carousel*) and would maintain an important career for thirty years, finally creating Otto Frank, the heroine's father, in *The Diary Of Anne Frank* (1955).

Then, too, Broadway was in an expansive mood in the 1920s, and some two hundred productions opened every year. So it was easy to overlook even a controversial title like *The God Of Vengeance*, especially because the hatred of gay people kept theatre critics from using the word "lesbian," dancing around it with euphemisms. The closest the *Morning Telegraph* got to it was

---

[**] By the rules of the ancient Greeks, who invented Western theatre, there can be only one protagonist per work. Other principals are the deuteragonist and the tritagonist, but the protagonist is the one the story is about—Oedipus, Molière's Dom Juan, Dolly Levi. We'll be observing that usage in this book.

"There are some themes that have no place on the stage," and many of the dailies refused to cover the show's obscenity trial.

However, in the four years between *The God Of Vengeance* and *The Captive*, lesbians no longer terrified the press. Now they were a novelty: the critics discussed Bourdet's play as if it marked the first depiction of gay women on Broadway. True, *The Captive* was talky and suave, which made it easier to tolerate than the melodramatic *God Of Vengeance*, a play living in a state of rage. *The Captive* was middle class, while *The God Of Vengeance* was sheer outlawry.

Still, *The Captive* was a show that the Joab Bantons of the world were born to close down—better, to punish. Arrest the producer, the playwright, the actors! Planning his raids, Banton created a bucket list that included many of Broadway's most interesting productions; that was their problem. Banton believed in a theatre that entertained, not in one that stimulated or inspired. Or, worse, informed. One of the shows Banton was after was *An American Tragedy* (1926), Patrick Kearney's adaptation of Theodore Dreiser's novel. It was critical of American society and therefore a major addition to Banton's list. But common sense warned him that overreach might outrage the public and sabotage his purification campaign.

So he settled on just three titles for his raids: *The Captive*; a sex comedy called *The Virgin Man*; and Mae West's *Sex*. And, make no mistake, West was the real reason for the legal blitzkrieg, for West was dangerous. Her world-view challenged the status quo—about sex, yes, but also about everything. In a way, she was a hetero version of your gay uncle, a bank of information about the world that was far more intriguing than anything you heard from your parents. West was a forerunner of Auntie Mame, telling you to stop conforming and live, live, live!

Banton wasn't the only official who heard fighting words in the concept of a free and outspoken theatre. Directly after the Banton raids, New York State Senator B. Roger Wales successfully introduced a law threatening prosecution of those putting on plays treating "sex degeneracy, or sex perversion"—indeed, any play that could be called immoral. Haters of the probing liberalism of art thrilled at the very vagueness of "immoral"; that could be anything they didn't like—*Alice In Wonderland*, Beethoven's Ninth Symphony, floor wax. Note, too, that if prosecution led to conviction, the theatre owner could find his house padlocked for a year. The genius of the law lay in its grandeur: it was so encompassing that it would never have to be applied, as thespians would censor themselves out of sheer self-defense. This so-called Wales Padlock Law remained a potent threat through the 1940s. Ultimately enfeebled through disuse, it nevertheless remained on the books until 1967.

The Banton raids had a comic side, though, for the assault on Mae West's *Sex* gave its author (as she herself admitted) the kind of PR money can't buy. The press was filled with her escapades during her week's imprisonment (with two days off for good behavior). Reporters told how she wore her own silk underwear rather than the city's standard issue, dined in state with the warden, and, on release, was greeted like an opera diva who had closed the season with a superb Carmen.

And West wasn't giving up yet. As I've said, *The Drag* was too controversial to resuscitate, so West wrote *The Pleasure Man* to utilize *The Drag*'s outstanding elements. One was a murder plot: the protagonist, a closeted gay man with a secret male lover, kills him out of jealousy. A second element was the drag ball itself, with not only fantastical costumes and queens ripping each other apart verbally but also an onstage band and musical numbers: the works.

So *The Drag* had become a musical. Formerly set in New York amid West's beloved Society, it was now a backstager laid in "a small midwestern town" and concerned with stage performers, whose lifestyle is arguably only a step or two from a drag ball, anyway. The protagonist was a straight man of the caddish sort who is castrated (to death) by the brother of a woman he has wronged.

West may have thought she had made *The Drag* less risky in its new form as *The Pleasure Man*. But it was still too flashy for Banton's taste, and the law came after this one, too. RAID MAE WEST PLAY, *The New York Times* reported. SEIZE 56 AT OPENING. But Mae fought for her show with an injunction, and everyone piled back into the theatre for the second performance, a sold-out matinee. Partway through, the cops busted the show again, making *The Pleasure Man* possibly the only Broadway title to have played 1½ performances.

West continued to work on Broadway on and off even after launching her Hollywood career, in 1932, but she no longer tried to bring gays out of darkness into Broadway neon. Yes, there was a sensationalist aspect to her use, in *The Drag* and *The Pleasure Man*, of cross-dressing parties and in-crowd repartee. It's arguably exploitative. And, sadly, at other times in her life, West would make bigoted assessments of the world of gay men.

Yet consider this exchange in *The Drag* between a judge and a doctor:

GAY-HATING JUDGE: People like that should be herded together on some
desert isle—
FAIR-MINDED DOCTOR: Why?
JUDGE: For the good of the rest of humanity.
DOCTOR: You'd need a large island, Judge. And again, why? What have they
done? Their crime isn't of commission or omission. . . . A man is what he
is born to be.

The doctor also reminds us that many prominent persons have been gay, forever and everywhere: "Kings, princes, statesmen, scholars, fools!"

Truly, was anyone else—in or out of the arts—expressing so cogent an argument for tolerance in *The Drag*'s 1927? True, you could say that West simply
had an affinity for outlaws, whether crooks or the oppressed. Still, whatever
her motivation, Mae West was the first Broadway star to make a case for homophile acceptance, which makes her unique among the innovators in this
chapter—Bert Savoy and his hissy campapalooza, Cole Porter and his impish
innuendo, Sophie Treadwell and the blunt naturalism of her queen and his
pick-up in *Machinal*, and even the people who put on *The Captive*. Brave
they must have been, yet its leading lady, the aforementioned Helen Menken,
declared after the show was raided that she wouldn't return to the production
even if its impresario successfully defended it in court.

Perhaps she realized that, after giving gay a bit of leeway as a curiosity of
the carnival side-show kind, the authorities were going to lower the iron
curtain. Typically, Julian Eltinge found himself all but fired from show business, as "female impersonation" was now illegal. Bert Savoy's fate was harder
yet: three years before the Banton raids, in 1924, Savoy was struck by light-
ning while walking along the sands at Jones Beach. One might almost see in
it a portent of things to come.

2
The 1930s

The Gays Who Came To Dinner

If the previous chapter was something of a prologue, our tour more truly starts now, and Eva Le Gallienne is an ideal first stop, as she was one of the most remarkable gays of the twentieth century: uncloseted, visionary, and the very last of the great actor-managers.

This now-forgotten occupation denoted an individual solely in charge of an acting company, as producer, director, and star: an auteur, to borrow a term from film. As an idealist, Le Gallienne instituted the revolving-repertory model—an expensive one, because you had to pay actors who didn't necessarily play every night, expanding the salary calendar. And repertory was tricky to sell to the average theatregoer, who had to check the schedule to find which day of the week they were giving the particular show he or she wanted to see. Worse yet, the manager (again, simply the old term for "producer") couldn't assemble a troupe of seasoned actors, because the established names wanted to freelance.

On Broadway. That's where the fame and money were. Repertory gave you training and experience, especially in The Classics. But a sound career profile meant working on The Street, which Le Gallienne avidly loathed. Broadway was a land of play boutiques, she thought. It catered to the whims of a dilettante public rather than enlightening devotees with work of real content, from Molière to Ibsen to Chekhof, as Le Gallienne did in her Civic Repertory Theatre, which lasted from 1926 to 1933. Put simply, Le Gallienne embodied art, not commerce. Theatre was a temple; the profit motive profaned it. Broadway was a place of money–changers, while repertory ennobled all who took part in it.

Now, what was Le Gallienne like personally? Tireless, resourceful, and very strong-willed. I'd call her the ultimate lesbian butch, because she was a born leader, and, in her romances, she had the ownership—the living quarters (including a house in the wilds of Connecticut), the money, the schedule, and (because she partnered with actresses) the theatre. She was a tough ringmaster, yet also protective of her charges. Le Gallienne's biographer, Helen Sheehy, interviewed actress Rose Hobart, who recalled how another player outed Le Gallienne to Hobart and said it was assumed that the boss had taken Hobart to bed.

Hobart told Sheehy that Le Gallienne "taught me everything. . . . She was my instructor on . . . what kind of human being you should be." Yet the lesbian thing was a shock. When Hobart went to Le Gallienne, the latter "took one look at me, and said, 'You've heard.'" But was there a problem? "Have I ever done anything to hurt you?" Le Gallienne asked. She hadn't, of course. Le Gallienne was a fascinating creature—not unlike the unseen charmer of *The Captive*, perhaps. But she never exploited her appeal to ensnare anyone.* Finally, Le Gallienne told Hobart, "I'm looking for beauty in my way, and it's not everybody's way."

Key words! Le Gallienne looked for beauty in great playwrighting, dedicated actors, even determined audiences who would find their way to the Civic, in a long-disused house down on Fourteenth Street and Sixth Avenue, far south of the theatre district. And location was crucial back then, for day-of-performance walk-in business sold far more tickets than advance sales. When a box office opened each morning, the house could be nearly empty yet reach Standing Room Only by curtain time—because of that walk-in business, which is why Broadway's playhouses were neighbors. Customers would roam from theatre to theatre, inspecting the photographs and signboards ("100 Performances!" or "'Comedy Hit!'—*Daily News*") and weighing their purchase. But nobody "walked in" twenty-five blocks away on Fourteenth Street. You had to need to see Le Gallienne's shows (though she did maintain a box office uptown to make it easier for her audience).

It really seems a bit hopeless, despite a theatre structure so large (it ran through the block from Fourteenth to Fifteenth Street) that the stage could be thrown open to the rear wall for a spectacular effect impossible in most of the uptown houses. However, Le Gallienne had wealthy angels, and she featured ensemble casts anticipating the Stanislafskyan naturalism of the Group Theatre, launched about five years after the Civic. In the end, Le Gallienne was so successful that, in the 1928–1929 season—a commercial disaster theat

---

* A still active legend tells that, when Le Gallienne actress protegée Josephine Hutchinson became Le Gallienne's lover, Hutchinson's husband named Le Gallienne as the co-respondent in a bitter divorce. In fact, this was a scandal invented by tabloid journalists. The divorce was amicable, and Le Gallienne's name did not come up in the proceedings.

because Broadway had built too many theatres and outstripped its public, leaving even good fare starving for support—the Civic sustained an astonishing 94 percent capacity.

True, this was partly because Alla Nazimova had joined the Civic. The infamous Russian beauty, recently a Hollywood movie star who had wrecked her career with a little too much infamy (such as filming *Salome* with a reputedly all-gay cast in designs that could have come from the Mad Hatter), was all the same a compelling artist. Le Gallienne saw the women stars of Broadway as personality merchants, such as Helen Hayes and her mannerisms, signing her portrayals as if distributing autographs. Nazimova, however, was an *actress*—and, be it said, one of the girls in the band.

As for Le Gallienne's own acting style, she worked an expansive technique that enabled her to disappear into her characters, from the White Queen in an adaptation of *Alice In Wonderland*[†] to Peter Pan to Camille. Look at photographs of Le Gallienne in costume: she's different in every shot, somebody else forever.

She was the opposite, then, of her colleagues. They were always themselves; she had no self. She was her roles. This is getting famous the hard way—yet President Roosevelt wanted to give the Federal Theatre to Le Gallienne as its chief.

This was one of the programs the New Deal's Works Progress Administration designed for artists, writers, and thespians, simply to keep our arts foundation alive during the blitz of the Depression. But note that even as the Wales Padlock Law still forbade even the representation of homosexuals on Broadway, the government wanted to give control of a national theatre system to a woman who was somewhat known to be gay. This wasn't just an honor: this was history.

But Le Gallienne saw a "federal theatre" as an expansion of the Civic Rep, while the Roosevelt administration saw it as a social safety net—at that, one to address a national audience with a miscellany ranging from children's shows and old-time melodrama to all-black Shakespeare and experimental

---

[†] Le Gallienne collaborated on the script—scrupulously drawn from Lewis Carroll's two *Alice* books—with Florida Friebus, a lesbian who was later nationally famous as Dobie Gillis' mother on television. *Alice*, the Civic's biggest hit in a transfer to Broadway, was virtually a musical, with ever-changing background scenery moved scroll-like on rollers from stage right to stage left, with flying, masks, puppets, and special effects when Alice had to swim through a lake of her own tears or grow taller after tasting a Wonderland elixir. The costumes, after the books' Tenniel illustrations, were very elaborate; the Humpty Dumpty actor was encased in a huge egg above his legs with a little hole in the center for his eyes, nose, and mouth, all dovetailing exactly with what was painted on the egg, a delightful effect.

agitprop. A lot of it would be amateurish populism, not the high-maestro playwrighting that Le Gallienne worshiped. She and the regime could not come to terms, and Roosevelt hired Hallie Flanagan to run the shop; an adept of experimental theatre.

This was in the mid-1930s, after the Civic finally had to close. Ever after, Le Gallienne kept trying to return to repertory, but—to repeat—the model is cumbersome. Her last hurrah found her as an actor-for-hire playing what she really was, a grand old relic who lived to act and acted to live, in Kaufman and Ferber's *The Royal Family* (revival, 1975). Still full of spit and vinegar, Le Gallienne tied herself in knots commuting to the Helen Hayes Theatre on Forty-Sixth Street (now demolished) while averting her eyes from its façade, where gigantic lettering bore the two words Le Gallienne hated the most in the English language . . . "Helen Hayes."

And all this occurred without faking a "lavender marriage." The Lunts did, Katharine Cornell and Guthrie McClintic did, Charles Laughton did. Even Mercedes de Acosta, a writer of everything but mainly the lover of every prominent lesbian of the early twentieth century, faked one. De Acosta's list of conquests took in such as Nazimova, Marlene Dietrich, our own Eva Le Gallienne, and, top of the line, Greta Garbo. Cecil Beaton was treated as a fatuous sycophant in television's *The Crown* (as the royal photographer), but he knew everybody and got into everything, and he paid de Acosta quite some compliment in his journal: "She was one of the most rebellious and brazen of Lesbians," partly because she would leave her New York apartment dressed as a kind of Baroque troubadour and with a white-painted face and hair moussed in midnight black. Tallulah Bankhead called Mercedes the Countess Dracula.

Perhaps the most cynical of the hetero-married gays was Cole Porter. After all, whatever love life the Lunts had and with whom was as clandestine as a state secret, and though Katharine Cornell's husband was as fey as a buttered popover, only theatre people knew him. But Porter positively radiated gay: he was smart and playful, extremely aware of (and friendly with) the boldface names of the day, and an admirer of fabulous women, the saucy and glamorous personalities that make show biz go. All this is the urban gay style—as was Porter's sexual worldview, favoring men who were neither saucy nor fabulous: trade.

Trade comes in many forms, from bordello employees to shady street characters to "real" citizens, such as the young technician at the Liberty Music Shop who went on house calls to repair your phonograph. Porter would rip out wires in the playing arm, then set up an appointment, though the fellow would know there is no way a record player can sustain an "accident" like that. Still, he'd go about his work, and Porter would offer him a cocktail. But all he wanted was beer; that's trade for you.

Why did Porter marry? Because he was strictly comme il faut, and style was his ethic, from the buttonholed carnation in his lapel to the swank drollery of his shows—*Gay Divorce* (1932) with fashionable Fred Astaire or *Anything Goes* (1934) on the power of celebrity. Porter's wife, the former Linda Lee, was something of a drip, though the usual word for her was "socialite." It's a vague term, though, denoting virtually any married woman who knows how to dress. It was Linda's dream that Porter would, one, go classical and, two, stop dating toothsome riffraff. A hypochondriac, Linda may have weaponized her ailments to sex-shame Porter, and his friends always knew when she had caught him in flagrante again, as she would hop back into her iron lung.

Porter had studied classical technique and once composed a ballet, but he stayed with pop, and we wonder how Linda felt about all the gay material Porter would slip into his lyrics. His music is superbly crafted, with many a rhythmic or harmonic surprise, and his words are perhaps the wittiest Broadway knew till after World War II. Still, Porter's worldview is subversive, though much of it is conveyed in in-jokes for the cognoscenti. He speaks especially to his fellow gays of the ecstasy and horror of love at its hottest, of its power to affirm the ego but also of its destructive impulses, its restive contradictions. "I Hate You, Darling," the Porter heroine pleads, or "Get Out Of Town [before it's too late, my love]," because love is so absolute it swallows one's very identity.

The sentimental love ballad is basic equipment in the thirties musical— think of "As Time Goes By"‡ or "There's a Small Hotel." But Porter's ballads are often obsessed or fatalistic. "Night and Day" pounds with longing; "[It was] Just One Of Those Things" actually celebrates the end of an affair. Other songwriters treat the romance that never ends, but Porter's sweethearts adopt

---

‡ This number is a real curiosity, introduced in 1931 in *Everybody's Welcome*, recorded a bit, and forgotten. But Dooley Wilson made it unforgettable in the movie *Casablanca*, when it went into national release in 1943. Play it, Sam—but Wilson couldn't record it, as the musicians' union was on its two-year strike. A few 1931 "As Time Goes By" discs were reissued, but they didn't sound at all like Wilson's sweet torch-like rendering, frustrating the public. Then Decca signed a separate peace with the union, and while branding the Broadway cast album as theirs—with *Oklahoma!, One Touch Of Venus, Carmen Jones, Song Of Norway*—Decca took down Dooley Wilson's "As Time Goes By" as well, preserved for us on YouTube.

the bumblebee promiscuity for which gay men are famous, anticipating a popular joke of the early Stonewall era:

Q: What do lesbians do on the second date?
A: Hire a U-Haul.
Q: And what do gay men do on the second date?
A: What second date?

Then, too, Porter constantly slips parish code words into his lyrics. We've already heard him talk of "queens," and in "I'm a Gigolo," from *Wake Up and Dream* (1929), the singer admits "Of lavender my nature's got just a dash in it." There's more than a dash in "Farming," from *Let's Face It!* (1941), which warns us not to "inquire of Georgie Raft why his cow has never calved." Aren't animals supposed to mate? Yes, though it turns out that "Georgie's bull is beautiful but he's gay!" The G word, no less! And note Porter's use of the venerable folk wisdom that all the pretty ones play for the team.

At that, in the essential thirties Porter show, *Anything Goes*, one of the hit tunes the piece was studded with, "I Get a Kick Out Of You," is the torch number of the girl who can't land the guy—almost a counterpart to the gay guy with a crush on the straight guy, a very basic situation in gay life that Porter would have been well aware of. It's a subtly lavish number, its refrain built out of quarter and half notes constantly alternating with triplets (though few singers observe Porter's notation correctly), giving the melody the air of flight soaring above earthly cares.

Ethel Merman introduced it in the show, because she loves William Gaxton while he's after Bettina Hall.[§] Thus Merman was trapped for a time in the "extra woman" category, available for laughs and songs. They called this type a serio-comic, meaning she has the talent but not the oo-la-la. Fanny Brice and Sophie Tucker were others such; they tended to play vaudeville or revue rather than story shows because they were too interesting not to star yet weren't right for the romance.

Merman was so interesting that she eventually got the guy, too. Still, she didn't turn soft, and in real life she was a phallic woman, a tough New York broad with the filthiest mouth on Broadway. Sailors ran blushing from the room. In fact, Merman exemplifies a diva type that gay men have played

[§] Bettina's sister Natalie also played leads in thirties musicals, so they broke up their gigs by genre: Bettina appeared in musical comedy and Natalie in operetta. And still no one could tell them apart.

courtier to since who knows when, and Porter adored her, not least for her pinpoint diction, benison to Porter's lyricist side. At rehearsals, he would blow a whistle if a performer wasn't getting the words across; he never had to with Merman.

Yet there was more to Porter's admiration for this particular performer—a love of the outsized, struck-by-lightning female talent that gay men cultivate, as with Bette Davis, Mary Martin, Tallulah Bankhead, Maria Callas, Carol Channing, Barbra Streisand, Bette Midler. All marvelous one-of-a-kinds, they defy in various ways the cautions of the culture. They don't "look" right or they "overdo." But they give the public everything they have, and they can be just as theatrical offstage as on.

Merman, for example, was blunter than a pawnbroker and grander than Napoléon, very aware of whom she had to respect and whom she could scold, and there was an excitement about her that Porter seldom felt among the international café parasites he hobnobbed with. In short, Merman was a Character. Whenever someone mentioned Mary Martin, Merman would immediately pipe up with "Dyke, ya know." She was uneducated but fast and shrewd in comeback. Long after her Porter years, during her brief and stormy marriage to Ernest Borgnine, Merman (who was in her mid-fifties at this point) returned from a TV taping so pleased with herself that she had Borgnine snarling before she got through the front door.

"What are *you* so happy about?" he caws.

"Well," she explains, "they just loved my thirty-five-year-old face, and my thirty-five-year-old figure, and my thirty-five-year-old voice."

"Yeah? And what about your sixty-five-year-old cunt?" he counters.

And she replies, "Nobody mentioned you at all."

Merman epitomized a term I coined decades ago, the Big Lady, but there was another gay performer type emerging in these inter-war years, the Beautiful Male—and Porter's next show after *Anything Goes*, *Jubilee* (1935), offers one in Mark Plant. It was *Jubilee*'s conceit—in Moss Hart's book—that a royal family of vaguely British hue would tralala off to romantic adventures. The King finds Elsa Maxwell; the Queen hooks up with MGM's Tarzan, Johnny Weissmuller; the Prince gets a sort of Ginger Rogers; and the Princess pairs off with Noël Coward. Plant played the Weissmuller role as Mowgli, making a personal appearance at his latest film clad in a bearskin that left most of Plant's flesh open to view.[**]

[**] The script says Mowgli is wearing "a loin-cloth and nothing else," but the Vandamm contact sheets of the original production show otherwise. Plant also attended a costume ball at the end of Act

The Hart and Porter Mowgli may have set the matrix for the Beautiful Male as a dope. Plant's entrance line is "Me Mowgli, me save girl from elephants!," and the formal speech that Hart wrote for him is inane. "Well, folks, here we are," it begins, going on to "I guess we're certainly all here, all right. Yessir, here we are," and so on. Then Porter steps in with "When Me, Mowgli, Love," perhaps the most bizarre song Porter ever wrote. The music tells of jungle drums lightly pounding, palm trees swaying, and a lot of heavy sex, and the lyrics report on Mowgli's erotic prowess, as an audience of elephants watch through opera glasses.

Keep in mind that the gym-expanded or even just well-toned physique, de rigueur in leading men today, was all but unknown in 1935, when muscle training was little more than calisthenics. And, as if Mowgli's establishing number were not enough to define his erotic bona fides, Porter wrote as well "There's Nothing Like Swimming" for Mowgli and the Queen, backed by the chorus boys, who encourage her to get into a daring mesh outfit. As the Queen was played by Mary Boland, the first name in the Dizzy Dame type so basic to Hollywood's screwball comedies, this was a comic piece. Its highlight was Boland's leap off a diving board, and Porter included a reference to "Neptune's Daughter," in-crowd slang for a gay man who chases sailors. But the number had a secondary purpose: to put the cutest of the ensemble men into swimming togs. Ultimately, the scene was dropped, as the show was running long—especially in its huge score, counting twenty different songs.

Summing up our position thus far, we have on one hand the ever-present threat of the Wales Padlock Law, clearly designed above all to block any depiction of gay life from public view. As that line in *The Captive* suggests, gay men and women had truly become the shadow people. Yet nature finds a way. And theatre people are the cleverest, most resourceful tribe in the population.

Consider Thomas H. Dickinson's *Winter Bound* (1929), the tale of two women living together in a rural northeastern setting. The pair offer tintypes of the iconic lesbian couple, the butch and the femme—yet it appears that they are celibate. Are they lesbians at all? Well, the butch, known as Tony as opposed to, for example, Dorinda, is brusque and athletic and dresses like a man. She's also given to saying things like "I know what you women are up against" (in regard to menstruation) and "I'd hate to think I was a woman."

One as Cupid, dressed in a white cache-sexe and wings, and he deserves to, all biceps and thighs. Bow, arrows, and a cunning little quiver completed the ensemble.

The show didn't run long, likely because it played the old Garrick Theatre, just east of Herald Square, by 1929 too far south and east of The Street to partake of that all-important walk-in business. In fact, *Winter Bound* eked out its short run only because a few critics noticed—and stated—that Dickinson seemed to be writing about lesbians, which must have intrigued the more progressive theatregoers. Much later, historian Kaier Curtin called Tony "the first 'bull-dyke' character ever seen on an English-language stage," yet when Curtin spoke of this to the original Tony, Aline MacMahon, he says she was outraged at the very thought.

If *Winter Bound* gives us a serious view of cross-dressing, Julian F. Thompson's *The Warrior's Husband* (1932) presents the comic one. The title alone, when first viewed in the theatrical listings, must have caused minority male hearts to flutter. But there is no gay here: the warriors are the Amazons of Ancient Greece. They do the fighting while the men do the housework, and as one of the Amazons was the twenty-five-year-old Katharine Hepburn in her breakout role, *The Warrior's Husband* made a splash.

Hepburn's big set piece was a physical battle with a Greek enemy, Theseus, played by Colin Keith-Johnston, an English émigré who played New York's Stanhope, the protagonist of the famous World War I play *Journey's End* (London 1928, New York 1929). Classy and heroic, Keith-Johnston was the perfect foil for Hepburn's blithely bellicose Antiope, and their armored wrestling match ended with Hepburn backing her foe against the set, forcing her body against his face-to-face, and grabbing his hair. It looked like rape, and a photograph celebrating the moment became the wallpaper of the season, an idée fixe for the media. Even your Aunt Prudence saw it.

You'd think that that shot alone would have made *The Warrior's Husband* a smash—and it played the Morosco Theatre on Forty-Fifth Street, the very center of walk-in-business Broadway. Yet the run tallied at only 83 performances.

Perhaps the public was uncomfortable with so many effeminate male characters making so many gender-reversal jokes. The show's male lead, Sapiens (Romney Brent), admonishes his spouse with "So! Woman's brute force has failed and you have to fall back on woman's intuition" when he isn't mincing about being afraid of everything. Actually, this personality was already a type, known as the "nance" (from "Nancy boy"), but nances really belonged on their home turf, the burlesque house, where the exaggerated gestures and phony caterwauling allowed the all-male audience to feel superior to these absurd caricatures.

The Broadway public, however, wasn't used to this gaudy persona, too un-real to be called even a stereotype. Ironically, Mayor Fiorello La Guardia's prudish war on burlesque forced its adherents to seek work elsewhere in show biz, including the stage, thereby popularizing burlesque's tropes. So by 1942, when *The Warrior's Husband* reappeared, now as the Rodgers and Hart musical *By Jupiter*, the audience was amused rather than offended.

By Jupiter was a smash, not least for its Sapiens, Ray Bolger, who inte-grated dance into his portrayal to make the character flighty and whim-sical rather than an outright nance (though some of the critics thought he did too much smirking). And we should note one *By Jupiter* lyric chal-lenging Cole Porter for Gayest Line a Musical Ever Got Away With, in "[Oh, how I miss] The Boy I Left Behind Me," the merry lament of Amazon soldiers. One of them admits, "The girl behind the spear has little sport." She'd be better off in the Navy, she explains, "Because a sailor has a boy in every port!"

Now and again in the 1930s, we find a playwright daring to include the odd gay character. Clifford Odets, a mainstay of the leftwing Group Theatre, turned the nance inside out in *Golden Boy* (1937), set in the boxing world and counting in one Eddie Fuseli a promoter who was crooked, violent, mas-culine . . . and homosexual. Or take Thornton Wilder's *Our Town* (1938). Critics have long thought that the local choir director, Simon Stimson, is gay, though Wilder simply makes him the town drunk, a grouch and a suicide. And Philip Barry's *Here Come the Clowns* (1938) featured a ventriloquist with a termagant wife who lives the life. "She was a sweet kid once," he recalls, but another character replies, "You mean before the girls came around. . . the little ones—the soft ones—the frilly ones—the girly-girls." He does every-thing but call them the femmes to her butch.

It appears that the trick to outwitting the Wales Law was to feature a single gay figure rather than presuppose an entire gay culture. Thus, the gay man or woman would be isolated—harmless, in other words, for there is power only in numbers. That's where Mae West crossed a line: she rev-eled in unveiling gay men's culture (at least as it was supposed to be). And in *The Captive*, the husband of the unseen lesbian speaks, we remember, of a world of "shadows." A world, mind you: an entire population rather than a few . . . what, malcontents? Eccentrics? So the workaround lay in setting a gay character or two against a "normal" heterosexual background.

And it came from England: Mordaunt Shairp's *The Green Bay Tree* (1933). Hearing the plot premise, anyone of today would assume that the show provoked another raid from the authorities: a wealthy gay man buys a young boy from his father to raise him as his ward in a life of aesthetic decadence. Now in his twenties, the boy is so comfortable in his sybaritic lifestyle that he abandons his likeable, sensible fiancée rather than give up his disapproving guardian's largesse.

And there is no way to see the guardian as anything but gay. His name is Mr. Dulcimer, "Dulcie" for short; I mean, come *on*. Shairp describes him as "a man who could fascinate, repel, and alarm," and introduces him arranging flowers and fussing over how they have been cut. More precious yet, he is taking his ward, named Julian, to the opera, but "I never arrive at *Tristan* till the second act." Gracious me, isn't he the aficionado, though, more Wagnerian than thou. Further, Robert Edmond Jones, one of Broadway's go-to designers, created the living room of Dulcie's flat as a kind of lair, with its grand piano, weaving loom, and artisanal lighting.

Note the source of the play's title, in the Old Testament, The Book Of Psalms 37:35: "I have seen the wicked in great power, and spreading himself like a green bay tree." The *wicked*—and after Julian's father shoots Dulcie to death, we see Julian settling into his legacy: to become the next Mr. Dulcimer. The butler (who is also gay) is about to bring in the flowers for Julian to arrange, so we have come full circle. A death mask of Mr. Dulcimer hangs on the wall, and as Julian smokes a cigarette, the lights dim till all we can see is the mask—smiling, by the way—and the tip of Julian's cigarette as the curtain falls.

How on earth did they get away with it? For the show won excellent reviews and enjoyed a five-month run, rather good for the day. Here's the secret: the playwright kept sex entirely out of the very concept of Mr. Dulcimer: his relationship with Julian was, so to say, purely secular. The play's subject is not eros but hedonism. Or so said the critics. The one exception was Robert Garland of the *World-Telegram*, who got to the play a week late. Noting that his colleagues thought *The Green Bay Tree* had "nothing to do with the way of a man with a man," Garland snapped back, "if it has nothing to do with that it has nothing to do with anything."

Noël Coward was responsible for getting the play to Broadway. He urged it upon producer-director Jed Harris and all but demanded that Julian be played by Laurence Olivier, an intimate of Coward's and the male half of the Second Couple in Coward's *Private Lives* in London and New York. Harris acceded to Coward's pleasure; in fact, he ignored *The Green Bay Tree*'s entire West End cast yet hired nothing but Brits for New York. Olivier's then wife, Jill Esmond (who had also been in the New York *Private Lives*), was the fiancée, James Dale Mr. Dulcimer, O. P. Heggie Julian's homicidal father, and Leo G. Carroll (later the befuddled hero of TV's *Topper* sitcom) was Dulcimer's butler. To add to the fun, Jill Esmond was gay, too, though it took her so long to figure it out that it almost doesn't count.

Julian is a much better role than the one Olivier had played in *Private Lives*, yet he still hated the whole thing, partly because Jed Harris was a monster but perhaps also because he felt too close to Julian through a certain lack of interest in sex, as Olivier mentioned in his memoirs. At that, Olivier had his own Mr. Dulcimer—Noël Coward, who developed a tremendous crush on the young actor and had a habit of ordering people around, even to coercing them into joining him in bed. "He can be very persuasive," Olivier warned his son, who shot back, "Did he persuade you?"

Even more successful than *The Green Bay Tree*—in fact a smash, at 691 performances— was Lillian Hellman's *The Children's Hour* (1934). Again, the play presents no gay subculture to antagonize the authorities; there isn't even a gay character in any effective sense for the first two acts. For this play is about not homosexuality but the art of the smear.

Anticipating the guignol frisson of little Patty McCormack's pigtailed serial killer in Maxwell Anderson's *The Bad Seed* (1954), *The Children's Hour*'s brat, Mary, can steal the show from the grownups in any revival. The leads are two youngish women who run Mary's school, the affable doctor engaged to one of them, and Mary's grandmother, the local beldame, who sponsors the school and can at any moment destroy it.

And destroy it she does, when Mary concocts, out of nowhere, the lie that the two schoolmistresses are sexually intimate. By this time in the storyline, we know how evil Mary is, how she manipulates adults and bullies her coevals, and we expect to see the adults tear off her mask.

But no: Hellman creates a superb second-act curtain as Mary threatens a schoolmate who stole another girl's bracelet. Now, this occurs in front of the four principals cited above, and while Mary's direly even tone warns the little thief that jail awaits her if Mary exposes her, the four seniors—in that maddening way that melodrama characters have of not seeing what is right in front of them—simply don't get the story the way we do. We watch in horror as Mary forces the other little girl to support the big lie:

ROSALIE: (*with a shrill cry*) Yes! Yes! I *did* see it. I told Mary. What Mary said was right . . .

And of course the grownups are staring at Rosalie, trying to absorb this. But we in the audience are fixed on Mary, who calmly and with almost expressionless satisfaction sits, mission accomplished. And the curtain falls.

It's a terrific cliff-hanger. Yet Act Three ushers us into a totally different play. The aftermath of the lie finds the old dame with all the power passing the falsehood on to the students' mothers, and they all pull their girls from the school. The two women sue for defamation, but their chief witness ducks out on them and they lose. All because of a lie.

Yes, that much is a plausible outcome. But then Hellman has one of the two women confess that it wasn't a lie: "I have loved you the way they said." Worse, she says she didn't really know till she heard the smear. "A child gets bored and lies," she says, "and there you are, seeing it for the first time." Is something as fundamental as one's sexuality so totally latent that you don't know you're in love with your best friend? You don't even have an inkling?

Of course, the actress can unify the disparate pieces of the play by foreshadowing this confession in subtle ways. Still, it comes out of nowhere, as if from a rejected first draft. Imagine that the work was going to be about lesbians, then the lesbian plot was abandoned for the theme of character assassination, then the lesbian theme was crowbarred back in. It reminds me—sorry, but this will sound bizarre—of Alan Jay Lerner's error, in writing the book of *On a Clear Day You Can See Forever* (1965), of assuming that a woman who has been reincarnated will naturally have ESP as well. However, there is no logical connection between the two.

That said, there is no arguing with a run of twenty months during the Depression. *The Children's Hour* was a sensation, and it even occasioned an intellectuals' querelle when the Pulitzer Prize committee ignored the theatre critics' recommendation of the Hellman to present the Drama award to a "polite" Edith Wharton adaptation. One of the committee even refused to see *The Children's Hour*, period. Nevertheless, Samuel Goldwyn bought the play for the movies.[††]

There was a major Broadway revival, in 1952, when a look at the destructive power of slander was most apropos, especially to the fanatic Stalinist Hellman. She directed the show herself, with Kim Hunter and Patricia Neal

---

[††] Goldwyn, a famous Mrs. Malaprop, loved filming Broadway hits. But when an aide warned him that this particular property involved lesbians (actually just the one), Goldwyn replied, "We can always call them Bulgarians." In the event, we didn't have to, for Hellman's own screenplay heterosexualized Mary's lie, and the film was released as *These Three*, to avoid association with the play's notoriety. A remake in 1962 restored the gay angle and Hellman's original title.

as the teachers and, in her original part, Katherine Emmet (by then seventy years old) as the beldame. The revival played 189 times, a respectable run but probably limited by the public's impatience with the subject matter—no, not the gay subplot. The smear plot. Just a year later, Arthur Miller's now classic tale of McCarthyist witch-hunters, *The Crucible*, suffered the same disappointing run—and Miller wrote of how silently wrathful *The Crucible*'s first-night audience grew once it realized what the story was going to be about.

Some readers may be wondering why the usual professional bigots weren't agitating for more censorship, as the Wales Law clearly wasn't successfully freezing out depictions of gay people. In fact, the bigots had been active throughout the early 1930s, finally reaching a climax when New York State Senator John J. Dunnigan, whom the *Daily News* called "a terrible man," sponsored a bill to create a theatrical censorship tsar, to be not elected but appointed. Herman Shumlin, the producer-director of *The Children's Hour*, mustered the theatre community to stir up resistance, aided by a great influencer, Helen Hayes. Eva Le Gallienne, we know, abhorred what she saw as a mincing, cutesy egotist, yet Hayes was a beloved figure, physically tiny but with the authority of a skyscraper. And when Hayes joined your side in a controversy, your side won: New York's governor, Herbert Lehman, vetoed the bill.

One play that a censorship tsar would have banned was the brothers Leslie and Sewell Stokes' *Oscar Wilde* (1938). London's own censorship tsar, the Lord Chamberlain, refused to license the play, so it had to be shown under private-club status for members only. In New York, however, producer-director Norman Marshall opened *Oscar Wilde* right in the middle of The Street for all to see—and be it said that the Stokeses were very direct in recreating Wilde's gay liaisons, his trials (one suing the Marquess of Queensbury for slander and the second as defendant for "unnatural acts," which resulted in Wilde's sentence of two years of hard labor), and Wilde's last days, in Paris.

So this time a play sited the gay figure not in the hetero world but within a gay subculture, with gay companions, one rent boy, and even a famous (indeed infamous) heterosexual, Frank Harris. Lord Alfred Douglas, son of the Marquess who had defamed Wilde as a sobdomite [*sic*]‡‡ and the favorite of Wilde's inamorati, also appeared, played by John Buckmaster, Gladys Cooper's son. But by far the most successful piece of casting was Robert

‡‡ This misspelling was the Marquess' error. The Stokeses left it out as confusing and irrelevant.

Morley in the title role (which he had created in London), a portrayal that enchanted New York, thus arming the production against bigots' attacks, as Morley's Wilde was the talk of the town, and important New Yorkers were eager to collect it.

Another strength of the show was its sampling of Wilde's famous lines—and the authors invented their own "Wildeisms" in such authentic style that one couldn't tell them apart:

LORD ALFRED: You would not believe what my father has put in this letter.
WILDE: I can believe anything, provided it is quite incredible.

Or, in the first trial, as Wilde, standing in the dock, is asked about the lads he consorts with:

QUEENSBERRY'S DEFENSE ATTORNEY: [This young man] sold newspapers at the kiosk on the pier?
WILDE: This is the first I have heard of his connection with literature.

Above all, the authors rounded out their Wilde so that the text awaited only a performer gifted with Morley's icy filigree in delivering the epigrams—and Morley even looked like Wilde. As the play moved from event to event, one began to notice that Wilde's love of making the important seem trivial and vice versa was a character flaw; it led directly to his catastrophic lawsuit against Queensberry. For when the court found Queensberry correct in calling Wilde a (in the Stokeses' version) "sodomite," it followed that Wilde was guilty of sodomy and must be tried and punished. Alas, when your life is a performance, you fall into the false belief that, when matters get dangerous, you can retire to your dressing room. Wilde retired to Reading Gaol.

The theatregoing community of course knew who Wilde was, but few knew the details of his downfall. So the play sustained suspense during the rather long trial scenes, giving the show extra oomph that enabled it to last 247 performances. True, its use of disconnected events left out too much, less a life than its pieces. And it never got to one of Wilde's spiciest bons mots, when he was arrested and rather roughly handled by the constable. "If this is how Her Majesty treats her prisoners," he said, "she doesn't deserve to have any."

Lord Alfred Douglas was not only a character in the piece but one of its enthusiasts, and he wrote a preface to the published text, pointing out how much was lost in "many masterpieces of dramatic art" by Wilde's brutal punishment and early death. "Let England bear the responsibility," he said, "for what she did to him."

Noël Coward has much in common with Wilde, including a fondness for sassy epigrams and a skill in expanding celebrity into immortality. As John Lahr observes in *Coward the Playwright*, The (so-called) Master "had his first Rolls-Royce at 26 and his first biography at 33," and "he knew what there was to know about stardom." The deft ones manage it, and a just-starting-out Coward schemed that Alfred Lunt and Lynn Fontanne would establish imposing acting brands, marry and work only as a team, and then appear with Coward in a comedy he would write specifically for them, to the point that the three of them weren't in the show. They *were* the show: *Design For Living* (1933).

Ironically, while Coward was openly neither gay nor not gay (his attitude was "You figure it out"), *Design For Living* is almost an explanation of why it's smarter to be gay than straight, at least if one is of the bohemian mind. In his first-night review, the *Times'* Brooks Atkinson noticed that the play gave the three stars supporting characters to play against, because "Mr. Coward needs a few dull persons to victimize": the straights! Here's Lynn on this matter: straight means having children, a permanent address, "social activities," and financial security:

GILDA: Well, I don't like children; I don't wish for a home; I can't bear social activities; and I have a small but adequate income of my own.

Given that "social activities" presumably means the ceremonies of middle-class hetero culture complete with demanding relatives, Gilda is in effect outlining the life of the outlaw: the gay. Gilda is an interior decorator, Leo (Coward) a playwright, and Otto (Lunt) a painter, yet more than artists they're scalawags, scorning the way almost everyone in *Design For Living*'s audience lives. They even seem to change sex partners among themselves— yes, Leo and Otto, too. Yet the show was a smash, a sell-out on its pre-Broadway tour and so SRO that Coward had to break his rule against playing any engagement for more than three months: he extended the run to five out of sheer public-relations appeasement.

One reason so many gay Britons moved to the U.S. was its comparative freedom of expression. The Wales Law didn't threaten *Design For Living*, but back at home the Lord Chamberlain was so reluctant to let Coward get away with this barely encoded slap at "normality" that it didn't play London till 1939, with Diana Wynyard, Anton Walbrook, and Rex Harrison—sharp actors but cast in roles written to exploit the deadly serious whimsy of Coward and his two pals. They're not just shallow: they're *intensely* shallow, because *Design For Living* doesn't run on its content (which is mostly hidden, anyway) but on its original stars' technique, their Wildean ability to utter gleeful drivel as if it were Scripture. In his review, Brooks Atkinson suggested that, in the theatre, "the most trifling things are often the most priceless," and in fact it mattered so little what the three leads were saying that, one night, Coward and Lunt accidentally played almost an entire scene with each speaking the other's lines.

Though English from top to toe, Coward was the first uncloseted Broadway star. Yes, Eva Le Gallienne preceded him—but she didn't project "lesbianism," at least to the untutored eye. Coward, however, didn't look, move, or sound like a straight man. Nor would a straight man have written Coward's operetta *Bitter Sweet* (1929), with its quartet of extremely minty young blades singing, "As we are the reason for the Nineties being gay, we all wear a green carnation."

Yes, it means what you think it means. And would a straight man have conjured up Coward's *Private Lives*, with its—sorry, no other word will do—brittle dialogue, as here between Coward and Gertrude Lawrence, exes meeting on a hotel balcony:

COWARD: [My new wife and I] met on a house party in Norfolk.
LAWRENCE: Very flat, Norfolk.
COWARD: There's no need to be unpleasant.
LAWRENCE: It's no reflection on her, unless of course she made it flatter.

I ask you, is this gay art or not, especially as delivered with a crisp lightness of tone? Modern revivals of Coward's plays are filled with earnest "organic" actors naturalizing the fragile characters; but the style needs the fantastical, the idiosyncratic, the high-strung peacockery of Wonderland.

Thus, *Design For Living* reaffirmed Broadway's first gay era, when the outlaws weren't always closed down. A few even were national figures, especially Alexander Woollcott, whose precise vocation no longer exists, something like unofficial Minister Of Culture. Woollcott's radio show, *The Town Crier*, actually began with the ringing of the bell and a few "Hear ye!"s, for Woollcott was the man with the news: about what books to read, what plays to see, what artists to idolize, and his listeners obeyed as if appeasing a pasha. No one else in America could sell a book or play the way Woollcott could.

He was as gay as a parade of candy canes, in the bitchy-queen style, but he had a cover story: a case of the mumps had supposedly made him asexual. This was medically implausible, but his public was content with the myth while his coterie knew better. Howard Teichmann's character study, *Smart Aleck*, imagines a Woollcott intimate saying, "Aleck Woollcott was a fag but nobody ever caught him."

He was portly and owlish, with his glasses and trademark mustache, yet soft and florid, Humpty Dumpty as a Beanie Baby. Witty, demanding, egotistical, scornful, he seemed always on the verge of a tantrum. Once, over drinks with *New Yorker* writer Corey Ford, Woollcott suddenly announced that he was going to stay at Ford's country place the following week. No one said no to Woollcott, so Ford put a nice face on it with "Well, that'll be nice." And Woollcott thundered, "*I'll* be the judge of *that!*"

A *New Yorker* profile called him "Big Nemo,"[§§] underlining the childish nature of his capers, and, as with Noël Coward, we have an influential figure in American life who in style and tone could not possibly be hetero. It's as though Americans could accept a gay personality whose flamboyance suggested not man-to-man sex but performance art.

And that's how Woollcott's audience finally got a glimpse of him, for playwright S. N. Behrman thought Woollcott so theatrical a creature that he appeared in two Behrman works in tailor-made roles, *Brief Moment* (1931) and *Wine Of Choice* (1938). Yet Woollcott on stage was a disaster, unable to project his voice in those pre-microphone days and so awkward in motion that he played almost all his scenes ensconced on a couch. And the plays themselves were minor Behrman, himself at best a minor boulevardier. Nevertheless, here was Woollcott for his many fans to experience in full true.

Then Moss Hart, who loved basing characters on celebrities (as in the aforementioned *Jubilee*), got an idea. Just as Woollcott burst into the homelife of the hapless Corey Ford, what about a play on that very subject? A comedy, of course, the latest in the series Hart had been writing with George S. Kaufman throughout the 1930s. They favored farce, with a load of characters crashing

---

[§§] After Winsor McKay's famous comic-strip hero Little Nemo, who dreams his way to magical Slumberland, filled with bizarre characters, only to wake up with a bang in the last panel. The suggestion is that Woollcott lived in a kind of fantasy world of eccentrics like himself.

in and out and a plot made of twists and chaos, Woollcott's own favorite environment as long it was he who was in charge.

However, rather than setting a Woollcott amid the culturati, Hart envisioned his monster staying with Midwesterners, unused to the quixotic hurly-burly of the elite. And while celebrifying, Hart added in tintypes of Gertrude Lawrence and Noël Coward. *Oh!*—and Harpo Marx, for a surprise entrance very late in the continuity. And the lead role, named Sheridan Whiteside, would be not merely modeled on Woollcott but a faithful rendition of Woollcott himself: the first time a full-fledged, brilliant, hysterical, bossy northeast urban razzamatazz homosexual queen was the protagonist of a Broadway show.

So Woollcott became *The Man Who Came To Dinner* (1939), in a bravura role seldom offstage in a very long and exhausting part. It's a wildly funny show, because that's what Woollcott was, which is why his friends put up with his implacable need for control. Here's Woollcott—okay, Sheridan Whiteside—making his star entrance, in a wheelchair because he has slipped on winter ice when arriving for dinner. The host family, servants, neighbors, and doctor stand there as The Man slowly surveys the assemblage. Then:

WHITESIDE: I may vomit.

One of the neighbors is so startled that she drops the present she has brought, some calf's-foot jelly:

WHITESIDE: Made from your own foot, I have no doubt.

There's more to the action than the way Woollcott commandeers this bourgeois household for his own subversive uses: his long-suffering, irreplaceable secretary has fallen in love with a local gentleman of the press:

WHITESIDE: I'm afraid you're that noble young newspaperman—crusading, idealistic, dull. [The guy is attractive, and in Woollcott's world, looks count,] Very good casting, too.

As for the secretary, Whiteside has this to say—and note how much he sounds like Michael, the protagonist of *The Boys In the Band*, thirty years later:

WHITESIDE: Don't look at me with those great cow-eyes, you sex-ridden hag.

That last bit is the love tap of the fast-track gay, though Whiteside can be spiteful even with friends—and his plot to destroy the secretary's amour is truly despicable. So Sheridan Whiteside—how well Hart and Kaufman caught the very flavor of Woollcott in that name!—is a rich role. It needs a comic who can play in the grand manner, and when producer Sam H. Harris left the casting to the two authors, they in turn left it to Woollcott.

He suggested John Barrymore—a great idea in theory, as Barrymore in his heyday had the temperament. By 1939, however, this one-time Hamlet was an old souse who couldn't remember two lines together. Woollcott's second choice was Robert Morley (our Oscar Wilde just a few pages ago), but they ended up with Monty Woolley, who had been directing musicals and then got up on stage himself in exotic roles—a quirky Russian in *On Your Toes*, a British royal in *Knights Of Song*. Woolley was perfect—he did the hit movie as well—and he was gay in the first place.

So was Moss Hart, sort of. But unlike Monty Woolley, who was well in with the Cole Porter set, the coterie of anything goes, Hart didn't want to be gay. He even went into psychoanalysis—very offbeat at the time—to find a workaround for it as the dutiful "straight" son to Kaufman, a father figure of crucial import to Hart's self-esteem. And Kaufman hated gays. His daughter, Anne, told me that Kaufman always avoided having to shake hands with the prominent gay director Hassard Short "because my father worried about where those hands might have been."

Researching *Dazzler*, a biography of Hart, Steven Bach spoke to a lifelong Hart intimate, an actor turned psychiatrist named Glen Boles. "Moss," Boles recalled, "was distressed by the occasional involuntary attraction he felt around young actors." And there was one in *The Man Who Came To Dinner*, the extremely handsome Gordon Merrick. (Another actor turned something else, Merrick would have unhappy memories of Hart that he made public, as we'll presently see.)

Even after Hart married and sired children, he was bedeviled by his "shadow" self. As late as the musical *Camelot* (1960), which he directed, Hart shared with Boles his fear of "taking out on [Robert Goulet, the show's Lancelot] how much I resented him for being attractive."

This aside, Moss Hart was a gay (or something related) success story, indeed a dazzler. It was said by the worldly that to get anywhere in New York during its cultural Golden Age, one had to know both gays and Jews, whether to spark a dinner party or to pillage for ideas on everything from how to dress to where to invest one's capital. Hart was one of those whose very appearance for cocktails with his wife, actress Kitty Carlisle, guaranteed a happy evening. He was smart, ambitious, and energetic, qualities common among northeast urban gay men. Today, someone like that would want to direct movies; back then, someone like that would want to enter the theatre.

He died young, because of a heart condition: in 1961, he and Kitty were about to drive somewhere when she heard a thump, as if something had banged against the car's trunk. It was Hart, who had collapsed and never regained consciousness. But he left behind the example of how a gifted young guy pursues destiny and embraces the public life of an artist, becoming a great influencer. People may not think of *The Man Who Came To Dinner* as one of the great gay plays, and of its three progenitors—Hart (whose idea it was), Kaufman (his collaborator), and Woollcott (the play's content), only one-and-a-half were of the tribe. Nevertheless, they remind us that an essential quality of the gay male is his power of observation, developed in youth, when it is necessary to scrutinize hetero models in order to imitate them in protective coloration, to defend oneself from being ostracized.

Woollcott was an observer; it was the most interesting thing about him. His insult comedy was a trivial sort of bonhomie: the real Woollcott is found in his ability to recognize patterns of behavior, almost as a psychiatrist does. He bullied his friends, but he understood his friends. Once, George S. Kaufman was explaining how his then wife, Beatrice, had taken a fancy to young Moss, George's new playwriting partner and thus a constant figure in the Kaufman household, as George almost never wrote a play by himself.

"You know," Kaufman was saying, "Beatrice tends to adopt these sensitive young Jewish boys."

And Woollcott replied, "Sometimes she marries them."

3

The 1940s

The Poet Of Big Characters

The Wales Law had become all but latent till, in 1942, it reared up like a stalking beast to close *Wine, Women and Song*, imprison its producers, and padlock the Ambassador Theatre for nine months. This was not a gay show but rather a salute to vaudeville and (mainly) burlesque, featuring stripper Margie Hart and comics Pinky Lee and Jimmy Savo, who, like their colleagues, had moved to Broadway after the closing of the burlesque houses. It worked for Gypsy Rose Lee, singing "I Can't Strip To Brahms" in *Star and Garter* (1942), a "classy" burlesque revue co-starring Bobby Clark and with some material by Harold Arlen and Harold Rome—top songwriters of proven caliber—that played for eighteen months. But the less "cultured" *Wine, Women and Song* had no such prestige defense.

Now alerted to the perils of the reinvigorated Wales Law, Lee Shubert created a ruckus when a gay show came along in 1944. Or no, not gay as such: more like an American version of *The Captive*. This was Dorothy and Howard Baker's *Trio*, from Dorothy's novel. *Trio* was playing its Philadelphia tryout when Shubert—who had not known what it was about when he pledged his Cort Theatre for its coming New York opening—suddenly panicked. He was right to, perhaps, for it was his playhouse, the Ambassador, that had been padlocked because of *Wine, Women and Song*.

What to do? Shubert was not an idealist but a businessman: he wanted to book *Trio* if it was good for business and terminate his agreement if it wasn't. He knew better than to try a sit-down with the authorities, so he invited New York's seven daily theatre critics to come down to Philadelphia and have a look. They found *Trio* completely lacking in obscenity or degradation: a rather homophobic young man (future movie star Richard Widmark) frees his lady love (Lois Wheeler) from another lady (Lydia St. Clair). One of the reviewers found *Trio* so inoffensive that he suspected a publicity stunt.

That it wasn't. Shubert continued to withhold his playhouses—and the Shuberts owned most of them—so playwright Elmer Rice, who was leasing the Belasco Theatre, offered his stage to *Trio*'s producer, Lee Sabinson. Oddly, the fascists of City Hall did nothing . . . at first. *Trio* opened, played for two months, and then, when Rice's lease was up for renewal, the City Commissioner in charge refused to grant Rice an extension unless *Trio* closed.

So *Trio* was killed, and the partially laissez-faire attitude of the 1930s was now over, probably because wartime always emboldens the censors: when it comes to government, everything is about control, and the governing class can never get enough of it.

Still, gay characters did turn up in a few postwar titles—a lesbian in Jean-Paul Sartre's *No Exit* (1946) and a few gay men in Keith Winter's *The Rats Of Norway* (1948), both foreign imports. Gays even figured prominently in a very strange piece that seemed modeled on the relationship between ballet impresario Diagilyef and his star dancer Nizhinsky. However, their play, *The Dancer* (1946), was no backstager but a murder mystery as the Nizhinsky (played by real-life ballerino Anton Dolin) applied his distinctive modus operandi of breaking backs to a prostitute, to his own wife, and then to the Diagilyef figure, played by Colin Keith-Johnston, whom we last saw tussling with Katharine Hepburn in *The Warrior's Husband*.

These were not successful productions—*Rats* and *Dancer* couldn't run even a week. But Moss Hart had a smash hit with his musical with Kurt Weill and Ira Gershwin starring Gertrude Lawrence, *Lady In the Dark* (1941). This one introduced the nance-like flaming queen to Broadway in Danny Kaye's women's-magazine photographer, as here running in after having just had a shoot with rugged movie star Victor Mature:

KAYE: Girls, he's God-like! I've taken pictures of beautiful men, but this one is the end—the *end*!

As we'll see, it was a provable belief right into the 1980s or later that playing a gay role could destroy an actor's career, albeit more in the movies than on Broadway. But Kaye left *Lady In the Dark* when it went on summer hiatus after five months, first taking a job in the Cole Porter show *Let's Face It!* (1941), then sailing off to Hollywood.*

---

* You can imagine the difficulty management had in replacing Kaye, given how innovatively queeny the role was (in its "real-life" scenes, that is: the character, like other *Lady In the Dark* principals, took on alternate personalities in the show's three dream sequences). Hart's first choice, Rex O'Malley, had just been playing the "Noël Coward" role in *The Man Who Came To Dinner*, as

Hart wasn't done yet with effeminate gays. In *Light Up the Sky* (1948), an *à clef* show-biz comedy, Hart based one character on Mr. Katharine Cornell, Guthrie McClintic, revealed as a simpering dearheart who says, at the slightest provocation, "I could cry." The mischievous Hart gave the role—with the wing-tipped name of Carleton Fitzgerald—to Glenn Anders, a former vigorous romantic lead by then specializing in playing softies.

But what about that famous British play about the closeted gay man whose new marriage is disrupted by the sudden arrival of the ghost of his former love . . . another man? Can even Noël Coward, the author of the piece, get away with this?

All it takes is a little front matter. Just make the former love the ghost of his dead *wife*, and *Blithe Spirit* (1941) will run for nineteen months. (In London, it played for five years.) There is even a hint of the gay husband's psychology when his second wife points out that he has been dominated by women:

CHARLES: You said . . . that I had been hag-ridden all my life! How right you were!

Of course, that is only a theory of how male homosexuality is implanted. But while Coward let another actor create Charles in the London premiere, Coward did take on the role for a time, as well as playing it on the U.K. tour—and Coward was known to some as gay, as we know. So Charles is gay. In New York, he was Clifton Webb, one of the most glass-closeted gays of his era. At that, writers today assume that Oscar Wilde's concept of "bunburying," introduced in *The Importance Of Being Earnest*, is a euphemism for gay lads throwing off their straight personae in rustic frolics with their own kind. And how is *Blithe Spirit*'s inconvenient Return Of The Loved One any different? On one level, all art by gays is gay art; you *mussst* come over!

Indeed, doesn't John Van Druten's work teem with what we might call gay-adjacent titles? English of Dutch descent, Van Druten moved to the U.S. specifically for freedom from the Lord Chamberlain's censorship, most immediately of Van Druten's play *Young Woodley* (1925), about a boarding-school student in love with the headmaster's wife.

John Hoysradt's replacement. O'Malley, who also appeared as the notably fey Gaston in MGM's Garbo *Camille*, should have been a shoo-in, but perhaps he was too suave for *Lady In the Dark's* photographer. Coward would have been, too. When *Lady* reopened in the fall, chorus member Eric Brotherson had been promoted to Kaye's old role

This is arrestingly anticipatory of *Tea and Sympathy* some thirty years later. *Tea* is on the short list of pre-Stonewall gay drama; no college course in the topic would be complete without it—yet *Young Woodley* is forgotten. It did finally get a U.K. booking, in 1928, three years after it played Broadway, but Van Druten was right on principle: better a system in which the theatre community angrily resisted authoritarian rule (as in New York) than a system in which the theatre community cooperated with it (as in London). So Van Druten remained in the U.S. to write for Broadway and became an American citizen, at liberty to spin out his "Yes, I'm not" gayish fare.

Take his *Old Acquaintance* (1940), whose tale of two women aging in frenmity is familiar through the Bette Davis–Miriam Hopkins film and its remake, *Rich and Famous*, with Jacqueline Bisset and Candice Bergen. For one thing, there is the notion of the barbed relationship that turns up later in *The Boys In the Band*, the bond of people isolated from the mainstream who must depend on each other even if one of them is treacherous. Van Druten's two leads are writers of fiction, but one is of niche appeal while her rival is the best-seller of cheesy romance novels.

Then, too, Van Druten created terrific opportunities for strong actresses. On Broadway, Jane Cowl played the artistic one (the Bette Davis role, later on screen) and Peggy Wood the spoiled selfish one, perfect for Miriam Hopkins, who often gave off a narcissistic vibe no matter what she was playing. Pauline Kael said of Irene Dunne that "she does something clever with her teeth that makes you want to slap her." Well, Bette Davis slapped Miriam Hopkins with a resounding crack on this very shoot. Yes, it was in the script. But it's still a "real" moment. To repeat: the gay view of show biz centers on Big Ladies, and not on, for instance, Laurence Olivier or Robert Preston.

This is different from the hetero idolization of women, epitomized in Goethe's apostrophe to Gretchen at the end of Part Two of *Faust*. Gretchen is young, pretty, plunderable; Goethe's idolatry is aligned with the strangely ennobling catharsis of copulation. It gives the poet his contact with the Divine. The gay idolatry, however, looks above all for personality and talent. The gay Gretchen is the Queen of Broadway (Ethel Merman, perhaps) or the greatest pop singer alive (Barbra Streisand, arguably).

Van Druten was definitely writing for gay idols. Consider as well Van Druten's *Make Way For Lucia* (1948), an adaptation of E. F. Benson's wickedly charming novels about two women warring over which of them will run the social life of their English village. They aren't frenemies: the pretentious Lucia (Isabel Jeans) barely hides her scorn for the clumsily upstart

Mapp (Catherine Willard), who ever schemes and invariably fails to bring Lucia down.

And note that Lucia's confederate is a closeted gay man, though the finicky Georgie (Cyril Ritchard, later famed as Mary Martin's Captain Hook, in another of his festively minty renditions) is asexual more than homosexual. And Lucia, she will tell you, is an artist—not at her mediocre piano-playing (she and Georgie duet, which is physically as close as they ever get) but at reigning over a social scene always subject to revolt. To use the symbology of that central gay play *The Boys In the Band*, Lucia is the Michael of her set.

Make Way For Lucia failed badly at 29 performances, too exotically Janeite in its village skullduggery for local tastes. But another Van Druten adaptation, from Christopher Isherwood's so-called Berlin Stories, *I Am a Camera* (1951), made an immortal contribution to the history of the musical in *its* adaptation, *Cabaret*. A gay patina has crept into the material over the years, first in the film of the musical, then in revisions of the musical itself. But note again that Isherwood's saga of a young Briton at loose in the sybaritic chaos of Weimar Germany—"Berlin means boys," Isherwood cried at the time—was closeted in Isherwood's two Weimar novels and Van Druten's adaptation. The Isherwood who tells these tales was gay, but his alter ego (on page and in the theatre) was presented as straight, enchanted by a fascinating woman, Sally Bowles.

So once again we have that unique homosexual character combination, the straight gay, wherein the straight part is a lie and the gay part is latent, peeking around the corner. They meet in the figure of this Sally Bowles, because gay men worship these divas of real life, women with a show-biz charm that has to be written about, filmed, staged. They're so irresistibly theatrical that even before they're cast they're in a show. Theirs.

Julie Harris originated the character in *I Am a Camera*, play and film, and a succession of fizzy personalities followed in *Cabaret*, finding ultimate completion in the film *Cabaret*'s Liza Minnelli. Less a Big Lady than a Big Kid, Minnelli played a Sally with bite, for the *Cabaret* movie was a Bob Fosse presentation, and Fosse liked tension. "Make them fear you," he would tell his dancers, of the audience. "Pick one out and stare at that face till the curtain falls." If it wasn't hostile, it wasn't art.

But Fosse was playful, too, one of the great creators of crazy-fun musical stagings. Think of *Sweet Charity*'s "Big Spender" and *Chicago*'s "Hot Honey Rag." Sometimes it seems as if musical comedy is essentially a gay form;

it's almost shocking to realize that Fosse was not only straight but a relentless hound.

Meanwhile, doesn't anyone want to make a musical out of Van Druten's gayest piece, *Bell, Book and Candle* (1950)? This one's about witches, and as the play unfolds we are hit with the suspicion that these "witches" are really gays. For example, as one character remarks:

They have their regular hangouts—cafés, bars, restaurants.

They have their own outfits, too:

[They] go about dressed up so that people will recognize them.

One thinks of the "clones'" of early Stonewall, in their white T-shirts, jeans, and motorcycle (or bomber) jackets and a bushy yet clipped mustache. Van Druten treats also youth's first stirrings of gay consciousness:

I always knew that I had something, but I thought it was artistic temperament.

The author even locates a temple of the New York congregation:

There's a place on Third Avenue . . .

which, at the time, was where many of the gay bars were located and where hustlers met johns, especially around Fifty-Third Street.

But wait. Couldn't all this be taken literally, as a fantasy about witches? And the answer is: yes, of course. But Van Druten was gay, and gay writers like to write about the world they inhabit and the people they know. It seems likely that Van Druten was using witches to toy with a gay daydream: what if you fell for a man who seemed oblivious and you had only to mutter an incantation to your familiar (in this case a cat called Pyewacket) to make him fall for you? The then-married Lilli Palmer (the witch) and Rex Harrison (her enchanted beau) played the leads, and the hit show sent out a tour with Rosalind Russell and Dennis Price, succeeded by Joan Bennett and Zachary Scott.

And there was a Pyewacket on stage, though animals are notoriously unreliable actors. Once, the cat scratched Palmer. Van Druten, who directed his plays, had a word of advice for anyone else casting a cat: it "should be fed before the performance so that it is in a more tranquil frame of mind." That's good to know.

If Van Druten found a way to bring gay life onto the stage using an evening-long euphemism, Tennessee Williams raised the stakes with at times brutally honest tales that could only have been the work of a gay man and did not euphemize. Williams himself was something of a professional gay, uncloseted in an almost amused way, as if to point out that homophobes are the most boring people in the room, so why would anyone care what they think? Ugh, here comes that dreary Philip Roth again.

Everything amused Williams, it seems, except when it didn't and therefore made him hysterical with paranoia. He could turn against close friends on phantom pretexts and was a perpetual traveler, as if trying to escape himself. If your home is what you are, you can always go to Tunisia, Rome, anywhere. And then you'll be somebody else. And despite his talent—his visionary worldview and lyrical observations make him arguably our most poetic playwright—he would start a script on just a premise without thinking it through first, as if he had to write a play to learn what it was about. This would lead to constant revisions, second and third thoughts forever. Yet when working without the guidance of a sharp director, Williams could end up with a misfire, as with almost all his plays after *The Night Of the Iguana* (1961).

But what creator really wants collaboration from a helpmate? Williams saw life as a battle between the artist and the realist; he, Williams, was the artist and the director was the realist. The latter represents power, materialism, certainty. The artist represents beauty, idealism, wonder. But here's the gay slant: Williams made the comparison physical, erotic, a kind of wrestling match between the top and the bottom.

The classic instance gives us Stanley Kowalski and Blanche DuBois in *A Streetcar Named Desire* (1947). Stanley says, "All right, let's have some rough-house!" Blanche says, "I want magic!" And note the rich symbolism of Williams' title, for New Orleans, the play's setting, does indeed have a trolley line that starts at Canal Street and terminates at Desire Street. And while the trolley takes Blanche to her destination on the literal level—the Kowalski apartment—Williams is mapping Blanche's voyage into a sexual fascination with the brutal but life-affirming Stanley, which will end in rape and madness. But Stanley is irresistible, a type so iconic in gay culture that he claims a taxonomy. The term, as I've said, is "trade." And in the battle between gay and trade, trade always wins.

Theatre buffs enjoy attending different productions of *Streetcar* to collect the various Blanches in their flowery flirtation game with men. Hinting, pushing, goading. The revue *New Faces Of 1952* included Ronny Graham's take-off on an unspecified southern playwright, whose latest heroine ends in tragedy for her terrible sins of "drink, prostitution, and puttin' on a-yuhs [airs]." Well, that's Blanche, and it drives Stanley crazy.

On Broadway in 1992, Jessica Lange, opposite Alec Baldwin, was restrained till the last few scenes, when, eerily, she began to unravel. By comparison, Gillian Anderson with The Young Vic, in the round but on an inane set so tall it had to keep revolving so the public could catch isolated glimpses of the actors, was wildly irritating, concertizing in roulades of fluty laughter till the audience had to feel as antagonized as Stanley.

Avatars of Stanley and Blanche recur throughout Williams, especially in his best-known plays, spanning *The Glass Menagerie* (1945) to *The Night Of the Iguana*, fifteen years later. Oddly (perhaps), Williams' outwardly gay characters are usually offstage (or dead), though the expressionistic *Camino Real* (1953), whose leads bear iconic names—Casanova, Lord Byron, Marguerite Gauthier (the heroine of the play we call *Camille*)—offers Proust's Baron de Charlus, gay in Proust and gay here. He speaks literally of "cruising" and of hoping for a sadomasochistic date with "a wild-looking young man of startling beauty" (as Williams describes him) who has been stalking him.

However, like expressionism itself, this Proustian cameo is exceptional in Williams. Instead, he presents the Beautiful Male figure, invariably straight, unshirting him in accordance with gay demands that show biz enthrall us with fantasy. Looks are not enough: gays (and others) want skin. Thus, in *The Milk Train Doesn't Stop Here Anymore* (1963), a professional widow living in an Italian villa is visited by "the Angel of Death," a handsome poet and mobilist who is seen napping naked in a grandiose bed with the blanket turned well down as the woman and her sidekick, "the Witch of Capri," coo over him. Paul Roebling, the most beautiful specimen in town, played the young visitor, and when the lights came up on the bedroom scene, the audience suddenly got very quiet.

The play itself was one of those unfinished pieces Williams would offer for production before they were ready, though it skated through the playwright's very serious thoughts on the mystery of death. Hermione Baddeley and Mildred Dunnock were wonderful as the two old women, but the gnomic script baffled them along with the audience, and director Herbert Machiz was no help to anyone.

The show flopped. It was a serious setback for Williams, as it began his "second act" of one ghastly bomb after another because the scripts were not fully developed. Rather, they were feral imaginings of a poet under the control of alcohol-drenched pharmacopeia. Or, to use strict academic terminology, he was stoned out of his mind, now protected only by interest in his older work. He had become the author of revivals.

Bizarrely, David Merrick decided to bring back *The Milk Train* just a year after its failure—not in a regional or other perhaps specialized theatre but right back again on Broadway, this time with Tallulah Bankhead and Tab Hunter. And now it *really* flopped. "The original production," Williams told James Grissom for *Follies Of God*, "possessed an ornate and absurd set, and the revival possessed an ornate and absurd cast." More absurd yet was the director, Tony Richardson, who reportedly ignored the struggling Bankhead while pursuing Hunter on- and offstage.

But then, Williams had made the Beautiful Male a fixture in Drama, whether as Marlon Brando casually changing shirts or Paul Newman (in *Sweet Bird Of Youth* [1959]) lounging in open-topped silk pajamas or Tab Hunter as a Europe bum who escorts rich women to a splendid death.

The Beautiful Male was, in fact, a figure that show biz had been flirting with all its life in one form or another; if Broadway could stage *Tarzan Of the Apes* (1921) with the hero in leopard-skin shorts, what couldn't Broadway show?

Now actors began to adopt weightlifting programs to enhance their appeal, and directors made the male torso a decoration of their stagings, most notably Joshua Logan, who turned the return of sailors from a rowdy shore leave in *Mister Roberts* (1948) into an eyeful of shining young men in various states of undress. They included an almost naked Ralph Meeker, Henry Fonda's understudy in the title role and one of the exponents of the new style in masculinity, less authoritative and more physical—from, say, Walter Huston to Marlon Brando.[†]

[†] Logan, an obsessed aficionado of the male physique, reached an acme of sorts in the locker-room scene in the Ray Bolger college musical *All American* (1962), showing footballers in shorts strutting about and creating a human pyramid. These were not traditional chorus boys but, if you will, "real" men, a strange patina to add to a foofoo musical comedy like *All American*. And back at *Mister Roberts*, Logan testosteroned up the sequence of the shore-leave return by hauling the sailors onto the set all jumbled up in a cargo net as if they were freight. None of them was wild about it, so when it came time for the "practical," Logan and his coauthor, Thomas Heggen (who wrote also the source material), had to ride in it themselves first, to allay fears.

Not surprisingly, Meeker played Stanley Kowalski, in the last seven months of its run and on tour. He was roughly handsome and fit, with a working-class charm tinged with menace: Broadway's New Man. Still, the immortal—meaning unchallengeable—Stanley is Marlon Brando, always thought of as America's greatest actor, the one that got away (from the stage). But his power lay in more than his hair-trigger instincts, his danger. There's a story that a college class in film history, about to screen the *Streetcar* movie made with most of the Broadway cast (though Vivien Leigh replaced Jessica Tandy's Blanche), told the professor that they knew Marlon Brando only from *The Godfather*, in his broken-down seniority. So when, early on in the *Streetcar* film, Brando changed his shirt, baring his torso, the class gasped at his physical beauty.

And speaking of another Brando role, in the movie *The Fugitive Kind* (from Williams' play *Orpheus Descending*), critic Foster Hirsch spoke of "this very Williamsesque male prostitute, this angel of mercy whose body affords mystical ecstasy . . . his torso arched in hustler-like poses."

Then, too, Williams wrote Stanley as a combination of tenderness and rage, an alpha male who has as much love in him as bluster—and a sense of humor as well. In fact, Williams saw *Streetcar* as a kind of disturbed comedy in which the fun is vexed by Blanche's specious rhapsodies about gentlemen callers and glamorous yacht trips. Attending various *Streetcar* productions, Williams used to annoy his neighbors by laughing at many of Stanley's lines, as when the unpacking of Blanche's trunk reveals ropes of pearls. "What is she," he asks, "a deep-sea diver?" It sounds like a line Neil Simon would use; I can hear Lou Jacobi's sarcasm in the very words.

In all, Stanley Kowalski was a Big Character, fascinating, rich, and dense, important in his realm, and irresistible to comparable Big Actors. The type was endemic to the ancient Greeks because of the grandeur of the subject matter and common in Shakespeare because of the magnificence of the poetry, but is relatively rare on the middle-class stage. That may be why Eva Le Gallienne favored the classics, as that's where we find many Big Characters. Eugene O'Neill has them, of course; he forced the issue by writing Big Plays—and of Williams' contemporaries, Arthur Miller and Edward Albee have a few.

Williams' own plays, however, are usually premised around Big Characters whose lives turn on sex and violence. *Streetcar* has a great deal of it, especially when the top shows the bottom who's boss. I once asked a friend, a gay escort, what his clients were looking for. He was a Big Character too, at least physically, and he said, "They all want to be kidnaped." Further, most of the outstanding gay artists, from Tom of Finland to A. Jay, focused on coercive sex. Comparably, when Stanley rapes Blanche, he "excuses" it with "We've had this date with each other from the beginning." And in Williams' *Suddenly, Last Summer* (1958), half of the off-Broadway double-bill *Garden District*, a major gay character (as usual off stage) is torn to pieces by a mob of hustlers. This was rash storytelling for the time, but Williams wasn't interested in the stately, reasoned-out themes of the well-made play. He once likened an evening of Ibsen to "eating a box of soap flakes."

Certainly, *Cat On a Hot Tin Roof* (1955), Williams' second-longest-running title and by now as popular in revival as *Streetcar*, is filled with Big Characters speaking in a highly inflected southern lingo. There is also another gay figure who is unseen (in fact deceased) yet a kind of Damocles Sword hanging over the action. The dead Skipper confessed his love to his best friend, Brick, who then ghosted him, causing Skipper's suicide. So haunted with guilt that he drinks as if working on his own suicide, Brick becomes an almost wholly passive character: an enigma. Because he repulsed Skipper out of homophobia . . . or gay panic.

Williams had been uncomfortable with the production and even with Elia Kazan, his most sympathetic director. Until the sensational Philadelphia tryout, Williams hadn't even liked the cast: Ben Gazzara as Brick; Barbara Bel Geddes as his wife, Maggie "The Cat"; folk singer Burl Ives as Big Daddy, gargantuan in both physique and temperament; Mildred Dunnock as the now fluttery, now steely Big Mama;‡ and Pat Hingle and Madeline Sherwood as Big Daddy's bitter, scheming older son and the son's vicious wife, the resonantly named Gooper and Mae.

They are like a dog pack fighting over a bone, yet Kazan felt the script went lame in the third and final act. For one thing, Maggie was too mean, though Kazan knew the audience would want to like her. And when Big Daddy accused Brick of being more or less Skipper's murderer, Brick retaliated by "murdering" Big Daddy: revealing that he is just about to die of cancer. Bellowing like a rabid beast, Burl Ives lurched offstage as the act curtain fell, and in Williams' script he never appeared again.

Impossible, Kazan told Williams. It breaks the First Rule Of Theatre: Exploit Your Stars. Ives was simply too Big not to take part in the third act. Further, Maggie needed to end the evening by reconciling with her estranged

‡ Fun Fact: She is universally called this by everyone, but she actually has a name: Ida.

husband, her Brick, so dear and so angry. As for him: why did he spend all of that last act just moping around without driving the action? In a letter, Kazan wrote, "God, Tenn, can't we bring that son of a bitch to life?"

How important was he? We never learn if he's gay or not, but then we never learn much about Brick in the first place. It's worth noting that, central as he is—and he is as well the Beautiful Male, spending the entire show in pajamas[§]—the role itself seemed so "lesser" in 1955 that the print ads gave top billing to Bel Geddes, then (in descending order) Burl Ives, "the Elia Kazan production of," the play's title, Williams' byline, Mildred Dunnock, and only then the Brick, Ben Gazzara, though he did get an "and" first.

Despite *Cat*'s success, Williams was not content with the revised Act Three—the "Kazan version"—because Williams felt Maggie and Brick were not reconcilable. It was the gay subplot, the suicide of Skipper, that got in Maggie's way, for she had tested his masculinity by bedding him, disastrously. As Williams saw it, the audience shouldn't want to like Barbara Bel Geddes. He had created too Big a heroine, too ambitious and guilty. It was she who killed Skipper, not Brick.

Then, too, as Williams saw the play's continuity, there was nothing left for Big Daddy to do after hearing his death sentence. Still, as long as he had to compromise his vision, Williams used designer Jo Mielziner's thrust stage to bring Big Daddy way down in front, almost into the public's lap, to tell an obscene joke about a zoo elephant getting a hard-on for a female. A child asks his mother what that strange, protruding object is, and she, unsure how to explain erections to a youngster, replies, "Oh, that's nothin'!" And here's the punchline:

BIG DADDY: His Papa said, "She's spoiled!"

The point of the episode was to show Big Daddy in fact playing the joke entirely to Brick, to emphasize their bond, in effect locking Maggie out of her intimacy with the husband who can't forgive her for killing his gay friend— because he, too, is guilty of that kill. Her act is his act, which shows us how complex the play's psychology is.

As for the joke itself, it was considered so shocking in 1955 that, two weeks after the opening, Williams had to put something less arresting in that slot,

---

[§] Modern productions prefer him topless, and at Britain's National Theatre, in 2017, both Brick (Jack O'Connell) and Maggie (Sienna Miller) each tried a bit of nudity.

to placate the city license commissioner. Still, *Cat*'s "elephant joke" became so notorious that *Theatre Arts*' critic Maurice Zolotow accused *Cat* of having been written "not by Tennessee Williams but by Stanley Kowalski." *Cat*, he went on, was "ugly, primitive, crude" and its characters were "faked for melodramatic effect."

The London *Cat* couldn't play at all till the Comedy Theatre reformatted itself as The New Watergate Club, giving performances for members only. Arthur Miller's *A View From the Bridge*—another piece with homoerotic vibes—took in thirteen thousand paying guests in the same "membership" protocol, but *Cat* brought in five times that. Our own Kim Stanley played Maggie, to Leo McKern's Big Daddy, while the inexperienced Paul Massie played Brick. But that's what director Peter Hall wanted in the part: someone naive rather than jaded: an innocent in the "I want magic!" role. Hall's company played Williams' original Act Three, not the Kazan-ordered revision, though both scripts use almost the same words at the very end, as top Maggie is tender with bottom Brick:

MAGGIE: Oh, you weak, beautiful people who give up with such grace . . .

So almost everyone in *Cat* except Brick is Big, and the last of Williams in his prime, *The Night Of the Iguana*, attracted the participation of one of the Biggest Ladies in American show biz: Bette Davis. As Maxine Faulk, the proprietor of a seedy Mexican hostel, Davis somewhat anticipated the raucous yet loving Martha of Albee's *Who's Afraid Of Virgina Woolf?* one year later.

Apparently, Davis didn't realize that the play was about not Maxine but the other three principals, broken-down tour guide Shannon (Patrick O'Neal) and the I Want Magic! figure of a sketch artist (Margaret Leighton) taking care of her ninety-seven-year-old poet grandfather (Alan Webb, many years before this one of Noël Coward's most enduring romances). If anyone can steal a show from Bette Davis, it's a ninety-seven-year-old blind poet—who, furthermore, gets to die onstage. This is not even to mention Leighton's very touching character, reaching at one point a key speech that left the Royale Theatre rapt in awe the day I saw it.

There was less sex and violence in this one, and the Beautiful Male was not much more than an extra, one of a vacationing German family. He was actor Bruce Glover (father of actor Crispin Glover), who gymmed up for the obligatory shirtless appearance—in fact, strutting in with his family in beach togs, which Williams directed to be a "Wagnerian nightmare."

It was not long in the rehearsal stage before Davis noticed that though her part was showy and set her off quite well physically in her tropical outfits, the others had The Roles. So she started acting up and looking for all sorts of ways to become impossible. Yet she was essential, being the production's box-office insurance.

We like to think of our greatest actors as valiant troupers—Eva Le Gallienne and Katharine Cornell were. But Davis was such a beast that she got *Iguana*'s director, Frank Corsaro, fired—and Corsaro was as expert as Kazan in plays like these. O'Neal became so maddened by Davis' antics that during one rehearsal he attacked her with his hands on her throat, and in the end she did open the show but left prematurely, as always when venturing into what Arlene Francis on *What's My Line?* would lovingly call "the legitimate the-atre." Davis' perennial excuse: illness. On the revue *Two's Company* (1952), her previous Broadway appearance, she blamed that rare malady Shut Up I'm Quitting Syndrome. On *Iguana*, it was a bad case of The Audience Wants Me To Failitis.

These Big characters were as basic to Williams' art as was his wish to delve into gay material, though less in gay people than a gay worldview of tops and bottoms, of Marlon Brando's bared torso and Blanche DuBois' hunger for the fabulous that we hear in "I want magic!" Williams' career was extraordinary in its first half, which helped lead on to the Stonewall Rebellion and gay civil rights, even if Williams himself had no apparent politics. But his second half, enfeebled yet inflamed by the drugs and alcohol he was virtually living on, obscures the heroism and vision of his youth.

Eva Le Gallienne saw it coming. "He didn't believe in the pragmatic habit," she told James Grissom. "He was like [his characters] who wanted magic, who got lost in dreams. We all know what happens to people who descend into magic, don't we?"

Grissom said he didn't.

Le Gallienne: "They disappear."

4

The 1950s

The Body Beautiful

Many years ago, a wise old queen told me that gay was invented in 1956, during Tallulah Bankhead's limited engagement of *A Streetcar Named Desire* at New York's City Center. Bankhead's Blanche DuBois was so potently homosocial that everyone who attended these performances was instantly struck gay, never to return. This included the candy sellers and ushers and, on Tallulah's good nights, even pedestrians passing outside the theatre.

But what of Oscar Wilde? Noël Coward? Even, say, Achilles and Patroclus?

"Performance art," the queen replied, dismissively. "Stylists. Phantoms." Not till gay favorite Tallulah met the most gay-related character in theatre history did the stars align proactively.

At the least, it was splendid casting, Blanche DuBois as the ultimate—as they were called then—"fag hag." Granted, Tallulah was an unusually strong-willed Blanche, not at all the traditional languid dreamer. The anonymous *Theatre Arts* reviewer covering the production felt "some of the nebulous shadings of Blanche's immensely complex character . . . were lost," and he thought Tallulah's "suggestion of a sense of humor" was way off for a figure embracing subterfuge and phony grandeur. Still, "the impact of the play came across," and when Blanche sent the antagonistic Mitch packing, Tallulah "gave it a fury" in "a moment to be remembered" as never before. Wrong or right, "This time Kowalski almost met his match."

Well, of course: Tallulah in general was boisterous, witty, reckless, fascinating, and thoroughly original, a real-life Big Character. Though bisexual, she married actor John Emery, and, one night out on the town, she insisted on picking up another man when Emery wanted to go home. By Tallulah's clock it was never too late for carousing, so as Emery stomped out of their cab, leaving his wife and the pickup behind, Tallulah called out, "Dahling, if I'm not home by five, start without me."

Impetuous, unreliable, droll—and all of it came through onstage, so when Thornton Wilder had Tallulah's Sabina in *The Skin Of Our Teeth*

(1942) open the show by ranting at the audience about how much she disliked the play, the public was bound to think that Tallulah was ranting for real. But *Skin* was a crazy romp; what of Tallulah in more stately work? "No intelligent playwright ever trusted her," Tennessee Williams told James Grissom, "because her pact was with the public." Especially the gay public, for whom Tallulah would give what critic Foster Hirsch termed a "coterie performance," tilted toward her supporters. "So exciting for the boys," Williams noted. And what presence she had: "She could upstage a crucifixion with the right dress."

Really, Tallulah was a magician, for—like Gertrude Lawrence—she had only to enter for everyone else onstage to be rendered invisible. But there was a catch to all this, because her gay fans treated her shows interactively, letting out gales of laughter at any line or gesture that could be received as a reference to anything from sex to booze. And the laughter wasn't random, as at a comedy. It was forced, a demonstration that the gay public understood more than the rest of the audience.

I heard this kind of laughter only once, at the old Met in 1964, when the curtain rose on the second act of Gian Carlo Menotti's *The Last Savage*. Two tailors were fitting the savage—bass-baritone George London—for his first suit, and as one called out London's expansive chest measurement, some five or six unmistakably gay voices deliberately shrieked in delight.

One could argue that this was a sign of rebellion, a pre-Stonewall manifestation of political defiance of the culture's entrenched bigotry. But it was a distraction to both performers and public, and by the time Tallulah got to that *Streetcar* revival, the laughter had the effect of sabotage. At one of her *Streetcar*s, Tallulah actually dropped character and stepped forward to say (as her biographer Joel Lobenthal quotes it), "Will you please, please give me a chance!" Further, Lobenthal interviewed cast member Frances Heflin for his book, and she recalled that the carnival atmosphere "broke her heart. She never did get over it."

Most actors are remembered in any real sense only if they leave a legacy of filmed performances. Alas, Tallulah's universally admired Regina Giddens in *The Little Foxes* (1939) went to Bette Davis in the movie. Nevertheless, Tallulah left behind such a potent myth that show-biz aficionados know her well. Playwright Doric Wilson used to dine out on the tale of when he was in a gay bar called Le Faison d'Or (The Golden Pheasant) and heard somebody behind him imitating Tallulah, with the bass voice and "Dahlings" and the strangely glamorous grotesquerie.

"That is the worst Bankhead imitation I have ever heard!" Wilson cried, turning around and facing, to his shock, the lady herself. "Re-ah-ly, Dahling?" she said. "I rather thought I had it down by now."

Everybody did, because it was so thick with mannerisms, so expectedly unpredictable. "Tallulah Bankhead the Incomparable" is how the City Center *Streetcar* posters billed her, and when she wasn't camping, she was a marvelous actress. But she did camp. Oddly, when rehearsing she set her madcap style aside, the total pro—as long as a strong director was in charge, such as Herman Shumlin on *The Little Foxes*. But with Tony Richardson on that revival of *The Milk Train Doesn't Stop Here Anymore*, Tallulah was in trouble.

Tracking down many *Milk Train* participants for his biography, Joel Lobenthal found them all defending Tallulah's helplessness in the face of a director who openly scorned her, not least for her early career as a star of light comedy in London in the days of Somerset Maugham. All that was worthless frivolity to Richardson, busily engaged in the nobler pursuit of getting into Tab Hunter's pants. Marian Seldes—everyone's favorite historical witness because she was smart, fair, and pleasant—had an important supporting role in this *Milk Train* that gave her a lot of stage time with Tallulah, and she told Lobenthal that Richardson waved away Tallulah's questions with "You're the actress." Then why have directors at all?

Even in specialized work that called for her unique improvisations, her campy chalumeau register, and "Dahlings," Tallulah was a legend fighting for life. Playing sketch comedy, singing (though she really couldn't), and cutting up, she served as emcee of a resuscitated *Ziegfeld Follies* in 1956, an elaborate production with a huge cast taking in not only singer Joan Diener and jokester David Burns but a chorus including Larry Kert, Beatrice Arthur, and Julie Newmar. The notion of Tallulah's hosting a variety show was so logical that, a few months later, *New Faces Of 1956* adopted it using a drag queen, T. C. Jones, "as" Tallulah. *New Faces* ran long enough to make an impression and get a cast album, but the real Tallulah and her fifty-six-person company shut down in Philadelphia without reaching Broadway.

What made this actress such a gay icon, not just for professional queens demonstrating at her *Streetcar* but gay men generally to this day? The answer is personality, of course, and everyone, straight or gay, reacts to that. But read how Tallulah herself defined it in her autobiography (cowritten with Richard Maney, and a huge bestseller, by the way): "inner fire, competitive spirit, defiance of the norm, solo effort," and, perhaps especially, "showmanship, in the ability to transform a liability into an asset." That isn't just "personality." That's the gay way of life, not least in "defiance of the norm."

Then, too, Tallulah maintained a strong association with camp humor. This is a difficult topic to pin down, as Susan Sontag inadvertently proved in her essay "Notes On Camp." It's a bold stab or a misfire, depending on one's view, as everybody recognizes the finished product of camp but nobody agrees on what the ingredients are.

Further, is camp under the control of the artist or is it the public that decides what's camp? Because even while *seemingly* enjoying the gig as proprietrix of the *Follies*, Tallulah knew that it wasn't how her career was supposed to have matured. She was trapped in dead ends—in TV one-offs and summer tours of tents and barns. "It's this or debtor's prison," she would explain; but what do these people do with all the money they earn when they're hot? That humiliating *Milk Train* revival, a run of 4 performances, was her last job on Broadway, and four years later she was dead.

Yet the City Center *Streetcar* was to have rehabilitated Bankhead's reputation; it would have moved to Broadway if the *Follies* contract hadn't tied her up. She really thought that a great role in a great play would save her sinking career. And there was wonderful Tennessee telling her how marvelous she was while telling everyone else she was wrecking his play.

To see Tallulah in her last days, one would think she was still getting a kick out of life, camping everything up because Tallulah is fun and camp is fun: a marriage. Still, you can be as much a victim of your coterie as its mistress: Lobenthal reports that, at the *Streetcar* opening-night cast party, with the laughter of the peanut gallery still echoing in Tallulah's ears, one of the party guests happened to walk past a room where Tallulah was hiding, to keep everyone from seeing her cry.

Tallulah had many affairs with women over the years, including even Eva Le Gallienne, an important historical link. Nevertheless, Tallulah's valence as a gay icon lies specifically in her appeal to gay men, as a contributor to the spirit of liberation. It's all but impossible to state why certain Big Ladies are so resonant with gays, though the element common to them all is talent. These are super-charged performers, taking us out of the cares of the day into the extraordinary. For straight men, this figure is about youth and beauty: again, Goethe's Gretchen, a poetic interpretation of the excitement of sex. But for gay men, the figure is about genius and fantasy.

And yet the camp thing is always lurking nearby; it is difficult to imagine gay art without it. Consider two pastiche musicals from this era, the British import *The Boy Friend* (1954) and the operetta spoof *Little Mary Sunshine* (1959). Each was the work of one gay man, respectively Sandy Wilson and Rick Besoyan, writers with the smart gay's typical powers of observation (especially of the workings of show biz). *Little Mary Sunshine*, a kind of *Rose-Marie* set in Colorado, offers not only a "Colorado Love Call" (to match *Rose-Marie*'s "Indian Love Call," including its melismas, as on "When I'm calling you-oo-oo-oo, oo-oo-oo"), but also mock-ups of numbers in *Florodora*, *Music In the Air*, *The Firefly*, *Madame Sherry*, and so on. *The Boy Friend* is comparable in its replica of a twenties musical comedy, and in both shows the characters utter bizarrely silly spoken lines.

But there is no camping. A note in *Little Mary*'s published script warns that "it should be played with the most warm-hearted earnestness" and everyone "should appear to believe in the perfect sincerity of their words and actions." Thus, when Little Mary's Corporal Billy Jester of the Forest Rangers (like unto *Rose-Marie*'s Mounties) is to undertake a suicide mission:

CAPTAIN JIM: You'll be a hero, Corporal.

BILLY: Me, sir?

CAPTAIN JIM: If it works.

BILLY: Are you sure some of the other fellows don't want to come along? I don't want to hog all the glory.

Yet the actors aren't playing in inverted quote marks or signaling to the audience that they're ribbing the material. The writing is playful rather than derisive.

Ironically, *The Boy Friend*'s American production office, (Cy) Feuer & (Ernest) Martin, decided that Wilson's gentle satire, faithfully curated by its original director, Vida Hope, would confuse American audiences, and Feuer stepped in to gag up the proceedings during the tryout. When Wilson and Hope objected, they were banned from the theatre, then found that critics and the public liked Feuer's version. *The Boy Friend* was a hit, not least because it revealed a new star in Julie Andrews, who turned eighteen after midnight of the premiere.

Trapped in a success, Wilson and Hope offered diplomatic remarks for PR purposes. Wilson's, quoted in *Theatre Arts*, ran as "Miss Hope was convinced that Messrs. Feuer and Martin know exactly what's required for New York."

Feuer jiggered *The Boy Friend*'s tone, but he stopped short of wholly camping it. No, that was a job for Ken Russell, directing *The Boy Friend*'s 1971 film version with his characteristic madcap overkill. Russell built a structure around Wilson's little valentine, catching a matinee of a third-rate English provincial *Boy Friend* tour; and a Busby Berkeley–like director's imagining what he could do with the numbers in his *Boy Friend*; and the backstage lives of the cast. The boys are femme, the girls are twisted, the actor-manager (Max Adrian) is a vain loser, and only the sweethearts (Christopher Gable, Twiggy) are sincere. It's a giddy assault on everything *The Boy Friend* believes in while pretending to like *The Boy Friend*: absolute camp.

Isn't camp a style unique to gay artists? Can creators like Russell take it on? Or do straights operate their own kind of camp?

But then, what is camp, anyway, beyond the "You know it when you see it" definition? We saw it starting back in the time of the first Broadway *Boy Friend* and off-Broadway's *Little Mary Sunshine*, for midway between them appeared one of the gayest shows of all time—gay in spirit and the way some gay men in particular adopted the mannerisms of its protagonist. The show was *Auntie Mame* (1957), drawn by the team of Jerome Lawrence and Robert E. Lee from Patrick Dennis' novel and directed by Morton Da Costa but above all starring Rosalind Russell. Broadway's most expensive straight play to that time because of all the scenery and costumes, *Auntie Mame* was the whirlwind adventure of a bohemian eccentric who is scatterbrained yet strangely right about everything as she raises an orphaned nephew while warring against babbitts and bigots.

Incredibly charming (and not least in Russell's portrayal), Mame is also a phony, role-playing when necessary, as in a southern excursion to nab a rich husband, and she adheres to the gay credenda of partying while staying thin, as when her young nephew startles her awake one morning:

MAME: Ask Ito to bring me a very light breakfast: black coffee and a sidecar. And you might ask him to fix something for your Aunt Vera: I hear her coming to in the guest room.

Whom does this remind you of? Isn't there more than a dash of the madcap yet ultimately persuasive Big Ladies we meet in Muriel Spark's *The Prime Of Miss Jean Brodie* (1961) and Graham Greene's *Travels With My Aunt* (1969), both filmed with a Mame alter ego, Maggie Smith? And note that one could easily see the younger Maggie Smith playing Auntie Mame but difficult to imagine Rosalind Russell as Jean Brodie or Aunt Augusta. Clearly, as time passed, the "Mames," so to say, became flightier, even . . . effeminate. The original Mame, by comparison, is almost butch.

Still, in any form Mame is the gays' best friend, as her life's motto of "Life is a banquet" comes off as "Live and let live." Dennis' novel even alludes at one point to Mame's "queer friends on Fire Island," and Mame calls them "some of the most amusing boys."* Further, some of the play's creatives were gay.

Auntie Mame's link with Patrick Dennis is especially relevant, as his novels tended to include at least one major gay character. And one of Dennis' books, the faux-movie-star autobiography of one Belle Poitrine (literally "beautiful bosom") called *Little Me,* was heavily illustrated with crazy photographs, many devoted to a character named Letch Feeley, a gym beauty who, as Belle's Hollywood co-star, appears with her in *Paradise Lost,* a filming of Milton. (Belle thinks it's his first name.) *Little Me* then offers a still from the movie, a sequence in the Garden of Eden with our Adam and Eve biting into the apple. They are completely nude with fig leaves obviously applied after the shot was taken, and this picture of Mr. Feeley left a powerful impression on three generations of gay men. Appearing in 1961, *Little Me* was another "piece of the puzzle" presaging the Stonewall Rebellion of 1969 and the sudden emergence of gay—the "shadow world" in *The Captive*—into sunlight.

There were Letch Feeleys live on Broadway, too, for (as I've said) New York's part-time bartenders and short-haul movers took up weightlifting to secure roles that demanded muscle appeal. Casting the musical *Wish You Were Here* (1952), about a grownups' summer camp and featuring an actual swimming pool, director Joshua Logan told the auditioning Thomas (later Tom) Tryon, "You can't sing, you can't dance, and you can't act. But with a body like yours, you're just what this production needs."

John Perkins, also in the show, had a speaking part as Harry "Muscles" Green, the campus athlete; he posed in swimming trunks with the campus flirt, Sheila Bond, for the show's poster, sheet music, cast album, and souvenir book, later going Euro-art in nothing but skimpy, low-waisted trousers for Jean Genet's *The Balcony* off Broadway in 1960 as the Executioner. And six foot five John Granger was another off-Broadway executioner in a European title, in 1962, in Michel de Ghelderode's *Hop, Signor!,* hotting up the stage in his white tights with white jacket open to the waist.

---

* "Queer," in those days, was a rude derogation; Mame herself wouldn't use the term. Note that these two bits I have quoted are from the novel and do not appear in the play.

Skin was everywhere all of a sudden. When the Provincetown Playhouse staged Robinson Jeffers' version of Euripides' *Hippolytus* (1954), retitled *The Cretan Woman*, there was such public interest that the limited engagement was extended, either because of Jeffers' new slant on the ancient tale (his Hippolytus rejected Phaedra not out of moral scruple but because he was gay) or because the Hippolytus, William Andrews, was irresistibly fetching in his peplum, cape, and sandals laced to the knee with no shirt.

Those not into Greek tragedy could try a boxing musical, *The Body Beautiful* (1958), with Steve Forrest having weight-trained for the lead. And as the MOAB of gay skin shows, *Li'l Abner* (1956) offered a pride of professional bodybuilders in posing shorts, making their first entrance strutting to music that sounded like the offspring of a gavotte and the missionary position.

Not surprisingly, there was a near-simultaneous reflection of all this on television, where ABC developed a group of western and private-eye series that reveled in shirtless hunks. Usually, of each show's stars, one in particular could be counted on for skin—Robert Conrad of *Hawaiian Eye*, Van Williams of *Surfside 6*, Ty Hardin of *Bronco*, and that towering inferno Clint Walker of *Cheyenne*. This sort of thing reached an apex in CBS' *The Wild Wild West* (1965–1969), with Robert Conrad again, dressed (although in the 1870s) in suits made of tight matador pants and a bolero jacket cut short at the waist, to display Conrad's spectacular bottom, tight and tempting. Many a gayling out of puberty first realized *what gay is* while gazing upon Conrad's rear, and a superb cut torso completed the picture when Conrad, subdued by bad guys, was revealed bound and shirtless, though why the crooks wasted time getting his clothes off was never explained.

With its penchant for macabre villains (one episode featured a troupe of homicidal marionettes), idiotically unbelievable plots, and screwy sci-fi gadgets, *The Wild Wild West* was if nothing else picturesque. However, its high-pitched violence made it the network's albatross, controversial yet too successful to cancel—though after four years of angry criticism, possibly motivated as much by the gay flavor as by the rough stuff, the network terminated the series. As the show's creator, Michael Garrison, was reputedly gay (though married and a father), *The Wild Wild West*'s continued life on DVD is a monument to the homoeroticism that was exploding in our popular arts in the years running up to Stonewall.

Meanwhile, and in sync with all this, was the output of Daniel Blum, who issued illustrated books on the theatre that somehow always found the cutest guys wearing not a whole lot. Blum's annual, *Theatre World*, would go to such absurd lengths in this that one photograph of the musical *Kismet* (1953) concentrated on famed muscleman Steve Reeves. True, he was in the show, though his work over the course of the evening amounted to little more than . . . well, appearing nearly naked in *Theatre World*.

Clearly, there was now a gay presence behind the scenes in the culture, suggesting, revealing, implying. Blum even included, in his *Great Stars Of the American Stage* (1952), the young actor Charles Nolte, though by then Nolte had been on Broadway in only two small roles and one lead, the title role of *Billy Budd* (1951), from Herman Melville's novella about a young foretopman of "strength and beauty combined" and the very essence of goodness. Melville gives Billy's type as "the Handsome Sailor," but he's far more than a work of art: "Ashore he was the champion; afloat the spokesman." Yet he has an Achilles heel, a stutter that paralyzes him when confronted by a deceitful aggressor.

Physically, Nolte's type was Big Blond Boy, with notable arms-and-shoulders development in the weight room. And, for added relevance, Nolte was gay, maintaining a lifelong partnership with fellow actor Terry Kilburn, known to many as Tiny Tim in MGM's *A Christmas Carol* (the Reginald Owen version), a recurring event on television at holiday time. It's hard to imagine this *Billy Budd* without Nolte, as the right look is absolutely essential. Quite aside from his acting ability, Nolte was an utter revelation in his uniform, rough white trousers topped by a skin-tight striped tunic to emphasize Nolte's upper torso.[†] Thus, he was the "Handsome Sailor" but uniquely so: naive and transparent. In effect, Billy's physical beauty is one with his moral beauty: you look like what you are.

The play's original title, when it was staged, in 1949, by ANTA's Experimental Theatre, was *Uniform Of Flesh*, and it's Billy's "flesh" that excites and outrages his nemesis, the Master-At-Arms of Billy's ship, Claggart (Torin Thatcher). This story gets gayer and gayer, for Louis O. Coxe and Robert Chapman's adaptation of Melville did not try to soothe Claggart's blatant fascination with Billy, unveiled several times so the audience can't pretend it didn't notice. Still, the setting is 1798 on a British warship, so Claggart has to . . . hesitate . . . a bit:

CLAGGART: (*To Billy*) I can feel it now, looking at you. A certain . . . pleasure.

[†] Though Nolte was never shirtless in the role, Benjamin Britten's *Billy Budd* opera has become a haven for the so-called barihunk to flash skin. It's so de rigueur that even seniors past their marketable youth are expected to model—yes, even in opera.

Was 1951, when *Billy Budd* opened on Broadway, too early for such sen-
sual aggression, even when it ends in tragedy? For Claggart falsely accuses
Billy of fomenting mutiny, Billy's stutter leaves him defenseless, he strikes
Claggart dead, and Captain Vere (Dennis King) hangs Billy for a very dispir-
iting curtain. I don't know how Melville really saw Vere (his own creation,
obviously), but to me Vere typifies the little soul terrified of big decisions.
Though Vere knows that Billy is Goodness and Claggart Evil, and though
Vere's panel of officers exculpates Billy of murder, Vere nevertheless employs
tortuous rationalization to further Claggart's project of killing off Goodness.
A loathsome, craven little pig in a Napoléon hat, Captain Vere stands stoi-
cally as Billy halts his crewmates' rebellion at his hanging by shouting, "God
bless Captain Vere!" before climbing the rigging to his doom.

And that, one might guess, is why *Billy Budd* ran a disappointing 105
performances after glowing reviews. Coxe and Chapman wrote a beautiful
script, so poetic as to border on the Elizabethan, but they had to respect
Melville, and Melville tells a sordid tale.

Meanwhile, this decade, the 1950s, offers us some honestly gay characters,
as opposed to Claggart and his enigmatic motivation, for he may be simply
Melville's symbol for evil's recognition of the power of goodness rather than
a homosexual protecting his hetero cover by trying to destroy the object of
his desire.

We can start with a gay couple in Wolcott Gibbs' *Season In the Sun* (1950),
set on Fire Island. This couple is pleasant enough in the short time they are on
stage, but while Gibbs didn't call them "fairies" (the favored derogation of the
day), he did say, in a stage direction, "They would have no trouble at all flying
in and out of windows." Worse, director Burgess Meredith had the two actors
involved, George Ives and Jack Weston, play with limp-wristed mannerisms.

As Gibbs was *The New Yorker*'s theatre critic, a legend grew up that his
fellow reviewers let this boring "comedy" off lightly with professional courtesy. No doubt they did, but it ran nearly a year, so somebody must have liked
it. In the end, *Season In the Sun*'s main talking point was its use of a future
star of major musicals from *Kismet* to *Man Of La Mancha*, Joan Diener. With
her trick belt-with-high-soprano-extension voice, Diener was wasted in this
talkfest, though the tropical setting did give her a chance to show off her—
quoting Gibbs' stage directions again—"rather surprising figure."

By far the most famous gay play of the early 1950s was Robert Anderson's
Tea and Sympathy (1953), on the harassment of a sensitive boarding-school
student. Artistically inclined, he makes the mistake of playing women in

the dramatic shows and goes skinny-dipping with a teacher who is himself suspect.

But the boy, Tom (John Kerr), is not the play's gay figure. His housemaster (Leif Erickson) is—and of course *he's* the apparent alpha male, stereotyping himself as a brute to put everyone off his track. Yet his wife (Deborah Kerr) is tolerant and compassionate; her role in life is to make things easy for the boys with the titular concept. It's not much to ask, really: she serves tea while listening to them unburden themselves of an anxiety or two. Shockingly (and this contributed mightily to the show's run of 712 performances), she helps Tom over his personal crisis by giving herself to him sexually.

Well, he has more than the usual adolescent anxiety on his mind. If everybody thinks he's queer, doesn't that mean he must be? We can imagine how stunned audiences at the play's first performances must have been, before *Tea and Sympathy*'s ending became notorious through word of mouth: the older Kerr guided the younger Kerr's fingers to her breasts as she opened her blouse, and while the auditorium grew so still you could hear the theatre mice talking over their itineraries, she uttered a genuinely classic final line:

DEBORAH KERR: Years from now—when you talk about this—and you will!—
    be kind . . .

Earlier, she had accused her husband of bullying Tom because of his own gay panic:

DEBORAH KERR: Did you . . . persecute in him the thing you fear in yourself?

That's a key line, explaining why gay-hating congressmen keep getting arrested in men's rooms. But perhaps even more important is what she says after "When you talk about this." Note what follows: "And you will!": as though she already knows that her self-sacrifice will eventually turn into smug locker-room talk, the "I had the housemaster's wife" speech during college bull sessions. True, Tom is shy and quiet, not the braggart type. Yet boys will be boys, and you can almost hear the other young men merrily crying "In your dreams!" as Anderson's curtain falls.

Tea and Sympathy occupies the official top slot in fifties gay drama. But Ruth and Augustus Goetz's *The Immoralist* (1954), opening four months later, was the real breakthrough. Based on André Gide's eponymous autobiographical novel, *The Immoralist* respected Gide's revelation of a life spent in the closet in a mariage blanc while aware of powerful sexual urges. But more: the Goetzes pictured a more or less happy homosexual subculture in Biskra, the Algerian town the protagonist has moved to from Normandy. The notion of happy gay men, even in an exotic setting, was extremely provocative in 1954—remember, the Wales Law was still on the books and *Trio* had been forcibly closed ten years earlier. Even so, *The Immoralist* ran no less than three months.

Again and again, from *The Captive* on, we see at least some of the general public attracted by gay subject matter, and *The Immoralist* also came with a fancy cast—the French Louis Jourdan in his usual impeccable English, Geraldine Page as his wife, and, playing an Arab boy who steals and teases and insinuates, James Dean. Already an accomplished actor, Dean had played a naive, bewildered lad in N. Richard Nash's western *See the Jaguar* (1952); now Dean switched to the opposite type, virtually taunting the cautious Jourdan with reports of "the orchards," where "they live like a thousand years ago. . . . Only boys and men are out there. Beautiful men."

Needless to say, all the standard production offices turned *The Immoralist* down. But Billy Rose, known for nightclubs and the Aquacade, was always willing to attach his name to prestigious projects. He reclaimed the Ziegfeld Theatre for the stage after it had languished as a cinema. He produced Oscar Hammerstein II's faithful adaptation of Bizet, *Carmen Jones*, in an eye-filling staging using color experimentally. He even included a ballet by Igor Stravinsky in a revue, *Seven Lively Arts*. Bert Lahr and Beatrice Lillie headlined, but Stravinsky's name alone created a stir.

Simply put, Rose liked doing what no one else would do, so he took on *The Immoralist*. Unfortunately, the director, Herman Shumlin, was not sympathetic to what the Goetzes wanted to portray. Ruth Goetz gave an interview to Kaier Curtin for his book *"We Can Always Call Them Bulgarians"* (from the aforementioned Samuel Goldwyn quotation) in which Goetz recalled Shumlin's telling her the audience "can't relate to a homosexual husband!," thus "distorting the theme of our play" to side with the frustrated wife, Page, against her woeful, wondering spouse, Jourdan. At Mrs. Goetz's urging, Rose fired Shumlin, and Daniel Mann took over.

It's a curious note to sound, for Shumlin was another of the many theatre folk who balance the boulevard fare (*Grand Hotel*, for instance, or the Gertrude Berg vehicle *Dear Me, the Sky Is Falling*) with plays of social inquiry (the original staging of *The Children's Hour* or tackling academic freedom in *The Male Animal*). *The Immoralist* should have been another feather in his cap. Yet even among thespians, there are people who can tolerate gay but do not comprehend it and, when they get too close to it, retreat in dismay.

There is a problem with *The Immoralist*'s script, though, in the way it leaves the protagonist back in Normandy at the end, offering his wife a sexless marriage. Not the Cole Porter kind, roostering about in the barnyard of secret delight. No, Jourdan will respect the bond of marriage, however celibate his mode:

MICHEL: I promise you one thing: whatever life we may have here, we will
    live it with dignity.

Boy, at that rate he might as well be straight. Even worse was the psychotic gay killer, available for viewing in Meyer Levin's *Compulsion* (1957), from Levin's nonfiction novel on the Leopold and Loeb case, the thrill killing of a teenager by two young men with, one needs to say, too many social advantages. In Levin's view, the more aggressive of these two killers dominated the shy one by toying with his homosexual longings: desperate for approval, the shy one would take part even in the murder of an innocent schoolboy.

That's already a bizarre view of gay liaisons; worse, Levin was another of those who dismiss homosexuality altogether as a phase of adolescence, something you're supposed to get over. So it's okay to be "confused," as long as you end up straight. Of course, this is the homophobe's idea of tolerance: gay is acceptable as long as there isn't any. Given that Levin hobnobbed with free-thinkers and artists, it's very strange that he maintained such a puerile fantasy.

Yet the play *Compulsion* was sophisticated—in its staging. The script was an epic, using fifty-one separate characters (many of the large cast doubled), a live incidental score composed and conducted by Cy Coleman, a ton of sets as event followed event for, sometimes, just a moment or two, and an overtime bill to delight the unions.

Set designer Peter Larkin created an ingenious playing area to whisk the eye from place to place without delay. In fact, Larkin had to, as *Compulsion* was a thriller, flying on the pace of suspense and jumping around in time to cover two different scenarios. One presents the comings and goings of the two killers, especially the fun they're having as they socialize in speakeasies with other young people. Simultaneously, the other scenario presents the legal case, from the view of law enforcement. Thus, we watch as the two murderers go on with their lives in a Chicago enthralled and outraged by their act even as justice gets closer and closer to nabbing them.

Of course, the audience in 1957, a generation and a half after the real-life story, knew the basic action of the traditional who, what, and how: the guilty pair will be exposed, tried, and sentenced to endless prison terms (though one did eventually win parole; the other was himself murdered by a fellow inmate). The public knew as well that, although crimes such as theirs invariably ended with execution, Clarence Darrow got them jail terms because of their youth. (And Darrow's likeness, under a different name, appears in Levin's play.)

Nevertheless, few if any in the house knew exactly how the killers were caught or what the evidence was—because they had planned what they believed was the perfect crime. The dominant one of the pair thinks he's too big to fail, but mistakes are made—and the shy one has dropped his eyeglasses in the swamp where the killing occurred. More pertinent, his typewriter has an ID fault, a broken letter p that prints under the line. He used this machine for college assignments shared with other students . . . but also for the ransom note (even though the crime was always to be a murder and not a kidnaping). There is even the suggestion that the dominant one has been involved in several other murders, as yet unsolved.

The very title *Compulsion* was imposing, as Levin's novel had been a best-seller, and the two leads, Roddy McDowall as the forceful killer and Dean Stockwell as the hesitant one, were really good. McDowall is remembered mainly as the nicest guy in Hollywood in the 1960s and 1970s; the one with the home movies at the beach; he knew everyone's secrets and never shared them. Along with a ton of movies and television jobs, McDowall appeared regularly on Broadway, usually in shows forgotten before they were remembered except for *Camelot*. There, his Mordred was ascetic and unknowable, a truly dangerous villain.

In *Compulsion*, however, McDowall was spirited and energetic in probably the best acting part he ever had, with a terrific scene in a nightclub where, while dancing, he takes a tumble and then rages at Stockwell when he tries to help McDowall up. "*You lousy slave!*" he screams—a concise summation of the role-playing these two indulge in and a signal to the audience that The Gay Thing might come with dangerous manias built into it.

The play was a sensation. My parents, who went only to musicals, comedies, the Old Vic *Romeo and Juliet*, and Tennessee Williams, wouldn't miss this one; once again, we see a gay play intriguing a large audience. Unfortunately for *Compulsion*, its running costs were unusually high, with all the stagehands and actors and a playing time well over three hours. Moreover, Broadway was soaring back then. Within the same few months as *Compulsion* there were premieres of *West Side Story*; *Look Back In Anger*; the Lena Horne musical *Jamaica*; *Look Homeward, Angel*; and *The Music Man*--each in its own way a magnet for attention. Even Eva Le Gallienne showed up, if for a brief run, as Queen Elizabeth (of course: the power role) in a Phoenix Theatre staging of Schiller's *Mary Stuart*, with Irene Worth in the title part.

In the end, *Compulsion* ran for 140 performances, too short a stay to pay off. Alas, even a PR episode didn't help, when Levin had a public spat with his producer, Michael Myerberg. This was standard Levin: earlier in the decade, Levin threw a crazed tantrum when his script for *The Diary Of Anne Frank* was rejected in favor of one that, he thought, sought to universalize what Levin saw as a uniquely Jewish saga. Now he claimed that the *Compulsion* playing at the Ambassador Theatre was not his *Compulsion*, but the work of an interloper hired by Myerberg, possibly to change the two leads from one gay and one gay-adjacent into two victims of anti-Semitism.

Oddly, Levin was not the first writer to set Leopold and Loeb on stage in a gay retelling: English Patrick Hamilton's *Rope* got there first, though Hamilton denied using the criminal case. *Rope* was seen here in 1929 as *Rope's End*, and while the play does not view the homicidal pair as gay, the sheer horror of what they did seems to need a psychological explanation— and the usual Psychotic Gays make a dandy paradigm.

Further, when Hamilton's play was filmed, by Alfred Hitchcock, as *Rope* again, in 1948, the two culprits were Farley Granger and John Dall, both gay men who always came off on screen as—in the old phrase—light in their loafers. This was true as well of *Compulsion*'s Roddy McDowall (though not of Stockwell), and both McDowall and Stockwell had been child actors, which stereotypically clouds their ID as men, at least in the minds of shallow thinkers.

In any case, no matter who plays the principal roles, playwrights cannot leave this ugly story alone. Indie stage culture has hosted numerous versions, almost always seeing the killers as lovers. There has even been a musical, Stephen Dolginoff's *Thrill Me* (2003), and an offbeat transgender chamber piece, *Leopold and Loeb: A Goddamn Laff Riot* (2003).

If straight playwrights Robert Anderson, the Goetzes, and Meyer Levin give us gay characters, it's ironic that gay writers themselves were avoiding "the gay question." William Inge, with four hit shows in the 1950s, before he lost favor and capped a series of flops with suicide, did respect the Beautiful Male syndrome, in the supporting role of a sexy young athlete modeling for his girl friend, a budding artist, in *Come Back, Little Sheba* (1950) and then using the type as the central figure in *Picnic* (1953). The jock posing for a physique study in *Sheba* is little more than a visual bijou. But *Picnic*'s Hal Carter is the only thing happening in the play, as a drifter who flurries both men and women in a Kansas backyard where lower-middle-class folks lead dead-end lives. Hal's energy so enlivens the place that it's almost terrorism.

Something of a sensation for a steaming love plot uniting Hal and the local belle, *Picnic* still attracts interest, and we're used to seeing directors cast gym-sculpted boy-next-door types as Hal, as if he has just returned from a season as a personal trainer at the Topeka Crunch outlet.

However, that's not the Hal Inge had in mind. Hal is no boy next door: he's a ruffian, well-intentioned but too loud and full of himself to charm people. He has anti-charm—so much so that, on *Picnic*'s tryout dates, Hal was offending much of the audience. His braggy arrogance disturbed not just the other characters but the public as well, so the script was amended with revelations of his unhappy backstory, to make him sympathetic.

Casting cute preppies in the part further gentles him down, but Inge, like many gays an admirer of extremely masculine uncultured men—again, "trade" is the scientific term for the type—wanted Hal to be a big, unruly slab of testosterone, not unlike a mid-American Stanley Kowalski, and Hal was played by our old friend Ralph Meeker (who, we recall, appeared as Stanley as well). But when Inge put *Picnic* together, he countered Hal with a boss'-son type, a sort of country-town Ivy Leaguer, named Alan. And Alan was played by the young Paul Newman. Now Hal and Alan will be rivals for the local belle, Madge (Janice Rule). It's the hot guy versus the safe guy.

An odd quirk in the storyline sets these three people off beautifully: Hal and Alan turn out to be old college fraternity brothers. Presumably, Hal was on campus through a football scholarship, and the fraternity pinned him because fraternities worship star athletes, as Hal is too roughhewn to make a natural college man. In fact, he's a born loser, a magnet for bad luck and failure in everything he does. And that's *Picnic*'s drama: will Madge throw away security and social position with the tidy Alan to run off with the hopeless, futureless Hal?

Note that Newman was suavely kitted out for his part in a white suit while Meeker was shirtless, doing yard work for a handout on a hot day. The comparison between the two created a visual cross-section for Inge's aperçu that the boss' sons of this world maintain the stability of manners and courtship. They celebrate the ceremonies of life, those gala protections that keep too much truth from getting in the way of our plans. On the other hand, the drifters like Hal lay down a chaos of sexual blitzkrieg.[‡]

In fact, when Columbia Pictures made the *Picnic* film (with William Holden as Hal, embarrassed to be playing a young man at a rather weathered thirty-seven), the studio plastered the nation's billboards with the key art of Holden's bare torso. This was more of the new information the popular arts were giving us on the ID of heroes. Were they made of the traditional honor and courage . . . or sexual charisma and nothing else? And if it's the sex thing, is this another gay observation, that sensuality is the sovereign motivation in people's lives, whether straight or gay?

Inge's next play of his great fifties quartet, *The Dark At the Top Of the Stairs* (1957), presented a highly novel bit of gay treatment in a look at a young boy of twelve or so who is clearly a gayling in the making. Charles Saari played this unhappy, poorly adjusted child of parents Pat Hingle and Teresa Wright, who with the boy's older sister comprised the Flood family of Oklahoma "in the early 1920s."

A loner who keeps a collection of photographs of movie stars of the day, the boy, Sonny Flood, has no friends of his own. On the contrary, the local kids heckle him with "Sonny runs home to Mama!" and "Sonny plays with paper dolls!" Sonny is cold to his father, who gamely keeps trying to establish some dad-son rapport; Sonny is not even consistently warm to his ever-forgiving mother, who knows that there is something Different about Sonny. But what is it?:

CORA: You're a speckled egg, and the old hen that laid you can't help wondering how you got in the nest.

Sonny has but one love in life, going to the movies. Surely Inge created this figure to look in on the early development of a child simply born to be gay. Interestingly, the one character in the play that Sonny responds to is a military cadet (Timmy Everett) in his crisp uniform, on hand to take Sonny's sister to a dance. Sonny, who wants to come along but is too young, throws

---

[‡] Ironically, Newman understudied Hal, a weird piece of miscasting—except that, in the 1950s, principal actors, unlike many of those today, seldom if ever missed performances. This allowed cast members in smaller parts to cover characters for which they were unsuited, given the dim possibility that they would ever go on. Yet Newman did in fact substitute as Hal for a short time.

a lurid tantrum, hurling himself to the floor to stamp his feet and pound his fists. But the cadet, strong and soothing, knows how to talk him down as no one else can.

Inge's art lay in revealing how the uproars of life are pasted over in the normal functioning of midwestern culture, and *The Dark At the Top Of the Stairs* has rather a number of them, including the cadet's suicide later that night. Yet the play's moving parts work together naturalistically: in Inge's world, you pay a price for everything you get, and you don't get much in the first place. *Dark* is a superb play, arguably Inge's best, but one wonders how many in the audience understood what he was creating in the person of Sonny Flood, or what the public thought when mother Cora virtually defined a certain kind of gay personality in telling Sonny he's "a funny mixture . . . in some ways, shy as your sister. In other ways, bold as a pirate." She could almost be preparing the way for the drag-queen hero of *La Cage Aux Folles*.

Meanwhile, Truman Capote was trying his hand at playwrighting. Unlike Inge, Capote was all but publicly gay, partly out of fearlessness but also because what else could he be? Straight men didn't pose for a dust jacket photograph in checked vest and bow tie lolling on a sofa looking at the viewer with the attitude of a malicious petit four. He was something new in lit: a little blond boy in shameless bangs, and he was new in theatre as well. Without any experience in drama, he himself adapted his novel *The Grass Harp* (1952) for Broadway, though the story's delicate atmosphere could not transfer well from fiction to live action.

In *Theatre Arts*, *The Grass Harp*'s producer, Saint-Subber, called the show "a universal play, about universal people." In fact, it's about quaint outliers who abandon society to take up residence in a tree house—depicted as a small platform sitting in a structure with great spreading branches. In a way, Capote could have been writing about the gay world, the "treehouse" being the otherworldly culture gays inhabited, segregated from oppressive hetero regulations.

The Grass Harp was a collector's item for aficionados, and in an all but reckless career move, Capote's next show was a musical, *House Of Flowers* (1954), with a book by Capote, music by Harold Arlen, and lyrics by the two of them working mostly by long-distance telephone. The producer was Saint-Subber again (now dropping the hyphen; and he would further modify his billing over the years to come), and he assembled an astonishing team, the kind that makes an eye-opening debut in a full-page ad in the Sunday *New York Times*' theatre pages: director Peter Brook, choreographer George Balanchine, and designer Oliver Messel, with the key art of a sinuous black woman ensconced in a mesh hammock, her right hand clutching a fan and her left arm raised in sensual grace.

Set in Haiti amid a business war between rival bordellos, *House Of Flowers* had an interesting cast as well, with Pearl Bailey and Juanita Hall as the hostile madams, winsome ingenue Diahann Carroll, and a host of sharp character players both black and white. By the time the calamitous Philadelphia tryout had ended, however, some of the team had departed, mainly in frustration at the way Bailey took over everything.

Finding its final shape in a kind of amiable chaos, *House Of Flowers* reflected the evil side of the short story Capote had based his libretto on, and by the end of the show some nasty parties actually tried to kill the jeune premier (Rawn Spearman), Carroll's inconvenient boy friend. Capote and Arlen got a number out of it, "Turtle Song"; they got numbers out of anything—bordello "flowers" waiting for customers; a cock fight; "Two Ladies In de Shade of de Banana Tree." It's a joyous and charming score, and while the show failed, the album was a hit.

But it's worth noting that, here again in *House Of Flowers*, Capote was playwrighting about gay life without a single gay character. The show's gay feeling inheres in its seductively fleshly nature. The title phrase refers not only to Bailey's bordello but to Spearman's lush courtship of Carroll, inviting her to live with him au naturel as a Haitian Adam and Eve. Some call it sex; he calls it love.

True, Carroll's ID number, "A Sleepin' Bee," is so naive and visionary that it later served as a theme song for the very young Barbra Streisand, introducing herself as a voice of pure *espressività*. Both music and lyrics are pre-sexual. But Carroll and Spearman were the innocents in a show jaded with appetitive hunger: Bailey's ID number was "One Man Ain't Quite Enough"—and Bailey herself was another of those Big Ladies that gay men idolize.

Musicals with a powerfully felt gay authorship are not all that uncommon. Think of *Jubilee*—as we've seen, its gay aura was unmistakable. But *West Side Story* (1957) is notable in having been written (by Leonard Bernstein, Stephen Sondheim, and Arthur Laurents) and staged (by Jerome Robbins) by gay men without an apparent gay sensibility—the giddy skylarking and undressing we recall in *Jubilee* for instance, not to mention its fascination with celebrity, always a hallmark of gay style.

Yet *West Side Story*'s Shakespearean source, *Romeo and Juliet*, does have some gay in it, in the relationship between Romeo and Mercutio. Many

critics see it as homoerotic—and such a liaison would not have been unheard of in the real-life Italy of the play's fourteenth century, when the physical infatuations of young men were (however technically illegal) culturally
tolerated.

This turns up in *West Side Story* only vestigially, as in the first book scene
after the First Number, "Jet Song," when Laurents' script shows us the surprisingly tender side of the bond uniting the Jets' best fighter, Tony (Romeo's
counterpart), and the gang's chief, Riff (Mercutio). Tony tells Riff he's finished with the gang and its comic-book cadre:

RIFF: Tony, this is important!
TONY: (*sarcastic*) Very important: Acemen, Rocketmen . . .

And note this pungent bit of backstory:

RIFF: Four and one-half years I live with a buddy and his family.

This is almost certainly in a tenement, so Riff must be sharing a small
bedroom—and most likely a bed—at an age of sexual experimentation. And
when Tony speaks of "the kick I used to get from bein' a Jet," the normally aggressive Riff suddenly gets—say the stage directions—"quiet":

RIFF: . . . or from bein' buddies.

One wonders exactly what Bernstein, Sondheim, Laurents, and Robbins
thought this scene represented. Four years and change is a long time for two
just post-pubescent males at close quarters behind a bedroom door. But then,
such episodes had to be finessed, for—as we will presently see—the critics
could be vicious toward writers who were trying to take the vibrations of gay
life out of their hiding places.

Of all the gay authors discussable in this book, one in particular typified
the gay personality yet was never household-name famous and is all but forgotten today: lyricist John Latouche. One problem is his constant changing
of composer partners: you need a consistent brand (such as Rodgers and
Hart or Kander and Ebb) to secure prominence. Then, too, all of Latouche's
musicals were either bombs or commercially unimposing succès d'estime.
The really wonderful *Cabin In the Sky* (1940), with lyrics by Latouche and
music by Vernon Duke, paid off only because of a movie sale to MGM.

At that, *Cabin In the Sky* is still a familiar title, because its black-folk-play basis always excites interest. More typical of Latouche's career was *The Lady Comes Across* (1942), also with Duke, and built around the British musical-comedy star Jessie Matthews. It came in having just lost Matthews to a neurotic paranoid episode—she was playing the victim of a spy ring and suddenly decided she was a spy, too. With its rent-a-nobody replacement, Evelyn Wyckoff; a disorganized script; and 3-performance run, this was an ignominious flop. However, Latouche had also spectacular flops, especially *The Vamp* (1955), Carol Channing's first chance to create a role on Broadway after *Gentlemen Prefer Blondes'* Lorelei Lee, in a spoof of silent-era Hollywood.

The usual out-of-town squabbling left *The Vamp* with a helter-skelter book (partly by Latouche) but a very interesting score with music by James Mundy—unusually at this time, for a show without a racial theme, a black man. Latouche gave his cast a veritable mouthful of lyrics, so wild with invention that any song played faster than andante was difficult to follow. Still, Latouche had a novel field to toy with, as there had been few musicals about the movies. In the second-act opening, "Four Little Misfits," the Mary Pickford, the gossip columnist, the Snidely Whiplash, and the cowboy hunk delighted in how their personality flaws paid off in upside-down Hollywood. Robert Rippy, the cowboy, was so dumb the only thing he could relate to was a horse; it gave his westerns lovable tang. "Let's be happy we are misfits," the four movie people carol, "be glad that we are frights." Because everything in the flickers is fiction. "Who cares if you can't spell your name," Rippy gleefully explained, "as long as it's in lights!"

An inconsistent lyricist, always at least capable and often truly brilliant, Latouche interests us here less for the quality of his work than for the quality of his presence, supremely typical of the educated urban gay male, smart and flamboyant with a tendency toward goofing around and camping up.

He was typical as well in his lack of an anchoring income. Ever since the 1600s or so, there have been homosexual odd-jobbers eking out a living on the edge of the arts in the cultural capitals. In modern times, he might be a chorus boy then stage manager, with a side in playing piano in bars or for auditions. Some become personal assistants to weighty figures or enter the literary world, reviewing performances and books, indexing, copyediting—and all use charm and wit to get on the free list for invitations to top parties and trendy artwork, from Eugene O'Neill premieres to Kirsten Flagstad opera to advance screenings of the latest Ingmar Bergman title.

John Latouche was a few notches above that, but always as a writer, permanently broke or thereabouts and thus taking on random commissions till he would overextend himself. Worse, the guy was lazy, which made him late with everything. Add to this a need to dominate and outbursts when thwarted.

So he exasperated all of his collaborators. Still, they loved him, as his impish spirit was irresistible. Strangely, he married early on (though his wife was gay, too; heigh-ho! the gang's all here). But then, Married Gay Men was a thing in Latouche's day, roughly the 1930s into the 1950s; it sometimes seemed as though half the gay men one knew were married.

Unlike other gay writers of musicals, such as Cole Porter in "sophisticated" musical comedy or Stephen Sondheim in the concept show, Latouche never pursued an identifying genre, perhaps because his wild imagination led him to extraordinary projects wherever possible—a modern retelling of *The Iliad* and *The Odyssey* as *The Golden Apple* or the uncategorizable *Candide*. But Latouche's first big opportunity was, for the time, very sensible: the grand finale of the Federal Theatre revue *Sing For Your Supper* (1939), "Ballad Of Uncle Sam." Extracted from the show in a life of its own as a populist cantata, the piece was renamed *Ballad For Americans*, a sensation of the day after a radio performance with Paul Robeson singing the solo lead.

As a lyricist, Latouche was worldly and wily, but *Ballad For Americans* is transparent and sincere. "In seventy-six the sky was red," it begins, "thunder rumbling overhead." From then on, in a mixture of recitative, song, and speech, the baritone soloist keeps daring the chorus to identify him. His clues, though, are as cloudy as those of a Norn, as in "I'm everybody who's nobody." Still, there's a nice touch of ID contrast when he lists his "everybody" as including Betsy Ross and Crispus Attucks, Quaker and atheist.

So who is he, finally? America!, as the music breaks into an anthem. If you're in the right mood, it's quite thrilling. *Time* magazine said of the broadcast that "an audience of 600 stamped, shouted, bravoed for two minutes [and] the [station's] Hollywood switchboard was jammed for two hours."

The concert had to be repeated, and RCA Victor rushed Robeson into the recording studio with the appropriately named American People's Chorus. For some reason, the album of two ten-inch 78s included a photograph of Robeson's wife and accompanist looking oddly out of sorts, though Robeson, towering over them, seems cheerful.

It should have proved a great launching pad for Latouche. But it was Robeson, the "face" of the music, who got the attention, not the lyricist or the composer, Earl Robinson. At that, this was an offbeat turn for Latouche, a sheerly celebratory piece from a talent bent on raising hell all over the place, confounding genre by inventing new forms or getting silly in the established ones. *Ballet Ballads* (1948) with composer Jerome Moross is more typical of Latouche: an evening of three very various one-act operas as much danced as sung.

The form of the "ballet ballad" was invented by John Murray Anderson (using those two words) for use in twenties revues, favoring adaptations of fairy tales or the like. Revues tended to feature a song spot or a dance number or a song followed by a dance, but the ballet ballads used song and dance simultaneously. Thus, Anderson mixed ballet with hoofing, classical composition with the Broadway musical. These "ballads" were above all arty—and that was John Latouche, too: a poet in a world of pop.

Latouche and Moross went on to write a full-length ballet ballad in *The Golden Apple* (1954), the aforementioned modernization of Homer. This is one of those Ultimate Musicals, inscribed in the cultist's Golden Book for its wondrous score, but Hanya Holm's choreography was an essential part of the production. You can almost "hear" the dancing in Moross' infectious rhythms, an ideal complement to Latouche's insanely inventive libretto. These aren't just songs, because *The Golden Apple* is through-sung, so Latouche's lyrics are the very fabric of the storytelling. They are more concerned with narrating than—as would obtain in a "normal" musical—sympathizing.

In fact, only the two sweethearts, Homer's Odysseus (here called Ulysses, the Roman version) and Penelope, are truly sympathetic in the First Couple sense, à la Curly and Laurey or Tony and Maria. *The Golden Apple*'s other characters are crazies of various kinds, a quality of playwrighting that I find very common among gay creators like Latouche. (Jerome Moross was straight.) Noël Coward was similarly inclined, and of course the casting talent pool back then offered not only bigger-than-life stars (such as, say, Carol Channing) but eccentric supporting players as well (such as almost everyone else in the cast of *The Vamp*).

Musical comedy in the 1950s was loaded with oddballs. Think of *Guys and Dolls, Wonderful Town, Damn Yankees, Li'l Abner, Once Upon a Mattress*. One of the reasons the Rodgers and Hammerstein shows seemed somewhat stolid when new was their general lack of these beguiling freaks. Even the Steinbeckian *Pipe Dream*, with a chorus of sex workers and layabouts, came off as short in nutso show-biz drollery.

But *The Golden Apple* revels in it. That makes it hard to revive today, because besides the intellectual brilliance of its use of Homer as America's journey from a land of yeomen farmers to an industrialized jungle of cities, its cast calls for a troupe of giddy maniacs. This is especially true of the second act's olio, the variety show popular in nineteenth-century American showbiz.[§]

The Golden Apple's olio corresponds to Ulysses' travel in the Aegean Sea after the fall of Troy. He is trying to get home but instead keeps encountering obstructions, and Latouche recalibrates these as destructive novelties of modern urban culture (and thus baffling to Ulysses' men). These take in a stock-market catastrophe on one hand and a madcap "Lady Scientist" on the other, sending one of Ulysses' crew into outer space with no way of getting back.

Like the acts of a lunatics' carnival, these episodes are designed to showcase the Mad Hatters of musical comedy—in the original cast, such comics as Bibi Osterwald, Portia Nelson, and even Jack Whiting, a former romantic lead who always did have a Heckle and Jeckle side. Unfortunately, when our modern "organic" performers attempt such roles, they play them straight and the fun collapses, as happened in the Encores! *Golden Apple* in 2019. As the show's original-cast album of 1954 attests, the people in these numbers should seem interplanetary, like crazies running amok.

Further, to tighten the irony of the destructive power of these sprightly goons, Latouche demanded that they be impersonated by characters Ulysses knows in his hometown, people we met in the first act. As each of these merry nemeses kills off one or more of Ulysses' squad, the hero is left with only Achilles for the last of the vaudeville acts and the very center of the show: Circe.

She's "the woman without mercy," the chorus tells us, to a jazzy strain: "Circe turns men into swine." Back in 1954, an educated public would have been following all of these parallels with Homer knowingly. But Circe is Latouche's twist on the myth, for Circe's stock-in-trade is not modernism but sex. True, that much is in Homer—but Latouche wanted her played by not one of the madcaps but by Penelope, loving and true, Ulysses' hometown bride.

[§] The olio formed the minstrel show's Second Part (the middle of the three acts) and can be seen in the 1936 *Show Boat* film during the *Cotton Blossom*'s performance of *The Parson's Bride*.

Why? Because Circe has the golden apple, not seen since Act One. The apple can grant wishes, and he who knows how to phrase them will gain power over the world. However, like the Ring in Richard Wagner or J. R. R. Tolkien, one must lose one's very selfhood to win that power. It's an evil trade, and Latouche insisted (in the stage directions of the published text of the musical) that Ulysses "give up what is most tender and alive in himself." That is, he will dally with Circe in the person of Penelope, treating his wife as a whore and outraging their sacred bond.

Yet he doesn't. When the villainous Paris, "with the excited stealth of a mugger," tries to stab Ulysses, Achilles takes the blow and the City of Modernism dissolves as Ulysses tosses the apple away.

Thus, in Latouche's view, this unique American hero has been, in Lincoln Steffens' often misquoted phrase, "over into the future." For Steffens, "it works." But Latouche's Ulysses rejects it, to return home to his pre-industrial farming idyll.

Unfortunately, Latouche's far-seeing visionary creation of a Ulysses (Stephen Douglas) was sabotaged. It wasn't Penelope (Priscilla Gillette) who appeared as Circe but the more sensual and scandalous Mother Hare (Nola Day). Perhaps the producers and director felt a degrading of Penelope would cross a red line, so on the show's premiere, at the Phoenix Theatre,** before an audience of boldface names, *The Golden Apple* won a fabulous ovation, yet Latouche was heartbroken. Keeping Penelope "pure" and Circe simply a wanton exploded his daring mythopoeia: sex is both wicked and innocent simultaneously. Can we separate love from lust? Again, we must ask, Is this an observation a gay man in particular would make, given the erotic freedom of bachelorhood?

The Golden Apple was all the same a big event in its day. It got so much PR that its Helen (Kaye Ballard) made the cover of *Life*, the key communications outlet in middle-America then. Of course it moved to Broadway, with a few cast changes among the support. It ran for four months at the Alvin Theatre, and everyone who mattered saw it. Still, it's the cult musical of cult musicals, simply too smart for the mass audience to take in comfortably.

It did lead Latouche to something big, though, for Leonard Bernstein and Lillian Hellman were just getting started on their *Candide* project, and

---

** *The Golden Apple* first played on off-Broadway, but the Phoenix (today a cinema) was a Broadway-sized house. It just happened to be on Second Avenue and Twelfth Street.

Latouche's ability to make an arty concept entertaining recommended him as the new show's lyricist.

Ah, but. It proved an uneasy collaboration, with three overpowering personalities; among Bernstein, Hellman, and Latouche, it is impossible to determine who would have been the least uncompromising. Further, Latouche's habitual laziness and those distracting side-projects of his drove his writing partners crazy.

In the end, Latouche wrote most of the first-act lyrics and then left the project. His successor, Richard Wilbur, not only finished the lyrics but rewrote much of Latouche, and one must admit that Wilbur's work is often better. When Latouche had the satiric Voltaire to play with, he was at his best, but a duet establishing Candide and Cunegonde's love, "Plain Words," found them searching for a way to say "I love you" in rather humdrum verses. Wilbur's version, to the same music, "Oh, Happy We," reveals their plans for the future, as Cunegonde anticipates travel, luxe, "the high life" while Candide looks forward to "a rustic and a shy life." Neither is listening to the other, a wonderfully dramatic conceit.

To be fair, Latouche's treatment of the love plot in *The Golden Apple*, by contrast, is poetic and touching; Penelope's pining solo during the Odyssey section, "Windflowers," is one of the most beautiful love songs in the musical's history, metaphorical yet deeply heartfelt. Still, *Candide*'s comparable mixture of mirth and emotion seems to have confused Latouche (along with everyone else on *Candide*'s writing team), perhaps because it doesn't blend the two. *The Golden Apple* is homogenized; *Candide* is disjunctive.

Thus, "Oh, Happy We" amuses—but the show's finale, "Make Our Garden Grow," a chorus sung by the entire cast looking (in the original production) as if it had crawled out of an air-raid shelter after a nuclear detonation, blows one away with its colossal sincerity. The song's premise comes straight from Voltaire and forms the last line of all: "Il faut cultiver son jardin." It's quite matter-of-fact in that blasé French way. Yet Bernstein and Wilbur made it stupendous.

And *Candide* isn't supposed to be stupendous. It's a genie's stocking-stuffer of a piece, even a scathing joke, and the musical's various authors did not succeed in pulling it together properly. Marvelous despite its flaws, it has been revised so often that it is now virtually a Frankenshow, concocted of spare parts.

Still, isn't a Voltairean joyride exactly what Latouche—or any witty gay writer—would naturally excel in? Gay art is often made of one part vivacity, one part quirkiness, and one part mischievous bravado—qualities we see at fierce work in that ultimate gay theatre piece *The Boys In the Band*. This is why Latouche's launching title, *Ballad For Americans*, is so utterly unlike the rest of him. The *Ballad* is, in effect, straight art, using "real" life because straights think they're the default setting for humankind, whereas gay art idealizes while camping it up.

Thus, *Tea and Sympathy* is typical straight art while *Cat On a Hot Tin Roof* is gay, with its almost unbelievable Big figures, its Big Mama and Sister Woman and her "no-necked monster" children, even its elephant joke about a giant phallus, which straights keep trying to ignore and gays keep wondering about. Aloud.

Are there exceptions to these overbroad generalizations? Yes, of course. Gay William Inge wrote almost straight, keeping to realistic midwestern tales of family problems. And straight Betty Comden and Adolph Green's musicals have a zany atmosphere with flashes of spoof opera and the barely suppressed hysteria of characters living theatrical lives.

Think, in *On the Twentieth Century* (1978), of upstart producer George Lee Andrews talking Madeline Kahn into his Somerset Maugham drama of the decadent Mayfair coterie:

ANDREWS: Half-brittle, half-sardonic, half-tragic...
KAHN: Yes, yes . . . Three halves . . . Bigger than life!

But hold: John Cullum, the Broadway genius whom Kahn deplores, wants Kahn for a sacred tale of the Magdalen. Comden and Green were experts at building a waggish premise into an explosion of crazy—the whole of their *On the Town* (1944) libretto grows out of a sailor's yen for a girl in a subway poster.

So, as the Maugham play unfolds before us upstage, Cullum and his associates, in garish Biblical dress, mix among the dressy Maugham players, to illustrate the choice Kahn faces—corrupt Society or holy redemption? Simply the appearance of these "early Christians" among the Mayfair sybarites was one of the looniest visuals in the musical's history, a kind of war between two hopelessly outdated theatrical genres and the very essence of gay whimsy, thought up by straights.

Let us let Latouche reply with his characteristic homosocial capers, even if his last work (before his death of a heart attack at forty-one), *The Ballad Of Baby Doe* (1956), is hard to categorize. Written with composer Douglas

Moore, it's an opera—but a show–biz opera, planned for Broadway (though the plans fell through) and boasting vastly more dramatic vitality than was typical of fifties American operas, most of which were old plays with an inert soundtrack attached.

Interestingly, Chappell published the *Baby Doe* vocal score in the format it used for musicals. And there was even a cast album when after the premiere in the opera's setting, Colorado, the piece made its way to the New York City Opera. Dolores Wilson created Baby Doe in Central City, but it was Beverly Sills who recorded her, and the role lay so well on Sill's voice (especially in its many high-flying lines) that Baby doesn't sound right with anyone else. Sills' Baby is unique—yet her fellow coloratura soprano Ruth Welting's party turn was an uncanny imitation of Sills in one of Baby's solos, "The Willow Song."

The Ballad Of Baby Doe is a magnificent work, not only for its vibrant music and intriguing storyline but for its effortless conjuring up of a vanished America, that of the miners who left hopeless lives back east to become silver barons out west. Latouche cleverly weaves history into his tale—based on chronicle—of the wealthy and powerful Horace Tabor, who divorces his cold fish of a wife, Augusta, in a passion for the young (thus "Baby") Elizabeth Doe.

Using constant changes of scenery, Latouche takes us through the meeting and romance of the central pair, the anger of the discarded Augusta, the scandal of Baby's wedding with Horace in a Catholic ceremony though she had a (divorced) husband still living. All the while, we watch as the nation moves to adopt the gold standard even as Tabor clings myopically to silver, till at last his dream drags him down and he has nothing left in all his life but Baby.

Madcap though he was, Latouche could organize his artwork with great, sturdy foundations, and he centers *Baby Doe*'s action on the symbol of a silver mine, the Matchless. It comes up within seconds of the first rise of the curtain and is mentioned repeatedly thereafter as the heart of Tabor's obsessive personality: for silver, for Baby. In a way, she *is* the Matchless Mine, his fantasy, his undying love. Thus, Latouche had a prefabricated storyline that was literally fabulous: the fable as an American myth, built around those Big characters that opera and the musical love.

Fittingly, Latouche thought up a shocking end to his tale, all the more so because it tells us what really happened to Tabor and his Baby. He had made her swear never to let go of the Matchless, and after his death the penniless Baby moved into a hut adjoining the mine and was found there, over thirty years later, frozen to death.

While Tabor is the figure the history navigates around, Baby gets the best music. Her solos range from parlor ballad to Letter Song (as she writes to her mother) to an eloquent defense of her "forbidden" love for the married and much older Tabor, and the opera ends with yet another solo, an elegy comparing love to youth. They are the same, Baby sings, even as the shawl that had covered her head slips back to reveal her as a white-haired ancient. Behind her, the Matchless Mine comes into view, her tomb. As Baby shivers, it starts to snow, and there the curtain falls.

It is noteworthy that Latouche wrote so raptly of so intense a romance and, again, a controversial one, for gays of the 1950s were well aware how hard it was to come by. The legal difficulties alone were all but prohibitive; simply meeting worthy partners was nearly impossible for anyone not in the arts (where the gay scene was much more open). Think of that moment in the movie *Far From Heaven*, set in these same 1950s, when the closeted Dennis Quaid breaks down and steps into a gay bar: a dark, dreary collection of middle-aged losers. (We'll be meeting *Heaven* again later on, as it became a musical in the 2010s.)

So it could be argued that Latouche could see more clearly than many other writers the obstacles in the path of love if a couple doesn't suit The Norms, and he has Augusta Tabor, in a sorrowful and well-intentioned meeting with Baby, explain to her replacement as Mrs. Horace Tabor why so many people hate her: this young woman reminds them of what they missed experiencing "in their narrowness." Baby's enemies are "locked up inside themselves." Is this a gay man assessing the motivations of some straights? As Augusta phrases it, "Great love is freedom, and they fear it."

Unfortunately, this marvelous piece has a flaw that has kept it on the fringe of the repertory: Douglas Moore couldn't hear any music in Augusta. He does have the measure of her general tone: finicky, imperious, conservative in the extreme. But the melodies Moore wrote for her, even in her big solo near the end, "Augusta, Augusta, How Can You Turn Away?," lack interest.

And this despite Latouche having given Moore the words of a rich character, a passionless woman who understands and even secretly empathizes with passion in others. Her orthodox views tell her to treat Horace and Baby vindictively. Yet at length her humanity overwhelms her pride, and she blesses the pair with forgiveness.

Baby instinctively responds to this; it is one of her outstanding qualities that she is free of that narrowness that Augusta speaks of. Baby is an adventuress in the best sense, open and daring in an epoch of closed minds. But

Horace rages at Augusta, blind to her sympathy as he is blind to everything but his obsessions. In an odd way, one might say that Horace is the only character in the opera who doesn't comprehend what the opera is about—like, if I may extrapolate, the only guy at the gay ball who doesn't like gays.

Thus, Latouche's character interplay is not only expert but imaginative, a rich dramaturgy for the feckless American operas of the 1950s. Here was a writer who (after *Ballad For Americans*, anyway) was always ahead of his age. The density of personality in *Baby Doe* would be at home even in a Sondheim musical.

Speaking of musicals, we find numerous references in them to gay at this time, though only in passing. We even hear the word itself. For example, Rodgers and Hammerstein, of all people, opened *Pipe Dream* (1955) with a gay innuendo of sorts. The scene is the combination living quarters and laboratory of the show's hero, Doc, a marine biologist—and note that Doc was played by William Johnson, a bearded, conventionally masculine guy. As the curtain rises, Doc is enjoying a "morning after" a one-night stand; his date is still asleep. The action starts when Doc's buddy Hazel (Mike Kellin), a ragamuffin and wastrel in the typical Steinbeck manner, comes in for some man to man banter that leads to a highly Steinbeckian concept of Live and Let Live, "All Kinds Of People." So far, so good: Doc is fine company, Hazel is lovably screwy, and the song is wonderful.

But then Doc's date Millicent (Jayne Heller) awakens, takes in Doc and his pal, learns that Doc had left her slumbering while he went out to get samples of marine life, and decides to feel neglected. She thinks she knows why, too:

MILLICENT: Hazel! Maybe that explains the whole thing!

So Millicent, who immediately storms out, has taken Doc and Hazel as an item! It's an offbeat way to establish tone in a musical, especially one that was universally faulted for euphemizing its sexual content.

Consider: *Pipe Dream* was based on Steinbeck's novel *Sweet Thursday*, filled with the raffish folk of Monterey, California, that Steinbeck loved writing about. One of the leads was a bordello madam (Helen Traubel), and part of the action was set in the bordello, girls and all. Many were those who said the bordello was like a sorority house—yet there was Millicent taking Doc and Hazel for boy friends.

On the other hand, *The Nervous Set* (1959), on the beatnik lifestyle, was so hip that it troubled to print a glossary in the playbill, defining *the fuzz* ("law enforcement"), *to wig* ("flip, enthuse, gas"), *pad* ("apartment"). *Nervous*, strangely, was "contemporary," as if angst were now the normal human condition. "Man, we're beat," the cast reported, as if that explained everything. But no one needed a trot for a line in the song "New York" about the Plaza Hotel's being "not too faggy." The allusion was to the men's bar adjoining the Oak Room, a notorious gay meeting place (though probably few knew that the bar had undergone a gay purge sometime before). A forgotten show, *The Nervous Set* once maintained a presence in cabaret for its "Ballad Of the Sad Young Men," perpetuating the stereotype that gays are full of misery and doom. Not surprisingly, this musical is seldom if ever revived today.

Meanwhile, slipping over into the early 1960s, we find our trusty Noël Coward's *Sail Away* treating the topic with his usual haughty honesty, in the advice of an Arab souvenir seller in the Casbah. Earlier in the show, Charles Braswell (who, as Beauregard Jackson Pickett Burnside, would introduce the title song in *Mame*) appeared as a ship's purser, singing "The Passenger's Always Right" to his beleaguered stewards. Now Braswell was playing the Arab, singing "The *Customer's* Always Right"—with new lyrics to the same bouncy music as before. To the tourists who "yearn for secret joys," everything is for sale: "Offer them girls, offer them boys." In 1961, this had to be a shock, at least to some. But remember, Coward was the one who introduced "gay" into the musical's vocabulary, in *Bitter Sweet*'s aforementioned "Green Carnation."

And now it was *New Faces Of 1956*, Leonard Sillman's recurring revue specializing in presenting talents new to Broadway, that uttered the word that dare not speak itself, for here was Jane Connell touting a new must-see vacation spot in "April In Fairbanks." Yes, it's central Alaska that tempts the discerning traveler. The old haunts—your Paris, your Grecian Isles—now lack flavor. As for Rome, Connell reported with a guilty giggle, "The Piazza Di Spagna is no longer gay."

It's an in-joke of a pun. The square at the foot of the Spanish Steps (you've seen them in *The Roman Spring Of Mrs. Stone*; Vivien Leigh's house stands at the top of the stairs to the left looking up) was in fact the Hustler Central of Rome, where devotees of love-for-hire came to arrange the night's entertainment.

How often had *gay* (in this context) been used in musicals before this? After Coward's joke in *Bitter Sweet*, we recall Cole Porter's jest about the sexuality of the bull of "Georgie Raft" in *Let's Face It!*'s "Farming." But that was fifteen years before "April In Fairbanks," and I don't know of any other use of the telltale word than those cited here. But should we be surprised? Yes, the musical as a form loves to tweak the feelings of the puritans and regulators that rule the state, not to mention their stooges in the press and popular media. Still, for decades *after* this *New Faces*, the gay movement fought to change "faggot," "queer," "Sapphic," and the clinically disdainful "homosexual" into the word that gays themselves used—and the advance was slow.

Even in the 1970s, everyone knew about the word but would still turn shy around it. One day in Lehman Engel's BMI workshop in writing musicals—the academy that helped many shows reach Broadway—Lehman was speaking about his forthcoming book on the lyrics of Broadway. His research had uncovered an oddity, he said: one word in particular was used more than any other, and he asked us to guess what that word was.

Some of us knew it had to be "gay"—albeit in its old meaning of "glamorously lighthearted," irreplaceable in the vocabulary of operetta in particular. But none of us uttered a word.

5

The 1960s

You Shouldn't *Wear* Heels When You Do Chin-Ups

Suddenly, gay characters were everywhere on Broadway, though mainly in plays by Britons. According to West End legend, the nineteen-year-old Shelagh Delaney wrote *A Taste Of Honey* after seeing a play by Terence Rattigan and finding it just too pouffy, my dear. Anyone can write a better play than that, and I will, right now.

More precisely, Delaney thought Rattigan's world lacked reality, at least the kind Delaney had experienced. "Kitchen-sink drama" was the derogation for what she had in mind, and her play looked at the unhappy relationship of a working-class mother and daughter. In a central event, the now pregnant daughter, abandoned by her lover and quite alone in life, is taken in by a sympathetic gay man. Frances Cuka (pronounced "chewka") and Murray Melvin played the roles in London; on Broadway, in 1960, it was Joan Plowright and Andrew Ray.

Those with a taste for the more colorful and shiny workmanship of Terence Rattigan himself could enjoy *Ross* (1961), on T. E. Lawrence's bizarre masquerade as an enlisted man in the Royal Air Force and filled with espionage and war crimes, including Lawrence's rape on the orders of a Turkish general. John Mills—Hayley's father and one of the most versatile actors of the time—played a superb Ross; Alec Guinness had preceded him in the part in London the previous year.

And Charles Dyer's *Staircase* (1968) also dared go where American playwrights feared to, telling of two old queens bickering and laughing and being sorrowfully devoted to each other the day before one of them must face legal action for cross-dressing. In London, they were Paul Scofield and Patrick Magee and in New York Milo O'Shea and Eli Wallach. But note the star power of the movie version: Rex Harrison and Richard Burton. The poster showed the two dancing, with a one-word caption: "Whoops!"

Frank Marcus' *The Killing Of Sister George* (1966), seen here in virtually a replica of its London original, offered butch Beryl Reid and self-effacing

Eileen Atkins (much later the go-to in sophisticated, sarcastic grandee roles Maggie Smith didn't play) doing much the same that O'Shea and Wallach did in *Staircase*: successfully maintaining a live-in relationship in a state of reckless warfare.

Reid played a nurse on a BBC radio soap opera, fearing that she was about to be written out—and we actually heard the sound effect of the fatal moment, as George's moped is crushed by a truck just before the third-act curtain rose.

Playwright Marcus toyed most wickedly with the audience, who were just settling in for Act Three when they heard noises of the rural world at peace, Sister George's motor humming along the country lane as she sang a hymn. Then a big truck's heavy zoom assailed the ear, its driver drowsy and impatient. His partner in the truck's cab cried, "Look out!," followed by a crash and "Fred! We hit her!" All of this was still a relay of the radio broadcast as a farmer ran up and took in the scene with "Holy saints! It's . . . it's Sister George!" And the driver replied, in his north-country patois, "It *were . . .*"

Here was a superb bit of black comedy, and worse was to come, for after the curtain rose and Act Three began, the BBC official who had broken the news that Sister George was to be made redundant now offered poor Reid a new role: as Clarabelle the Cow on *Toddler Time*. And the BBC woman walked off with Atkins. "You're going to be . . . my little girl," she said. Young Atkins was expert in playing the femme who is as much in control as the butch, and Reid won much praise for her rich, crazy, angry Sister George, so vituperative that she constantly threatened Atkins with violence and in fact attacked a pair of nuns in a taxi.

Marcus' main concern was to lay bare to us what an "unequal" gay relationship might be like, with one partner dominating—roughly, not subtly—and the other playing along, even called "Childie" as a nom d'amour. In the end, though, Reid was left with nothing. "I love you," Atkins finally told her, "and that's why I've got to leave you." The curtain came down on the radio presenting a ceremonial farewell to Sister George and her "forthright, practical no-nonsense manner"—an amusing euphemism for the bull dagger style in general. Utterly bereft, Reid now readied herself for her next role and began to moo—"a heartrending sound," Marcus directs—and the show was over.

Few American works treated a full-scale gay relationship like the one in *Sister George*. More common was a bit of this or that in passing, as in James Goldman's *The Lion In Winter* (1966), famous for the very popular film version with Peter O'Toole and Katharine Hepburn as Henry II and Eleanor of Aquitaine holding a Christmas court amid vast skullduggery and Plantagenet infighting. Robert Preston and Rosemary Harris played the pair on stage, but even these very accomplished performers failed to spark the fireworks we enjoy in the movie. "It's the twelfth century," says Eleanor, "and we're all barbarians."

Yet *The Lion In Winter* has a central scene that plays as farce, wherein Henry jousts with his guest, King Philip of France, while Henry's sons hide behind the drapes, now popping out and now sneaking back in. "You're a stinker and you stink," cries the loathsome Prince John after hearing his brother Geoffrey betray him. And Philip betrays Richard, another of the princes—actually the most famous of the three: Richard the Lionheart. And it's quite some betrayal, for Philip asks Henry, "How stands the crown on boys who do with boys?" Ah, but Philip tells Henry he was merely playing a game of political sex. Dick diplomacy. "Imagine," he says, "snuggling [up] to a chancred whore," whereupon Richard roars out from behind a curtain with "No! It wasn't like that!"

So we have a minor facet of gay life, opportunistic (rather than genuine) bisexuality. And elsewhere in the decade, Hugh Wheeler (an expatriate Englishman) brought up, in two plays in 1961, the delicate matter of the gay crushing on an unattainable hetero. *Look: We've Come Through*, in which Ralph Williams doted on Burt Reynolds, ran only 5 performances but Wheeler's *Big Fish, Little Fish* was more successful at a three-month run. John Gielgud directed this intimate look at a middle-aged publishing editor (Jason Robards Jr) who maintains a small social circle of losers who depend on him for sustenance and selfishly turn on him when he gets a wonderful job offer that will take him away from them.

One of his coterie, played by Hume Cronyn, typified Robards' group with his loving support cut with a tart tongue.* Late in the continuity, Robards confides in Cronyn with a dire story in Robards' past, and Cronyn then tries to match him with a confession of his own:

CRONYN: We've never talked about this. . . but. . . but . . .
ROBARDS: Jimmy, do you think I didn't know?

---

* This was Cronyn's first acting job on Broadway without his wife, Jessica Tandy, after they inaugurated their professional partnership in *The Fourposter* (1951). *Big Fish, Little Fish*'s two women's roles weren't meaty enough to need Tandy, but the Cronyns were soon sharing bills again, and were still a team in *The Petition* (1986), thirty-five years on.

Cronyn is stunned:

CRONYN: You knew and didn't mind?
ROBARDS: Who am I to mind? People are the way they are. And that's how it
     ought to be.

Note the very precise echo of the lines I quoted from Mae West's *The Drag*,
wherein the fair-minded Doctor educates the bigoted Judge. Gay himself,
Gielgud would have directed sensitively. But Cronyn had a gift for locating
the awkward humanity in life's walking wounded, and he tuned the moment
with such hapless finesse that, at the performance I saw, the audience froze,
embarrassed for the character yet thrilled by his interpreter. To quote an
Italian idiom, it put wings on the play's feet.

   Some shows treated gay within a straight context, however, as something
slightly foreign, as in yet another British import, Joe Orton's *Entertaining Mr.
Sloane* (1965). Here, an amoral young man moves in on a household through
murder and seduction. He has a heavy to deal with, sort of the head of the
place, but he's an easy make for a boy with charm. The subject is exercise, and
Sloane blithely feeds the hungry older man the tidbits he longs to hear:

ED: A little bodybuilder, are you? . . . Do you (shy) exercise regular? . . .
     Stripped?
SLOANE: Fully.
. . .
ED: Do you wear leather . . . next to the skin? Leather jeans, say? Without . . .
     aah . . .
SLOANE: Pants? [i.e., undershorts]
ED: (*laughs*) Get away!

Or there would be the blackmail plot, as in two titles of 1960, *The Best Man*
and *Advise and Consent*, in which a homosexual encounter during military
service could destroy a politician years later. In *Theatre Arts*, *The Best Man's*
author, Gore Vidal, said he wanted to give the noble politician knowledge
about his rival that, unveiled, would wreck his candidacy for president. But,
for dramatic interest, it had to be something so low the good guy "would de-
test exploiting it." How bad could it be? Said Vidal, if he "had stolen money,
got a girl pregnant, run away in battle," and so on, it wouldn't be bad enough.
Only one thing, in 1960, was that bad: the gay stuff.

Of true-to-life, really out there gay people, however, there was little. Most of what we saw were fantasies, literary conceits, or melodramatic plot twists—except down in the West Village at the off-off-Broadway venue of the Caffe Cino, founded in 1958 by Joe Cino and run by him until his death, in 1967. Cino was gay and a theatre buff, so he threw open his space to virtually any writer with an idea.

Most of these writers were gay, it seems, and while their ideas were not limited to parish topics, when they dealt with gay life they could be refreshingly direct and organic. Honest, really: because that's what Cino's clientele needed. They could find the conceits and twists uptown.

Perhaps, in those days, it took American artists to start creating gay theatre from the inside, if only because gay culture, though still legally sub rosa, was so highly developed. Yes, the British kept sneaking titles into the West End and thence to Broadway, from *Oscar Wilde* to *The Killing Of Sister George*. And as for gay culture, Britain had Polari, their own gay language, as we'll presently see. But Americans had the drag queen, in British show biz the mere bagatelle of a guy in a dress and wig but in American gay life someone exotic and spirited, a human Hail Mary play of cross-gender scrutiny.

Take, for instance, Lanford Wilson's *The Madness Of Lady Bright*, produced at Caffe Cino in 1964. "Produced" is a grandiose term for the stagings in its tiny playing area; everything lay in writing and acting. A somewhat short piece, *The Madness Of Lady Bright* is essentially the monologue of "a screaming, preeny queen" (as Wilson describes him) of "about forty" and thus reaching the tail end of his sexual negotiability. The scenery gave the basics of his studio apartment, including a practical phonograph and telephone but most notably a wall of signatures "in every conceivable size and writing medium": his tricks.

Technically, Leslie Bright (played by Neil Flanagan) is not a drag queen. He's a middle-aged gay man. But his speech patterns sail along in a style that drag queens made their own—volatile, scornful, needy, raucous, victimized by everything, and constantly referencing high and low art—in this case the ballet *Giselle* on one hand and on the other the theme tune Bert Parks would sing at the Miss America Pageant. Whatever a figure such as Leslie Bright does has a hat and cane on it, metaphorically, so Bright is above all a child of show biz. He doesn't just live: he performs (which is arguably not just the drag queen's format but that of the tuned-in urban gay like the ones we will shortly meet up with in *The Boys In the Band*).

But note that the play itself "performs," for Wilson's imaginative drama-turgy gave Bright two foils, nice-looking young people—his opposites, right? They are Boy (Eddie Kenmore) and Girl (Carolina Lobravico), not literally present in Bright's apartment but rather theatrical devices, there to comment on Bright's observations and interact with him and even each other:

BOY: Last night. Did you go out for a while?
GIRL: Oh, yes. I went for cigarettes.
. . .
BOY: I looked over expecting you to be there—and there was nothing but loneliness.
LESLIE: (*To himself*) loneliness. . . . You know nothing about loneliness.

Because they're young? Cute? Straight? In the Boy's big moment, he stands in as Bright's favorite long-ago trick, a hustler, friendly but elusive. This is for money, Leslie. To the Girl, this date for hire explains the eternal glitch in the escort's business model. And yet:

BOY: Some pansies live a sane life and some don't. Like anyone else, I suppose.

Yet it is Wilson's aperçu that gays like Leslie Bright most definitely *aren't* like anyone else; the entire show reveals how the parish fosters personalities more intensely derived—more eclectic—than those in the outside world. *The Madness Of Lady Bright* uses deliberately limited means to open up an entire cosmos, *The Captive*'s "shadows" now radiant in light. It must have been fas-cinating for the Cino's audience to watch bits of their own lives unfolding as Bright paces his tiny apartment on a hot summer day, going over his past, his wishes, his now depleted catalog of options, knowing that he has no one but himself. "Take me home," he pleads at the end, when the Boy and Girl have vanished. "Take me home. Take me home . . ."

It is almost as if gay culture in the 1960s was half bleakly surviving and half camping around in desperation. Yet gay Jerry Herman could make a musical out of outstanding gay/not gay source material in *Mame* (1966), reveling in Patrick Dennis' aforementioned aunt and her eagerness to celebrate. She can make a party out of nothing (in "It's Today"), of her lust for novelty (in "Open a New Window"), of her ability to rise above catastrophe (in "We Need a Little Christmas"), in her frenemy socializing that anticipates *The Boys In the Band* (in "Bosom Buddies"), and only at length admitting defeat in a torch song ("If He Walked Into My Life"). Yet she conquers that, too, warm, lovable, ageless. Really, she's the antithesis of the Leslie Brights of the world.

And note that Mame herself was Angela Lansbury, soon to be a parish favorite as beloved as Bette Davis or Katharine Hepburn—and Lansbury was nicer. She had already appeared in a Sondheim musical, *Anyone Can Whistle* (1964), with an entrance number ("Me and My Town") modeled on Kay Thompson's glamour-jazz arrangement for Judy Garland's scene in MGM's *Ziegfeld Follies*. *Whistle* ran only a week, but the cast album placed Lansbury as a comer.

And of course she was the perfect *Mame*—but casting the show was tricky, as everyone seemed to understand that this musical would not only be a smash but was bound to glorify Broadway's next Big Lady. Rosalind Russell had owned the non-singing Mame on stage and film, but Herman's music lay beyond her abilities. And while she supposedly said she turned the singing Mame down, *Mame*'s creatives in fact never approached her out of fear that she would say yes.

It appears that some on the team favored Dolores Gray, one of The Street's finest singers. And Dolores had the chic; but Dolores was cold. Mame is many things, from scatterbrain to front-liner in the war against narrow minds. But she is above all warm and loving. Judy Garland would have been ideal, while we're talking gay faves, if she had been reliable. She wasn't, and would have flopped the show by missing performances. Even when she did turn up, she could be a wreck. "I'm what's left of Judy Garland," she habitually told new people in her life.

So it had to be Lansbury. Yet the producers wanted a star, and Lansbury, in 1966, had no more than niche fame. They made her audition multiple times, even as Jerry Herman kept insisting that no one else would do.

Still, after Lansbury did indeed punch out as a top star in *Mame*, others replaced her successfully during the show's nearly four-year run—Janis Paige, great fun though somewhat earthy for a sophisticate; Jane Morgan, a wonderful vocalist who as an actress was . . . a wonderful vocalist; and Ann Miller, always great company though somehow she seemed never to understand anything in her roles except the choreography. Stories about backstage life in musicals tend to be gay stories, fostered by the subculture, and the prime *Mame* anecdote takes place around the spring holidays, when one of *Mame*'s cast asks Ann what she's doing for Passover. And Ann replies, "Oh, I never do game shows."[†]

[†] She would be thinking of *Password*, but the tale is unbelievable, anyway. Ann Miller wouldn't be doing anything for a Jewish holiday, so why ask? Some of these show-biz stories must be viewed as entertainment only, inventions by people hoping to discredit someone famous.

Dizzy Ann? Isn't that really because of the many silly roles she played? Ann had her thoughtful side, in fact. As she told interviewer David Johnson, "Mame is Woman. And you have to fit her to your own personality. I'm playing me, Ann Miller. There's a lot of Mame in me." True, Ann wasn't exactly right for Patrick Dennis' visionary socialite, especially with the "That's How Young I Feel" ensemble dance restaged to give her some exhibition tapping. (Lansbury and the others discreetly slipped offstage at that point.) The tap stuff made it easy for gays to make Ann Miller an official parish mascot, thus all the jokes, for beyond the Passover story there was Ann's bright, straight, scary black hair (as in "Ann twirled and seven chorus boys went to the hospital for stitches").

Still, she was one of those amazing show-biz survivors, dating back to the 1930s. When, in 1998, she delivered the American musical's designated Survivor Anthem, "I'm Still Here," in the Paper Mill *Follies*, starting way upstage and steadily progressing from left to right and left again while moving ever closer to the audience, one had to admire the sheer show biz of her, the all but wanton oomph she brought to everything she did. She suffered a complicated personal life, but nothing defeated her. She was a natural, and that's why she had a gay following: the talent.

But we should pause here to examine the quality of gay humor, because there is arguably a lot of it in straight writers. When does the gay voice as such first sound? Here's a possible start—Neil Simon's Broadway debut, *Come Blow Your Horn* (1961), spoken mainly in the urban Jewish idiom:

ANGRY FATHER: Are you married?
SYBARITIC SON: No.
ANGRY FATHER: Then you're a bum!

The son, ethnically emancipated from Jewish folkways, communicates in standard American. But now and then he slides into the clever sarcasm we are about to hear a great deal of in *The Boys In the Band*. The son is educating his younger brother in the ways of the playboy, and the brother is dating a modern-jazz dancer named Snow Eskenazi. Simon deftly establishes the name *Snow* a few times to prepare a gag, and here it is. The doorbell rings:

OLDER BROTHER: Ah, that must be Nanook of the North!

Note the reference to an old movie that (in 1961) nobody saw but everybody had heard of. This is absolute gay humor, fondling a spicy bit of bygone show biz: automatic camp. It's fizzy yet risible, like a fan who ignores Hollywood's boldface names to attach himself to Gale Storm.

Or consider this bit from Simon's *The Prisoner Of Second Avenue* (1971), a look at a man beaten down by the tumults of modern life. The second act opens with a groan of a laugh: the apartment living room, established in Act One, is now a wreck, tossed by robbers. The thieves have made off with virtually everything:

HUSBAND: They took the television? A *brand* new color television?
WIFE: (*dryly*) They're not looking for 1948 Philcos.

Again, this is *informed* irony: one has to command some cultural perspective just to place a long-vanished electrical-appliance brand.

So: is this style of humor gay in origin or adopted by gays? Is it a New York kind of humor? But much of the modern gay style was developed in New York. Oppressed groups often create their own communications system; English gays actually devised a language, the aforementioned Polari. Used also by theatricals, circus people, and other "outlaw" groups, Polari was more a collection of secret words than a fully executed dialect, but all the same, when spoken quickly—on a bus, in a park—it could keep eavesdroppers from understanding what gays were saying to each other.

For example, *vada* meant "look" or "look at. "*Bona* meant" good." *Eek* meant "face." *Om* meant "man."

Today, seeing a looker approach, Simon might nudge Graeme and say, "What do you think of that one?" But back in the age of Polari (which ended when Britain decriminalized homosexuality, in 1967), Simon would instead say, "*Vada the bona eek of that om.*"

And some of the dialogue in *The Boys In the Band* (1968) almost bears that quality, an air of "We have our own way of communicating whether straights like it or not." Moreover, nearly any activity, no matter how ordinary, can be dressed up in a joke, as when someone picks up a ringing telephone with "Backstage, *New Moon.*" Again, the jest turns on the archeology in digging up a twenties operetta.

But much of the fun is insult comedy. Someone says he's flying to the West Coast and someone else replies, "You still have that act with a donkey in Tijuana?" *Boys'* author, Mart Crowley, intended his play as serious—sociology, drama, enlightenment. Yet the comedy ran away with it. In the end, *Boys* is at once wildly funny, drastic, moving, and maybe a tiny bit unbelievable, yet so reflective of what gay life was like in New York in 1968 that the show is almost a documentary.

There are numerous ways to describe it. For example, it takes place at a birthday party with the guests, all around thirty years old, presenting a gay "foxhole," as in the diverse personalities common in early fifties World War II movies—the nice guy, the edgy guy, the rustic, the hot shot, and so on. Here we have the straight-appearing gent (Hank), the slut (Hank's boy friend, Larry), the effeminate rowdy (Emory), the unattractive queen (Harold, the birthday boy), the hustler (known as Cowboy), the unachiever unable to cope with anything (Donald), the Ivy League black (Bernard), and the troop leader, bitchy but nice enough until he drinks (Michael).

Or the play might be taken as a study in how internalized homophobia destroys character, for Michael, notoriously a mean drunk, gives Act One its suspense curtain by pouring himself a drink. This promises a second act full of Michael's rage—at everyone, especially himself. Gays were so used to the hatred directed at them that they absorbed and nourished it without realizing it.

The English émigré Quentin Crisp, long a Manhattan celeb and renowned (from the television film *The Naked Civil Servant*) as a pioneer in gay liberation for being open about his sexuality despite legal terrorism, was an example of this Stockholm syndrome. Crisp would stun his fans at public gatherings by calmly stating that gays were inferior and pathetic. I saw him do it. His listeners expected Pride and instead got Prejudice. And Crisp had not adopted the bigotry without realizing it. He did realize it. He agreed with it.

So is *Boys* about a birthday party getting rambunctious or about how a younger, snappier sort of Quentin Crisp acts when liquor loosens his tongue? Or is it about the density and power of gay friendship? For when Michael turns on just about everyone in the room, he is most vicious toward Harold, one of his oldest and closest friends. And Harold rips into Michael in a scathing pushback; one expects the relationship to die forever on the spot. Yet when the party finally closes down and Harold leaves, he utters the play's key line: "Call you tomorrow."

It's key because, while all of these men are isolated by society, unlike Lanford Wilson's Leslie Bright they are not suffocating in loneliness. They support one another. Better: Harold understands Michael, flaws and all, and without one or two friends who truly know you to the core, you might as well be alone.

Of course, a party in itself is no more than a setting. The meat of this meal lies in Act Two, when a raging Michael forces his guests to telephone the one man they truly loved and confess that love to him: to humiliate themselves with the truth. And isn't that what the theatre has been devoted to since the Ancient Greeks, what our official Greatest American Playwright, Eugene O'Neill, was obsessed with: facing the truth?

Paradox break: in a subculture that can survive oppression only by living a lie—the closet—honesty is self-destruction. Yet some of the guests make that terrible phone call. Bernard is nearly comatose after it, though he spoke to not the straight boy he loved but the boy's mother. There's race and social class mixed up in it as well; this is one very heavy conversation:

BERNARD: Why did I call? Why?

Why? Because living a lie is the death of the soul. No wonder Mart Crowley regarded *Boys* as a serious work that some mistook for a boulevard‡ comedy with star turns, hunks, and a twist ending for the tourists. Yet it really is comparable in its own way to O'Neill's *The Iceman Cometh*, of course without the arty O'Neillian grandeur.

Edward Albee mistook it. When he, Richard Barr, and Clinton Wilder created The Playwrights Unit to showcase new writers, *Boys* was offered to them, but Albee thought it a Broadway sort of thing, gag-ridden and contrived. "Lousy" was the word he used, because although he acknowledged *Boys* as "highly skillful work," he felt its queeny repartee and "Oh, Mary" Emory would cripple the fight for gay civil rights. Yet the Playwrights Unit *Boys* showcase was a vast success, doing turnaway business every night. When Barr decided to move the production to the commercial level, at Theater Four (on West Fifty-Fifth Street between Ninth and Tenth Avenues, an area so dangerous that Crowley called it "a senseless-killing neighborhood"), Albee declined to take part. He chose, he later said, "principle over principal."

But surely he appreciated Crowley's one Albee-esque character. This is the traditional "uninvited guest" figure, the stranger who throws everything into chaos. In Albee's hands he is something of a menacing or Absurdist

---

‡ From the "boulevards" in north central Paris, where the middle-class theatres were located. Thus, a boulevard attraction is more *popular* than *artistic*, unlike the classics on view at the Comédie-Française or the Opéra.

invention; Crowley's stranger is less dire, though he is violent at one point. And he offers yet another way of describing *Boys*, for into our gathering of merry men comes a straight (but is he?) who provides Crowley's surprise climax.

Alan, the newcomer, is the ninth member of the cast, Michael's old college friend who may be having some interesting problems with his marriage. He seems attracted to Hank, and physically attacks Emory, the flamboyant queen:

ALAN: I'll kill you, you goddamn little mincing swish! You goddamn freak! FREAK! FREAK!

"Pandemonium" is Crowley's laconic stage direction, as some of the guests rush in to break it up while the audience tries to figure out if Alan's assault on the "gayest" character on stage reveals Alan's fear that Emory is his reflection. It's a great moment from the dramaturgical standpoint, because suddenly *everything* happens, not just Alan's attack: birthday boy Harold arrives, Cowboy sings "Happy Birthday To You" and kisses him, and Michael starts his drinking. "Ominous" is too mild a word for this first-act finale, because it's filled with memes that will need exorcising in the second act. Cleverly, Crowley starts it exactly at the moment when the first act ended.

Is Alan a closeted gay? A bisexual? Some straights love the notion of bisex, as it's a way for them to deny that any man or woman is absolutely gay, born that way forever. Why, look at Cole Porter, they'll say. Yes, he was impish and sophisticated—the gay style—yet he married a woman.

Well, ha, let me tell you about the marriage of Cole and Linda Porter. He was comme il faut and she needed an escort in order to go out in the evening. They were conservative people; conservatives married. And the number of times the two of them had sex with each other was: zero. How do I know? The ghost of Noël Coward told me.

And where does that leave us with Alan? He's married, too, with a pair of daughters. Is it a sham marriage? If not, why has Alan, who lives in D.C., suddenly arrived, very upset, in Manhattan, turning to Michael, the only friend he can talk to about . . . what? About how he has been uncertain all this time and is now what Quakers (in a very different context) call "convinced," ready to convert to being openly gay?

But here is where Crowley springs his big surprise, one that *The Boys In the Band* has been inexorably driving toward from the very first scene: Alan plays Michael's telephone game. Yes, he agrees to call his great love and make confession. Michael makes sure everyone knows who Alan's great love is, too: Justin Stuart, another old college friend, as closeted at that time as Michael and Alan were. But Justin is out now (fun fact: Michael and Larry have both had him), and Justin told Michael that he and Alan had sex.

Several times.

And then Alan cut Justin off.

Michael throws all this in Alan's face as we watch, Alan furiously denying it. Can we believe him? Michael doesn't:

MICHAEL: One time, it's youth. Twice, a phase maybe. Several times, *you like it!*

Yet Alan will make the call? *Really?* This section of *Boys* must be one reason why Edward Albee scorned it. This telephone business is so. . . hammy. So gluttonous. (Albee thinks.) Yet the audience is frozen in delicious alarm, as Michael looms like a vengeful deity who will see his adherents abase themselves in worship or resign their souls to torment and confusion. Alan places the call and says:

ALAN: I love you and I beg you to forgive me.

Ha! Then Michael grabs the phone with "Justin! Did you hear what that son of a bitch said?" Two beats. Then:

MICHAEL: . . . Fran?

It's Alan's wife, not Justin Stuart. Now Alan will return to her. He says, "Thank you, Michael." And leaves.

Whew, that was a close one. But close to what, exactly? Is Alan straight, after all? His marriage could still be a sham. Or was Justin Stuart making it up about him and Alan out of wishful thinking? Crowley makes it impossible for us to know, because love and sex are the most abstract elements in human life. No one can analyze how they work, and all the studies, from Kinsey on, only compound the mystery. In effect, Crowley is saying, I won't tell you the truth about Alan because there's nothing to say except that—allowing the exception of Hank, who left his wife and children for Larry—the boys in the band appear to be exclusively gay.

Gore Vidal famously said that there is no gay, only "homosexualists." In other words, bisexuals with a tilt rather than people with a congenital and exclusive interest in their own gender. What Vidal didn't understand about gay was what Crowley makes so much of in *The Boys In the Band*: its sense of *community,* the faultless or questionable or rococo friendships of the gay world, which the narcissistic Vidal had no use for. Gore Vidal's community was Gore Vidal.

Interestingly, when *Boys* began its run of 1,001 performances at Theater Four, the production PR emphasized this sodality of friendships. With a photograph of the actors, the ad's log line read, "Spend a marvelous evening with eight of the boys." Eight, we note, not the full cast of nine: Alan is not in "the band." Whether or not he is a natural outsider, he has rejected the community.

In a different vein, the poster for the movie, in 1970, addressed the nation at large with the shock value of showing gay guys at their sport. Under a photo of Harold was "Today is Harold's birthday." Next to that was a photo of Cowboy: "This is his present."

At Crowley's insistence, the film carried over the entire original stage cast, directed by Hollywood pro William Friedkin. (The play had been staged by Robert Moore.) Notably, Friedkin did not present an adaptation. He did open up the action with a strictly visual prologue—no dialogue—showing the principals in the hours just before the party: Donald driving into town in his Volkswagen, Michael buying last-minute accoutrements, Alan getting off the plane, Larry having a grand old time socializing at the venerable Village bar Julius while solitary Hank fumes. And Friedkin restaged the play's entire mise-en-scène, to let the camera help narrate. Otherwise, Crowley's play was not filleted. And, for realism's sake, *Boys* was shot in what Michael's apartment would look like. In fact, it was Tammy Grimes' duplex and its terrace, with some scenes shot in a studio duplicate.

Fifty-one years old at this writing, the movie holds up wonderfully because the actors really look like their characters—Keith Prentice's Larry handsome enough to be a real Anytime Annie; Cliff Gorman's Emory so lovably irritating in his pullover and Bermuda shorts; Robert La Tourneaux's Cowboy madly beautiful and nothing else; Laurence Luckinbill's Hank so used to being with straights that he seems like one himself. Remember, he's the one that the gay-averse Alan immediately takes a shine to, and later, when Alan wants to flee this party of doom, he begs Hank to come along with him. "You can pass for straight," he seems to be saying. "Like me."

Michael is the key role, the closest thing this ensemble piece has to a pro-tagonist (again, in the Ancient Greek sense of the subject of the plot). He is hard to cast properly, as he's the band's alpha male yet suffers from a poorly integrated ego system. He needs company yet rages at it, and thinks you can sin with mad abandon as long as you aren't late for Mass. Back in 1968, vet-eran theatregoers found the Michael of Kenneth Nelson a surprise, as he was associated with frothy musicals. Some aficionados had the cast album to *Seventeen*, with Nelson as Booth Tarkington's teenager courting a visiting belle in his father's tails and imitating her risible dog, Flopit. What on earth had got into Nelson in the seventeen years between *Seventeen* and *The Boys In the Band*?

Gay life had got into him—and almost all the others as well, so the pro-duction was cast realistically. The air of glowering resentment when Alan shows up was very real, virtually an anticipation of Stonewall. Mart Crowley would admit in interviews that he based some of the characters on people he knew well, which suggests that the Rebellion of June, 1969—which occurred during *Boys'* original run—was something like the culmination of how Crowley's characters felt about the state of gay in the American nation.

The excellence of that original cast is actually shocking, as many first-rate performers weren't willing to play such overtly queer roles. This explains why most of the cast were unknowns. Kenneth Nelson was unusual in having a rel-atively prominent track record, which besides *Seventeen* also took in having created the Boy in *The Fantasticks*. Nelson wasn't a household name even among the theatregoing class, but he was well known in the industry, and he was genuinely risking his career. Indeed, straight Laurence Luckinbill's agent, though gay herself, cautioned her client that he might never again be offered a decent role if he played Hank.

For others in the cast, however, *Boys* was just another gig: and actors need work. Cliff Gorman had been odd-jobbing before *Boys*, for instance appearing as one of the "frauds" on *To Tell the Truth*. His acting stints sited him on the lower depths, such as playing hotels in the Catskills in tiny troupes doubling and tripling roles in, say, *Arsenic and Old Lace*, *Night Must Fall*, and so on. The weekends might host Steve and Eydie or, in the more modest inns, newbies so soggy they would never even make it to has-been, and Gorman's group would go on during the week, to uncomprehending audiences. In an interview in *After Dark* magazine with Alfred Zelcer, Gorman recreated these unhappy gigs with his usual satiric worldview: "Cats and dogs would walk on stage, they'd page people through the loudspeakers (*shtick: Lawrence*

Welk): 'Mr. Horowitz got long distance . . .' right in the middle of the play." To Gorman, then, *Boys* might be perilous, but it *was* New York and the audience would comprehend.

That first *Boys* showcase offered no salary. However, as usual with such productions, the Playwrights Unit sent out cards to agents, scouts, and the like, advertising Gorman's participation. That was how the actors got "paid," and also how the public was mustered.

Gorman recalled that, twenty minutes into Act One, the house was "screaming with laughter." The cast took it for a fluke. "Somebody's doing *shticks* in the back of us." One night later, the show began its session of turnaway crowds, and one night after that, despite a rainstorm, "There was a line twice around the block." *Boys* was held over from five nights to fifteen, and the theatre-world buzz was incredible. Off-Broadway, here we come! Then: nothing. One of the play's few straights playing the swishiest character, Gorman had to wonder if *Boys* had been just another gig, after all.

It took three months for the show to reach Theater Four. But its impact was such that it sent out two national tours in 1969, very well cast and—typifying public curiosity about the subject matter—playing houses three or four times the size of Theater Four, such as the Forrest in Philadelphia and the Wilbur in Boston, standard pre-Broadway stops. Regional companies, too, were keen to stage *Boys*; it seemed as if every urban American had access to it.

Then the movie went international, even to Russia, where the title was translated as оркестранты—literally "orchestra players," in the meaning of the play's title but not its spirit. Of course, there had been gay characters in movies already, but they were often ambiguous, like Lee Van Cleef and Earl Holliman in *The Big Combo*. The *Boys* movie offered a full cast of gay males, not only defiantly gay (as Hank puts it, "I don't care who knows it") but set amid the details of gay culture.

Those details unfortunately did include the self-dramatizing misery Michael suffers from—"the icks," he calls it. And he says, "If we could just . . . not hate ourselves so much." This naturally antagonizes many gays, who don't hate themselves and don't know any gays who do. Yet Crowley was recording the life as lived *at that time*, and there were indeed gay men who deeply regretted what they were, some because of the legal hurdles and others, like Michael, because of psychological glitches of mysterious origin.

Further, as the years passed, detractors found other faults. For instance, when the mood changed in Act Two and the party got dangerous, why didn't the guests just leave? There are a number of explanations for this; one relates to Michael's odd relationship with the guests. Besides Alan, who blunders in from Somewhere Else, only Harold and Donald are in Michael's social loop. The others—as Michael tells Donald in the show's first minutes, "are really all Harold's friends." So they're not sure how to deal with Michael, especially once he goes on his rampage in Act Two. This also explains why Donald, who at first appears to be a major principal, does almost nothing during the actual party. He's there as Michael's supporter—and seems to be best enemies with Harold, though we never learn why.

Again, Crowley leaves a lot of our questions unanswered because much of gay life then was a mystery even to those who lived it. However, the 2018 Broadway revival, like the original production filmed with its stage cast, smoothed over some of these glitches. The line about the guests being Harold's—not Michael's—friends was cut, and Jim Parsons' Michael was softer than the high-strung Loki that Kenneth Nelson created, making the telephone game more of a challenge than a torture.

As for the ever-quarreling Hank and Larry, the original's Laurence Luckinbill was more aggressive and Keith Prentice's Larry more casual while the revival's Tuc Watkins seemed more resigned and Andrew Rannells rather belligerent. Still, there is only one way to play this show; these differences are of emphasis, not of kind. It is what it is: a birthday party used as a microcosm of gay life, with queen and trade, honesty and camp, love and lust.

And with the icks as well—but the revival unmistakably reinstated the work as a classic; cheers for the full-cast curtain call rang with the realization that *Boys* is a crucial part of gay history. And note that the troupe in 2018 was all gay in real life, openly so despite the same old warnings from agents that a job like this will cut an actor's potential for other jobs.

On the other hand, even back in the day Leonard Frey not only enjoyed rehashing his *Boys* experiences to anyone who would listen but loved pointing out that he knew actors who turned down the *Boys* workshop only to join one of the tours or as replacements in the New York run. Further, Frey had no trouble finding work after *Boys*, if only because he had—he felt—The Role. "Harold," he would point out, "has the best entrance and the greatest exit since the Lunts. And when I sweep out with my birthday gifts and the Cowboy, I still have the best line of the evening."

That line—the "Call you tomorrow" to Michael—binds the action, because Harold is the show's truth-teller and, as I've said, the plague of gay life in Harold's and Michael's time is the lack of truth: the survival through dissembling. Just as Harold is open about how poorly he does in the looks sweepstakes, he is open about Michael's addictions. I repeat: Harold *knows* Michael, and everyone needs that one person, smart and fair enough to understand us. Michael may be the showiest role in the cast, but Harold ·quietly holds the show in fee. "Everyone said this play would wreck my career," Frey would explain, "but it was the greatest thing that ever happened to me."

Not only that: Frey became *Boys'* exegete, armed with set answers to skeptics' questions. Why didn't the party guests leave when Michael got nasty? Because, Frey would say, it was pouring rain outside and they had to wait for it to clear up or get drenched. And why did Crowley paint all gays as miserable? He didn't, Frey would counter. Of the nine characters only three—Michael, Donald, and Alan—are unhappy, and we don't know that Alan is gay in any case. Emory and Bernard are unhappy after they play the telephone game, but they are clearly happy in their lives otherwise. In fact, after *The Nervous Set*'s "Ballad Of the Sad Young Men," *The Boys In the Band* is a relief. Gays don't need clueless straights to tell them how they feel.

I've spent extra time on this work not only because it is rich in meaning but also because it was the most influential play in gay history: it freed everything up. If *Boys* could be a commercial hit, anything was possible from now on—including an odd little era of nude theatre on off-Broadway starting in the 1969–1970 season. Simultaneously, hardcore gay-porn films stepped out of the underground to play in cinemas in the Broadway area on a plan new to show biz: if it's gay, it will pay. Amusingly, the actors in these films were the hunks one had seen in the bars or out on Fire Island's two gay compounds, The Pines and Cherry Grove. The print ads would herald "all-male cast," the first dog whistle of the Stonewall era, and the accompanying photos were skin-oriented. This public explosion of heretofore taboo material hit so suddenly that, to befuddle possible censors, one title was coyly advertised, in this spelling, as *STUDy FARM*. Still, the shot of a shirtless boy wrangling a snake left no doubt in the minds of the gay bien-pensants.

The nude plays, however, were not comparably pornographic—for the most part, at least. Here are just a few of the titles, each one different from the others: Gus Weill's *Geese* (1969) tackled both genders, one to an act, in tales of young people Discovering. David Gaard's *And Puppy Dog Tails* (1969), a four-hander, offered a partnered couple, the top's old Navy buddy, and the queen from next door, after *Boys'* Emory a staple of gay drama, present to pass saucy remarks. The cast was oddly interesting: the top of the partner couple was played by George Reeder, a chorus dancer in musicals from *Li'l Abner* to *A Funny Thing Happened On the Way To the Forum* who had replaced Sydney Chaplin in *Funny Girl* before Johnny Desmond's contract started, a rather classy résumé for an off-Broadway attraction. And the Navy buddy (Ken Kliban), who was bi but explained that the gay part didn't count as long as you didn't kiss, was in real life the brother of the famous cartoonist B. Kliban.

More of those Fire Island hunks turned up in Gerry Raad's *Circle In the Water* (1970), whose Shakespearean title promised more thematic depth than the script delivered, though this look at sadistic hazing games and hero worship among military-school cadets did flirt with exploring the secrets young men hide about their sexuality. "No one under 18 admitted," the print ads warned, with a photo of two of the cutest cast members apparently naked and either loving or fighting—it was hard to tell. Charging extra for the first eight rows of seats (thus to enable CinemaScope viewing of the skin), the production gave a series of previews without ever posting a date for the premiere. When business was exhausted, the show simply closed without having opened.

Lee Barton's *Nightride* (1971) not only opened but got reviewed by the *Times'* first-string critic, Clive Barnes. He thought this tale of a young, idealistically uncloseted musician who wants to make songs out of an old and burned-out playwright's private love poems was flawed but very much of the moment: "It is a serious play about homosexual life that makes no apologies and reveals no regrets."§ Further, Barnes greatly praised Lester Rawlins' portrayal of the playwright, "magnificently rich and controlled . . . a performance that, whatever few reservations you have of the play, demands to be seen."

Rawlins was an established actor, a veteran of much Shakespeare and even a Best Featured Tony winner. But Chandler Hill Harben, the looker playing the musician, had just done one of the hetero nude shows, a revival of the forties folk play *Dark Of the Moon*, and that and *Nightride* made him typecast as "erotic only" among the gatekeepers. In fact, Harben, a fine actor, got those parts because he was physically beautiful, not "erotic," whatever that means. Still, no one believes the beautiful can act. Even today, Marilyn Monroe's Warholian ID—her profile picture, so to say—fails to give her credit for her superb work in *Bus Stop* or *Some Like It Hot*.

Despite the drawbacks, some actors now decided to grab the opportunity to go erotic. Alan Castner, a looker who had danced on Broadway and played

---

§ The *Times* insisted on using the clinical term *homosexual* in place of *gay*, a crude ban that ended with the retirement of the gay-hating executive editor A. M. Rosenthal, in 1988. Ironically, his gravestone reads—with presumably inadvertent double-meaning: "He kept the paper straight. "

Riff in the Lincoln Center *West Side Story*, in 1968, agreed to play Larry in one of *The Boys In the Band's* national tours, and then went All the Way in one of the few nude shows to play Broadway, Robert M. Lane's *Foreplay* (1970). The (of course simulated) love scene between two men (the other was Sam Stoneburner) alienated at least one actor who refused to join the cast, Broadway or no Broadway. However, later that season, Keith Michell and Diana Rigg went nude in an English import, Ronald Millar's *Abelard and Heloise* (1971), albeit in subdued lighting.

The difference between the two shows' skin scenes, obviously, is that straight revelation is merely exotic while the gay version is taboo. Further, *Foreplay* was one of the first of numerous Stonewall-era titles to deal sympathetically with a married man leaving his wife for another male. We recall Louis Jourdan's coming out in *The Immoralist* only to vow to lead a sexless life. But after the blunt naturalism of *The Boys In the Band*—which many forget ends with two of the party guests copulating (unseen) in an upstairs bedroom—celibacy began to seem fantastical.

The most sensationalized of the nude shows—but also the most seriously *written* of them—was John Herbert's *Fortune and Men's Eyes* (1967), another title quoting a line from Shakespeare. Yet Herbert's setting forbids poetry: a cell in a reformatory, where Herbert autobiographically reveals the louche social interactions of the incarcerated, an endless predation by the strong of the weak.

The Canadian Herbert (a pseudonym, for protection from vindictive officials), robbed by hoodlums, pressed charges, but as he had been in drag at the time, the state turned the case against him in favor of the crooks, and he ended up, as his play's young Smitty does, learning survival skills in the lions' den.

Author Herbert makes much of little, in a single set with only five players. Terry Kiser (later the mostly dead title part in the *Weekend At Bernie's* films) played Smitty, bullied by Rocky (Victor Arnold) and mentored by the pugnaciously effeminate Queenie (Bill Moor). Easy to stage, the piece traveled the world in some fifty-five productions in many languages, though at first it seemed that everyone who read the script thought it socially important but commercially impossible. Then, too, it was a rich proposition, not easy to categorize: was it a gay play, a prison exposé, a parable about how flexible the notions of good and evil become under pressure?

In New York, *Fortune and Men's Eyes* lasted an impressive 382 performances, at the Actors Playhouse. But two years later, Sal Mineo directed a revival in Los Angeles that interpolated a brutal rape scene wherein Rocky teaches Smitty who rules the cell block. The event was part of the original storyline but occurred offstage; Mineo staged it.

In a number of press interviews, Mineo defended his decision to make the rape explicit. To interviewer Stephen Lewis, Mineo pointed out that the rape marks an intense turnover in Smitty's worldview. Herbert's text, Mineo said, tells us that Smitty "is grabbed and pulled offstage, and that's [all we see]. How could anyone . . . know what he was subjected to? [The spectators] have to see it themselves. The nudity doesn't shock them, but the act [of rape] itself does. Most people are terrified."

Mineo himself played Rocky, to the Smitty of a very young and unknown Don Johnson, though when the production came to New York, Bartholomew Miro Jr. was Rocky and Mark Shannon the helpless but then (after he masters jailhouse power protocols) conquering Smitty. Michael Greer, the go-to in dramatic drag parts, played Queenie, and this time the show ran only 231 performances despite all the PR the rape scene generated. (Author Herbert inadvertently fed the beast by repudiating Mineo's version, in the *New York Times*.)

One wondered if the revival and its bitter honesty about prison life was another piece of Mart Crowley's legacy, as gay subject matter in all its aspects had become the topic of the day. In a way, *Boys* was a Zeitgeist play just as the Stonewall Rebellion, one year later, was Zeitgeist history, while the quiet and all but unnoticed uninstalling of the Wales Padlock Law, one year earlier, was a Zeitgeist legal development.

One Big Broadway show—the kind with major brand names involved—flirted with gay nudity. This was *A Patriot For Me* (1969), on the adventures of a real-life double-agent, the Austro-Hungarian traitor (and closeted gay) Alfred Redl. The heralds boasted top credentials: written by John Osborne, directed by Peter Glenville, and starring Maximillian Schell. David Merrick produced it,** because of a long-standing alliance with Osborne (Merrick put on six of his plays) and a love of Osborne's knack for creating controversy, because socio-intellectual bowwows sold tickets.

Further, the promise of a full-scale drag ball involving officers of the Dual Monarchy promised to lure customers; the main drag queen was to be Dennis

---

** He offered the production under the aegis of the David Merrick Arts Foundation, founded to give Merrick some financial advantage in mounting uncommercial works of artistic importance, from Tennessee Williams to *Marat/Sade*. Ironically, many of Merrick's "commercial" titles bombed while a few of the Foundation's offerings were hits.

King, a notable leading man ever since he created Big Jim in *Rose-Marie* in 1924. Yet more: *A Patriot For Me* demanded a lavish production, designed by visual aces Oliver Smith and Freddy Wittop, and fielded a huge cast constantly changing costume to reappear as multiple characters. (Tom [later Tommy] Lee Jones, in his Broadway debut, played six parts.) Yet the production garnered just so-so attention, and it closed after 49 performances.

Where was the public that had flocked to gay shows in the past—*The Captive, Oscar Wilde, Trio*? Had *The Boys In the Band* sated their curiosity for the time being? But *A Patriot For Me* was more homophile even than *Boys*, for not only was Redl gay: so was much of the Austrian military, at least in Osborne's retelling. His famous plays can be small-scaled and talky, but *A Patriot For Me* is as big as a small country and dizzy with plot and sub-plot— so much so that it compromised Maximillian Schell's relationship with the audience.

Here is a role of grand proportions: a professional warrior suffering from feelings of inferiority, a gay among straights, an outsider from the regions surrounded by well-born Austrians, a prey to blackmail (by the Russians), and at last a suicide. However, Osborne's crammed, confusing storyline fails to tell us what is driving Redl, and Schell's dry, compact performance seemed more a reflection of European anomie in the years leading up to World War I than a revelation of an individual's character.[††]

In fact, wasn't Osborne more interested in his kaleidoscope of history, politics, and ruling-class social life than in Alfred Redl and his affairs with handsome young men? But then why write a play about Alfred Redl? The show's first scene found Redl strangely moved by a young officer forced to duel with a bully. Both duelists were very attractively cast and stripped to the waist, as is the custom among the military when settling an affair of honor. So with *A Patriot For Me*'s first minutes we were already enjoying views of the Beautiful Male, as if Tennessee Williams or even Joshua Logan had seized the stage.

The duel ended with the young officer dying in Redl's arms, a valid start for a play about Alfred Redl, and a strong opening for Schell, who had created the role in London four years earlier and no doubt had given it some thought in the meantime. But then Osborne started piling up the political subplots,

---

[††] The same problem obtained in a Hungarian film of 1985 supposedly inspired by Osborne's play, *Colonel Redl*. Despite a two-and-a-half-hour running time and the insight of the accomplished Klaus Maria Brandauer in the lead, Redl comes off as perfectly inscrutable.

and by the time that drag ball came on, the public was wondering what this spectacle was about. Was it real or was it Memorex, a history play whose only purpose was to enable Osborne to trot out his latest bêtes noires for extermination?

And yet that drag ball was clearly Osborne's very reason for writing the play. He set great store by its wild parade of color and camp and was meticulous about the kinds of drag to be employed, from the "bum boys" who "spend between 3 and 6 months preparing an elaborate and possibly bizarre costume" to "the men who positively dislike women and put on drag" to "make them appear as odious, immoral and unattractive.‡‡ Redl and a few others of the military wore full-dress uniform, as if The War Of the Austrian Succession had married a Fellini movie, and all together the drag ball was one of the wildest ten minutes in the history of the Imperial Theatre.

The last scene of Act Two—the one just before the drag ball in the play's three-act continuity—showed a very different side of gay life. The setting is simply "A bare, darkened room" (a small inset at stage right, in the Broadway staging), where Redl is in bed with a handsome young soldier named Paul, who then gets up and opens the door to let in four of his fellows. They beat Redl savagely while Paul dresses, meanwhile stealing Redl's valuables, even his crucifix. As the soldiers leave, Paul helps the bloodied Redl up with:

PAUL: Don't be too upset, love. You'll get used to it.

And he leaves as the curtain falls on the second act. So which of these two scenes is the key one—the luminous drag ball in celebration of the secrets of the elite; or the mugging, demonstrating the powerlessness of the minority?

At least Osborne really did delve into the gay experience. At one point, Redl takes as his lover a young lieutenant (Michael Goodwin), then loses him to a countess (Salome Jens). At length the boy's two owners, so to say, have a confrontation in the first scene of Act Three, a tense exchange that's like the big choral rouser that restarts a musical after the intermission.

---

‡‡ This alleged misogyny of gay men is a favorite fantasy of certain heteros, and, for all that, few men have been more abusive of wives, girl friends, and his one daughter than Osborne himself. He would wed interesting women (including Mary Ure, an actress of great charm), then cheat on them even while trolling for the next bride. "Will you marry me?" he wrote Penelope Gilliatt, during one marriage and several affairs. "It's risky, but you'll get fucked regularly." Yes, Osborne had a playful side, but he threw his daughter out of the house when she was seventeen and never spoke to her again. Once, they accidentally came face to face; Osborne walked right on without even a nod.

Osborne doesn't waste time, as always in this vast Rubik's Cube of lust and glamour: the curtain rises on Redl and a youth in bed. The latter gets up "very quietly, almost stealthily":

REDL: Don't take my cigarette case, will you? *Or* my watch. There's plenty of change. Take that.

Within seconds, Redl hears that the countess has stolen his lover in marriage—and now she comes in for a *scene à faire:*

REDL: You'll never know that body like I know it. . . . The backs of his knees, the pattern on the soles of his feet. . . . His thick waist, and how long his thighs are compared to his calves, you've not looked at him, you never will.

Because she lives politically, as all the elite do, while he lives for art? It's an extraordinary scene, not least because Redl and the countess have been lovers themselves. Whence comes all of this sexual overlap, though? There were rumors about Osborne's bunburying throughout his life, but there are always such rumors in the world of the theatre, where everyone is masked and gossip passes the laws. With so much bed-switching in *A Patriot For Me*, the play could be taken as an allegory of thespian life.

Anyway, it would seem that Osborne wrote *A Patriot For Me* as a more universal metaphor: he wanted to show what happens to "minority" people in a majority-run society. The theme is isolation. As one of Osborne's generals puts it:

HÖTZENDORF: Outsiders['] whole creed of life must be based on duplicity— by necessity.

This explains Osborne's title, drawn from a remark made by Francis II, the last of the Holy Roman Emperors: Redl isn't a patriot of the Austria-Hungary that merely tolerates him with contempt, so he becomes his own nationality, working in his own interest.

The Alfred Redl that Osborne conjured up is a genuine show-off part. Indeed, Schell had recently been touring Germany as Hamlet, a character not entirely unlike Redl, but the actor was a bit short in the combination of fire and ice that Osborne's writing called for. Actually, Merrick's production, different from the one in London, generally lacked spirit. Director Peter

Glenville was concerned mainly with the pomp and intrigue of Osborne's layout, much less with its personality. In effect, *A Patriot For Me* is a wild and crazy piece that can be mistaken—as it was here—for a stately historical pageant.

All the same, *A Patriot For Me* occupies an important place in gay theatre history, for the London staging had to battle the censorious Lord Chamberlain, who so hated any depiction of homosexuality that he demanded vitiating cuts. The required alterations took in not just single lines to be omitted but the dropping of the play's three most important scenes—Redl's first gay mugging, the drag ball, and a tumultuous love-duet encounter between Redl and his latest partner.

There was the usual workaround for this: to declare the Royal Court Theatre a private club and present *A Patriot For Me* to members only. However, this would severely curtail business and precluded transfer to the West End. Worse, this loathsome sneak of a Lord Chamberlain tried to have the production prosecuted. But this aroused such general disgust—enhanced by such influencers as Laurence Olivier and critic Harold Hobson—that the Chamberlain's office was shackled, in 1968, and completely lost its censorship powers forever.

6

The 1970s

Did You Go To Oberlin?

I still remember how shocked I was to encounter *The Lord Won't Mind* in stores, with its flashy orange-and-yellow-against-black cover art and, inside, a narrative about two young gay men who mate, fight, and reconcile. And no one committed suicide. Camp thespian Charles Busch later likened it to "the fat, juicy romance novels that housewives have been devouring for years."

That was exactly the plan. *The Lord Won't Mind* wasn't the typical "tortured gay" story or the other prevalent kind, such as Christopher Isherwood's *A Single Man*, which never got around to anything vitally gay beyond his being attracted to straight men. It's a loser's book; worse, it's written in Isherwood's habitual flat tone, devoid of imagination. His hero was a Pinocchio who never became a real boy: because his version of gay was so dull and lifeless. On the other hand, as Busch notes, *The Lord Won't Mind* was saucy stuff, with lots of sex and show biz.

Its author was Gordon Merrick, whom we know from several chapters ago as a former actor, playing the juvenile in *The Man Who Came To Dinner* and dealing with co-author Moss Hart's immense crush on him. Merrick wrote it into his novel, though his treatment of his Hart-like director makes him predatory in a very un-Hart-like way. More persuasive is Merrick's clearly autobiographical struggle to smash open his closet door and accept that he and his lover deserve the same rights that straights do.

That was shocking for a novel of 1970, as was its success, including several months on the *New York Times* bestseller list, unheard of for a tale of gay men *being gay*. A Stonewall-era infrastructure was developing, making *The Lord Won't Mind* a Zeitgeist novel. There was even a Zeitgeist magazine, *After Dark*, which first appeared in 1968, like *The Boys In the Band*. "The Magazine Of Entertainment" was *After Dark*'s cover sobriquet (later expanded to "The National Magazine Of Entertainment," to match its reach), and it covered theatre, film, pop and classical music, cabaret, fashion, and travel. Countless photographs emphasized attractive, undressed men; the selection of illustrations was as homoerotic as *The Lord Won't Mind*.

Thus, a twelve-page article (in 1978) on the renovation of Atlantic City offered eight pages of gorgeous guys (and gals) in swimwear. Or a quickie photo caption would tell of some actor appearing in some show—but the photograph was sex: "Robert Altmann prepares for the role of Harper in *Naomi Court*, which opens August 2 at the Intersection Theatre in San Francisco," and there's handsome, built young Altmann in just athletic shorts, up in the air exercising on the rings. Yet *Naomi Court* is not about gymnastics. Similarly, "Paul Charles plays Mark in *A Chorus Line*" heralds fine young Charles in some meadow, completely nude save for a fancy coat draped over his right side, artfully hiding his genitals yet showing a hint of his patch.

So *After Dark* was among other things a skin mag back when skin mags were of necessity niche material. But *this* mag's stated territory of show biz and fashion gave it a mainstream profile. At that, it ran many excellent interviews with performers of various kinds, and it seems there was no one too big to talk to them. Indeed, the editors incessantly threw parties honoring major celebrities, compiling guest lists of the great, the near-great, and Sylvia Miles.* For a "morning after," many pages bragged in thumbnail photos of the invited. Like the newspaper gossip columns of the old days, these party spreads told you who was famous this month, linking gay with fame, a genuine coming-out for the shadow world.

For twelve years, *After Dark* was in effect the magazine of gay liberation, till a revolution in its editorial direction (in 1980) heterosexualized the content. Not only was the design changed and pompous think-pieces favored over the hot-cha interviews, but the skin shots—the very ID of the enterprise—were gone. By 1981, the magazine was "Back—the way you liked us!," as the covers proclaimed. Even so, it had betrayed its mission. And the Zeit had moved on; within a few more years *After Dark* had run out of its own time and ceased publication.

In many ways, Stonewall culture was taking shape, and in New York gay was a village: from opera and brunch-time mimosas to Pines weekends

---

* An actress who never really made it despite two Oscar nominations, Miles was a New York pet for her shameless but good-humored vulgarity. She achieved heroine status for dumping food on vicious drama critic John Simon at a New York Film Festival after-party. In the legend version, it was a plate of spaghetti, which suggests a thrilling mess, but in fact it was everything—cold cuts, coleslaw, potato salad, and so on, culled from a teeming buffet. "Baggage!" Simon cried. "I'll be sending you a bill for this suit!" To which Miles replied, "Good! It'll be the first time it's ever been cleaned!" She was a Big Lady personality in a small-time career.

and going cowboy or leather man at the Eagle, because one kept seeing the same guys everywhere one went. The look was ultra-masculine and the style No Smile, Few Words, though the women somehow didn't maintain a comparable subculture; the genders were allied but separate. Thus, the men were partial to uniforms, if only in fantasy, while the butch women might affect the plain look of a laborer—something we'll encounter later, in *Fun Home*.

Meanwhile, the etiquette was constantly changing. One couldn't bluntly ask someone if he was gay, but a euphemistic solution became popular for a bit in around 1971: you'd say, "Did you go to Oberlin?" It would baffle the straights—why that school?—but a gay would instantly get it, responding with his own version of "Yes."

Suddenly freed to explore the Gay Thing, the theatre upped its now forty-five-year-old commitment to discovering the existence of gay people. Show-biz exposure always leads to minority rights: when Florenz Ziegfeld hired Bert Williams for *Follies Of 1910*, it was the first time a black performer had a part—a major one, at that—in a white show. It was too avant-garde to take at first, but a generation later, when Ethel Waters again integrated the white revue, producers saw the possibility of racial inclusion, with significant black participation in *Beggar's Holiday* and *Finian's Rainbow* in the 1940s. A generation later, the crusade for black civil rights expanded into the national culture generally.

Now it was the turn of gay people. Initially, the proliferation of gay characters would not only naturalize the subculture for those unfamiliar with it but even open up a conversation of what gender is made of, though this often led to controversy. Thus, in the cable television series *Deadwood*, a somewhat Shakespearean western of the mid-2000s, a serial killer of prostitutes, himself a combination of prissy and creepy, manages to cut the throats of three women he has hired, and when their madam is asked why he did it, she replies in an exasperated tone, "I don't know, I'm not a man." Not "I don't understand crazy" but rather "Only men do this kind of thing, so ask them."

But we're advancing too fast, because back in the 1970s, gays were still partly stuck in stereotype mode. Silly comedies like *Norman, Is That You?* (1970) and *All the Girls Came Out To Play* (1972), favorite dinner-theatre fare, visited Broadway very briefly with their cliché fantasies of queer behavior. Actually, *All the Girls'* handsome hero, played by super-blond television star Dennis Cole, wasn't even gay. But everybody thought he was, so he made out like a bandit with happily surprised neighbor-hood women.

Tubstrip (1973) was a kind of *Boys In the Band* set in a bathhouse, with the usual gay foxhole. Just as *Boys* has the queen, the slut, the "straight-appearing" gent, and so on, *Tubstrip* had its own assortment, complete with an S & M master and his slave. And *Tubstrip*, too, offered a "secret" vintage romance, as the baths' manager—the show's protagonist—nurtured a high-school crush on a man who now turned up as a Vietnam vet, uniform and all. Also closeted and married.

Jerry Douglas wrote and directed *Tubstrip*, using the pseudonym of A. J. Kronengold as his writing credit, a common practice in gay plays of the day, as we saw with *Fortune and Men's Eyes'* John Herbert. However, *Tubstrip* really was no *Boys In the Band*. First of all, it counters *Boys'* angst by showing gay men basically just joking around, and Douglas' script lacks Crowley's wit. What *Tubstrip* had was nudity and the clever casting of various renowned parish hunks, at different times Calvin Culver, Dean Tait, and Jim Cassidy. The show's tone was set in its first moments, as the lights came up on the bathhouse's main room with a little pool down-stage, the space empty save for a wicker chair suspended from the ceiling, which turned to reveal the hero—the Cal Culver role—sitting in it, moody and pensive. Then another player rose up out of the pool, completely naked.

In its farcical structure of the bathhouse customers running in and out, *Tubstrip* was much ado about very little, but it did at least follow *Boys* in achieving a national profile. It played New York's Mercer Arts Center, its run curtailed when the ancient Broadway Central Hotel, which housed it, collapsed, killing four of the inhabitants and injuring others. After an emergency booking elsewhere in town, *Tubstrip* toured the country from Boston to Los Angeles, then closed out 1974 back in New York at the Mayfair Theatre. This was really just an old ballroom in the Edison Hotel, with the stage at one end and rows of folding chairs.

That run ended quickly, and *Tubstrip* hasn't been heard from since. But another farce set in a gay bathhouse has enjoyed revivals and was even filmed, by director Richard Lester. This was Terrence McNally's *The Ritz* (1975). Farces are like machines made of disguise and surprise, and McNally's moving parts were a mobster (Jerry Stiller) out to kill his brother-in-law (Jack Weston), who is defended by his wife (Ruth Jaroslow). For extra fun, a menacing hunk of a detective stalks in as gay hearts throb, but he turns out to have an absurdly squeaky voice.

Meanwhile the bathhouse habitués stroll in and out, led by the all-knowing Chris (F. Murray Abraham) and joined by an excitable show-biz wannabe named Googie Gomez (Rita Moreno). She nurtures a running gag in the person of her worst enemy, one Seymour Pippin. In Googie's worldview, the race of men can be divided into *either* producers who can make her a star *or* Seymour Pippin. So of course, twenty seconds before the final curtain, the detective tells us that his uncle—*Seymour Pippin*!—is about to re-enter Googie's life.

Critics have compared McNally's construction to that of Georges Feydeau, a real compliment. But Feydeau farces are really only funny in their middle act, when all the frantic activity occurs; McNally's farce is funny (and very active) right from the start. Much of his humor lies in his setting three very old-fashioned Italian–Americans in an avant-garde gay setting, for instance in encountering men dressed as fantasy icons:

WESTON: (*To a patron*) What unusual pants. They look like cowboy chaps.
PATRON: They are cowboy chaps.

An opera buff, McNally directed the sound system to play the titanically menacing five chords of Scarpia's theme in Puccini's *Tosca* at the end of Act Two before the second intermission. But his most personal moment was allotted to F. Murray Abraham's Chris. Trim and lightly gymmed in his bath towel, Abraham was something like *The Ritz*'s spokesman. His attitude was typical northeast urban jaded circuit-rider, but he got serious on a line so arresting (especially for the early Stonewall years) that I've quoted it in three previous books. This is the fourth:

CHRIS: I'll tell you something about straight people, and sometimes I think it's the only thing worth knowing about them. They don't like gays. They never have. They never will. Anything else they say is just talk.

Interestingly, Weston, who has thus far been supremely befuddled by everything, has a positive reply:

WESTON: That's not true.

but Chris snaps right back with:

CHRIS: Think about it.

Even today, *The Ritz* is revivable, though it needs a really flavorsome co-medienne for Googie Gomez. The aforementioned star of *Tubstrip* Calvin Culver co-produced (and played the detective in) a staging in 1983, in the discotheque Xenon (today the address of the Stephen Sondheim Theatre), with Holly Woodlawn, too soft a talent for Googie. The production was arresting for its use of veterans Dolores Wilson (again, the original Baby Doe in Douglas Moore's opera some thirty years before) and comic Joey Faye. Also on hand was the professional queen Michael Greer as Chris, substantial casting in itself.

This revival failed. But the career of Cal Culver is instructive enough for us to pause here. Born with all the physical graces, Culver was intelligent and creative. He odd-jobbed while trying to promote thespian employment, and though he did get very minor roles, for example understudying in *And Puppy Dog Tails* or an under five in the 1972 Ingrid Bergman–Pernell Roberts revival of Shaw's *Captain Brassbound's Conversion*, Culver was mainly an *After Dark* "actor-model," the magazine's term for a fine young lad open to suggestion.

Indeed, Culver's most notable position in the subculture's hierarchy of the time was as the lover of the novelist Thomas Tryon, whom we remember auditioning for Joshua Logan for the musical *Wish You Were Here* in Tryon's acting days. The Tryon–Culver liaison was a meeting of minds, as both men knew how easily portals swing open for the looker. It's the character actors of life who have to hustle; the beauty has only to show up to prosper. But while Tryon found his niche creating eerie novels on the prestige level, Culver mistook gay liberation for gay-sex liberation.

So his most notable gig was in the porn film *Boys In the Sand* (1971), appearing under the nom de sexe Casey Donovan. Shot in Fire Island Pines, the movie consists entirely of self-contained sex scenes without dialogue, yet as the first widely seen release of its kind, it was much praised despite Blanche DuBois lighting and action often caught through the branches of what looks like J. R. R. Tolkien's Mirkwood Forest.

It wasn't long before Culver's stage presence was officially erotic rather than vocational, which trapped him in events like *Tubstrip*. When *The Children's Mass* (1973), by *The Boys In the Band*'s original Donald, Frederick Combs, was announced for the Theatre de Lys, Culver's head shot dressed the first print ads. Yet when the show opened, he was gone, replaced by Gary Sandy. At that, the play, exploring the world of the cross-dresser caught up in New York's drug-a-disco scene, played only 7 performances.

Thus, Culver was just another of the beautiful boys with a matchless smile who thronged New York in early Stonewall, where the lesson of the age was that porn doesn't generally lead to Broadway and Hollywood. Porn leads to more porn. Resourceful enough to try running a guest house in Florida, Culver found that he was just another of the many has-been actor-models, and he died in 1983, of the usual reason.

It's a discouraging tale, especially as every season expanded the opportunities for actors willing to risk career disability to play gay roles. Most arresting, gay characters could appear in plays that were in fact uninterested in their sexuality. They weren't really "gay characters": they were characters who simply happened to be, among other things, gay.

Two such were principals in Lanford Wilson's *Fifth Of July* (1978), produced like so much of Wilson's work by Marshall Mason's Circle Repertory Company. William Hurt, as a paraplegic Vietnam veteran, formed a couple with Jeff Daniels, the two as important as anyone else in this ensemble piece. Yet none of the others treated them as gay, or as anything. To quote Congreve's Millamant in *The Way Of the World*, gay was starting to "dwindle" into normal, ordinary, unremarkable. It was a correction of sorts to the high-fashion exotics of *The Boys In the Band*—but would it have been possible if *The Boys In the Band* hadn't done the heavy lifting in the first place?

Even so, Hurt's role became a magnet for young leading men. When the production moved to Broadway with cast changes, in 1980, Christopher Reeve played the vet, and Richard Thomas, who replaced Reeve, repeated the part on television, in 1982. Playing these "ordinary," even colorless gays is not as easy as one might think; neither Reeve nor Thomas was as gripping as Hurt had been. More important, though, we have reached a point at which gay characters are not only not career killers but perhaps confer tolerance prestige on the straights who play them.

Musicals of course got into the act, very colorfully in *Applause* (1970). This is the show *not* based on the movie *All About Eve*, as it was written when it had the rights only to the very slight short story that *Eve* was based on and couldn't use the eccentric figures the film invented, from George Sanders' honey-tongued traitor of a critic to Marilyn Monroe's starlet, whom Sanders introduces as an alumna of "the Copacabana [he very quotably pronounces it "Copacabanya"] School of Dramatic Art."

Applause finally acquired permission to use the film's details, but only at the last minute, by which time the authors had given the piece a flavor of its own, not least in Charles Strouse and Lee Adams' score, well beyond what was heard in the movies' 1950s. The music swerved into the past just once, in "Who's That Girl?," when heroine Lauren Bacall saw herself on television in one of her old movies. Elsewhere, *Applause* sounded like a combination of the Tijuana Brass and the Swingle Singers, a very seventies tinta. But "Who's That Girl?" was pure 1940s, in its boogie-woogie-swing feeling and Bacall's constant use of forties buzz terms— "floydoy," "hubba hubba," and the like. Here was a Big Lady who had come to the musical from other places in showbiz: a Novelty Star who fell right in with the way a happy musical comedy plays.

This paid off handsomely for the gay issue as well. One of *Applause*'s innovations was the replacing of the movie's Thelma Ritter with Lee Roy Reams, as Bacall's personal assistant. And when Reams couldn't join the gang on some festive junket, he explained, "I've got a date." So Bacall hit us with a surprise:

BACALL: Bring him along!

It was a shock because we hadn't known that Reams was playing a gay guy, and Bacall's utterly accepting reply—coming, we note, from an actress who in real life had a lot of street cred as a celebrity nonconformist—helped establish gay as a community that was more than psychological or political. Rather, it was coincidental, simply here on the planet along with everyone else.

Again, the stage was opening up, in all sorts of ways. Even historical chronicle was explored, as in four more or less off-Broadway items. The stormy, near-homicidal relationship of poets Rimbaud and Verlaine came to life in Christopher Hampton's *Total Eclipse* (London 1967, New York 1973), and a musical, *Dear Oscar* (1972), offered a look at Wilde's heyday, a surprisingly innocuous piece till a gentle yet loaded "farewell" number for the protagonist, "There Where the Young Men Go," reminded us that the subject was sex. The only interesting thing about the show was its authorship by two women (a very rare event for the time), Addy O. Fieger for the music and Caryl Gabrielle Young for book and lyrics.

William M. Hoffman, later to write the first of the prominent AIDS plays, *As Is*, dared to Go There with *Gilles de Rais* (1975), in which soap-opera star George Reinholt played one of the most repellent figures of the second millennium, the thrill killer of countless young boys in fifteenth-century France. *After Dark* commemorated the event with a photo of Reinholt, apparently nude in secretive lighting, gazing raptly at somebody's severed head in his hands.

GAYS ON BROADWAY

A Scrapbook

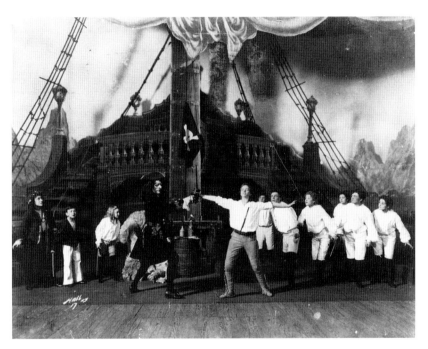

Maude Adams

Above, the classic shot of Adams in trousers as James M. Barrie's ageless imp Peter Pan in 1905, in the climactic battle with Captain Hook (Ernest Lawford). Probably the biggest star at the turn of the century—she could sell out during Holy Week—Adams was so reclusive that her public was spellbound at her shows trying to figure out who she really was. One of the boys, says *The Gay & Lesbian Theatrical Legacy*, without actually using the G-word. Instead, Kim Marra writes, "She engaged in two long-term same-sex domestic partnerships." And, in *Great Stars of the American Stage*, Daniel Blum dons dark glasses to say only, "She never married."

Eva Le Gallienne

Born in England, educated in France, and with a poet for a father, Le Gallienne is the most distinguished of Broadway's gay women, not only as actor but producer, director, and playwright as well. Unlike the stars who made their roles into themselves, Le Gallienne became someone different in every show, even changing her looks. *Above left*, she is the White Queen in *Alice In Wonderland* (1932), with Josephine Hutchinson. Then, *right*, in a complete change of personality, she is Marie Antoinette in Marcelle Maurette's *Madame Capet*, concerning the final sixteen years in the heroine's life, from Versailles to her cell in the Conciergerie, awaiting the call to the tumbril. *Opposite page*, a show card for the 1947 *Alice* revival. Note Le Gallienne's co-author credit.

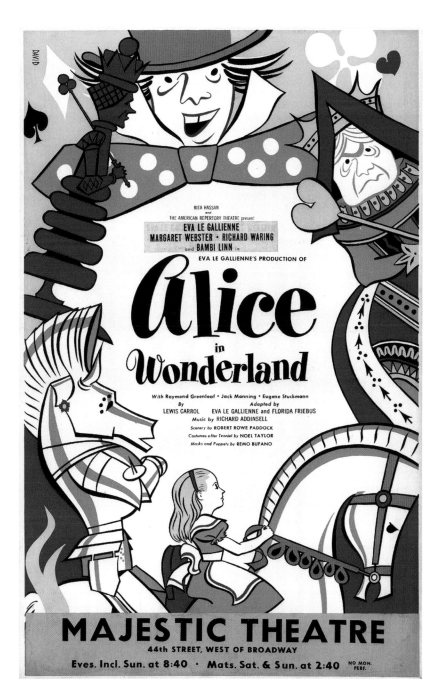

RITA HASSAN
and
THE AMERICAN REPERTORY THEATRE present

EVA LE GALLIENNE
MARGARET WEBSTER · RICHARD WARING
and **BAMBI LINN** in

EVA LE GALLIENNE'S PRODUCTION OF

Alice
in
Wonderland

With Raymond Greenleaf · Jack Manning · Eugene Stuckmann

By   Adapted by
LEWIS CARROL   EVA LE GALLIENNE and FLORIDA FRIEBUS
Music by RICHARD ADDINSELL
Scenery by ROBERT ROWE PADDOCK
Costumes after Tenniel by NOEL TAYLOR
Masks and Puppets by REMO BUFANO

MAJESTIC THEATRE
44th STREET, WEST OF BROADWAY
Eves. Incl. Sun. at 8:40 · Mats. Sat. & Sun. at 2:40   NO MON. PERF.

Katharine Cornell

Sustaining a marriage blanc with gay director Guthrie McClintic, Cornell had a very devoted public—one audience waited in its seats for four hours while she fought through a snowstorm to play. One wonders what they were thinking of Cornell's assumption of Shaw's Saint Joan, in the 1936 revival. Threatened by the Inquisition with a sadistic death (*above*; and note the presence of hooded executioners), she is asked why she wears men's clothes, fights and lives with soldiers. Why doesn't she stay home, cook, and clean? JOAN: There are plenty of other women to do it; but there is nobody to do my work.

Oscar Wilde

Despite legal harassment, theatre folk kept staging outspoken gay plays and audiences kept going to them. Many were forcibly closed, but not *Oscar Wilde* (1938), a British work and perhaps too classy for the censors to attack. Or were they appeased by the tragedy of his ignominious end, hard labor and then exile as a near-beggar in Paris? "I have had my hand on the moon," he cries, at the final curtain, comforted by absinthe and money from a friend. Meanwhile, let us admire the resemblance of the play's star, Robert Morley (*above left*), to the original (*right*).

THE PLAY OF THE WEEK: "THE GREEN BAY TREE"

(No. 1.) MR. DULCIMER (JAMES DALE),
Who Has Reared His Adopted Son, Julian (Laurence Olivier), in a Hothouse Atmosphere of Luxury, Is Shocked to Learn That His Ward Is Contemplating Matrimony, a Reaction Shared by His Cynical Butler, Trump (Leo G. Carroll). In This Scene From "The Green Bay Tree," at the Cort Theatre, Dulcimer Threatens to Cut Off His Ward's Allowance if He Persists in His Determination to Marry.
(All Photos by Vandamm.)

(No. 2.) JULIAN HAS GONE TO LIVE AT HIS REAL FATHER'S HOUSE,
Where, Under the Influence of His Fiancée Leonora Yale (Jill Esmond), He Is Industriously Engaged in the Study of Veterinary Surgery. He Is Bored and Very Unhappy.

(No. 3.) JULIAN FINDS THAT THE PURSUIT OF A PROFESSIONAL CAREER
Is Difficult After a Life of Ease, and Makes an Unsuccessful Plea to Dulcimer for a Resumption of His Allowance. Dulcimer Shatters Julian's Resistance and the Boy Consents to Return to His Old Life and at Least Temporarily Give Up His Idea of Marriage. Dulcimer, Realizing That He Has Won, Orders Trump to Prepare Julian's Former Quarters.

(No. 4.) JULIAN, HAVING DEFINITELY RETURNED TO HIS OLD LIFE,
His Real Father (O. P. Heggie) and His Fiancée Come to Dulcimer's House and Accuse Him of Exerting a Corrupting Influence Over Julian. The Father Demands That Julian Return to Him, but When Dulcimer Refuses to Give the Boy Up, the Father in a Frenzy Kills Him.

(No. 5.) JULIAN, NOW SOLE HEIR TO THE DULCIMER FORTUNE,
Assumes All of the Mannerisms as Well as the Mode of Life of His Former Benefactor, Much to the Satisfaction of the Cynical Trump.

The Green Bay Tree

Above, a scene-by-scene breakdown of another British gay play that Got Away With It, by Mordaunt Shairp. The captions reveal a distinguished cast; note Leo G. Carroll, later television's Topper, as the gay butler.

The Big Lady

Elemental in the history of gay playmaking and theatregoing, the Big Lady is a combination of extraordinary talent, outsized individuality, and unique appeal to gay men. These idols ruled during the Golden Age, and while everyone has his or her own idea of exactly when that was, it's definitely over now, as are the idiosyncratic personalities that gave it so much vitality. *Above*, Mary Martin leads John, Michael, and the Lost Boys in one of the video airings of the *Peter Pan* musical of 1954. Like her predecessor in the part Maude Adams, Martin didn't get into men's clothes that often, but they fit her to a T.

The Big Lady favored rococo attire, far from Mary Martin's Neverland casual. These performers were *stars*; they weren't people you knew in 4–H Club. *Above left*, Ethel Merman in the *Call Me Madam* movie, one of only two times she filmed one of her stage roles. Big Ladies were generally too Big for the screen (though Barbra Streisand managed the transition easily). *Right*, Merman is still grandly accoutered, with son Donald O'Connor and husband Dan Dailey in *There's No Business Like Show Business*, a Hollywood backstager about a theatrical family.

Why don't Big Ladies thrive in the movies? The broad gestures and pointed line delivery that enriches their presence in big Broadway theatres makes them seem insatiable on screen, greedy for attention. Most disappointing to fans of Gwen Verdon was Warner Bros.' *Damn Yankees, above*, with most of the stage cast. Verdon *(center)* was not photographed properly, and while her colleagues projected well enough in a somewhat cartoonish way, especially Ray Walston *(right)* as the devil, Verdon seems too stagey. Ironically, Tab Hunter *(left)* is the best thing in the film: most natural and very likeable, though all the Broadwayites on the shoot condescended to or ignored him.

Spoken drama is too realistic for the Big Lady, making do with the Grand Lady. *Tea and Sympathy* (1953) opened with Deborah Kerr (opposite John Kerr). After eight months, the two left, replaced *(above)* by Joan Fontaine and. . . Anthony Perkins, whose future as a "straight" husband and father would bring a new meaning to the word "gay." Note the dutiful illustration of the title concept.

One stage play without music did host a Big Lady, though *Auntie Mame* (1957), with its fantastical (and even campy) comedy and beguiling emotional tugs, is virtually a musical without songs. *Above*, Rosalind Russell models part of the heroine's fabulous Travis Banton wardrobe, as—to repeat—the Big Lady dotes on fashion. A smash hit with multiple stars on Broadway and on tour, *Auntie Mame* brought out a rota of dames with panache, from Greer Garson and Constance Bennett to Beatrice Lillie and Eve Arden. Most important, Russell's rendition of Mame supplied a matrix for the personality quirks of the queens of Stonewall, getting off hilarious mots while animating an imaginary cigarette holder.

Auntie Mame had its sentimental side, too, as, *above left*, when longtime staff Ito (Yuki Simoda) and Norah (Beulah Garrick) pay off Mame's Depressions debts with their life savings. Mame is overcome. Still, the story was not complete till it finally *was* a musical, with a Jerry Herman score, as *Mame* (1966). Angela Lansbury became a star in the part, with huge over-the-title billing and key-art caricature in the poster that ended forever Lansbury's twenty years of journeyman labor in show biz. *Above right*, Lansbury has just made her entrance as an official Big Lady in "It's Today," offering a great new reason for celebrating: just because. Mame is *philosophe.*

Above, more *Mame*, in the title song after the fox hunt. Then, *Mame* as a movie (below), as Robert Preston romances Lucille Ball, who was too old even behind Ponce De León lens filters and couldn't sing. Still, the character is one of the biggest in gay theatre. Mame is deathless.

The Beautiful Male

From Tennessee Williams to Christopher Durang, gay playwrights make a feature of young built guys, often shirtless. After *A Streetcar Named Desire*'s Stanley Kowalski, every man short of a character player had to tone up. *Above*, here's Edward Albee's *The American Dream* (1961), with Jered Barclay in the eponymous role and Sudie Bond's Grandma admiring his muscles. "They natural?" Grandma asks. The gym helps, he admits. Still, he was the goods right from the start: "Good profile, "he notes, "straight nose, honest eyes, wonderful smile." The romantic lead was always about looks, but gay drama sexualized the icon.

M. Butterfly

David Henry Hwang's flamboyantly exotic tale (drawn from the headlines) of how a cross-dressing straight man runs a "honey trap" on a another straight man (who thinks he's having an affair with a woman) is as much about East-West politics as about male-female gender relations. On Broadway, in 1988, John Lithgow and BD Wong played the leads, but Anthony Hopkins and G. G. Goei (*above*, in the PR brochure) assumed the roles at London's Haymarket Theatre in a replica of John Dexter's bizarre staging. Two men having an affair, yet neither is gay? Does the play's title explain this mystery? What does the M. stand for? Reader: all is explained in these pages.

The Nance

Above, we're back with a real gay—but he's still "performing" his life. The PR blurb (above) recalls the 1930s as "a time when it is easy to play gay and dangerous to be gay." Yet it was dangerous to play gay, too, for *The Nance* (2013) reveals that thespian freedom could be perilous. No one was certain how much the authorities were willing to tolerate from season to season, and Nathan Lane's prancy Chauncey Miles (*at center*) was bound by his belief in his art to push the boundaries. And that, really, describes what gay theatre has always been doing, from the "female impersonators" of the 1910s and 1920s right up to the various boys in the band. Writers use gay culture to explain humankind.

However, on a vastly more relaxed note and collaborating with Anthony Holland, Hoffman moved to colonial America for *Cornbury: The Queen's Governor* (1976), on a cross-dressing viscount who was an intimate of England's royal family, sent to run New Amsterdam to avoid scandal at home. As Hoffman saw it, Cornbury had all the characteristics of a modern-age gay before its time—fashion, style, repartee, shopping. When his financial advisor tries to get him to budget his spendthrift habits, Cornbury waves the lecture away with a lament about the colony's lack of chic. He yearns to have his portrait painted in his favorite accessories—the "silver-tissue manto," the "crimson velvet under-petticoat," the "rich fox muff":

FINANCIAL ADVISOR: The treasury is empty, my lord.
CORNBURY: *Sell Staten Island!*

Still, most gay fare busied itself with the dos and don'ts of the contemporary scene, such as how to react when the hustler (twenty-four-year-old Brad Davis) you brought home pulls a knife on you, in Michael Sawyer's aforementioned *Naomi Court* (1974). This was a two-act play, each act concerned with a different occupant of an apartment building about to be torn down; the play's title was the building's address.

True, hustlers were rare in seventies dramas. A more common theme was the "straight" husband who leaves his marriage to restart life with a boy friend. John Hopkins' *Find Your Way Home* (1974) presented Michael Moriarty as the new lover and Jane Alexander as the deserted wife, who created the evening's sole dramatic moment when she followed her errant husband right to Moriarty's apartment, thinking to confront the "other woman" and discovering instead a cute guy. "Filth!" she cried, to her husband. "You are—filth!"

In a way, this could have been an "untold tale" of *The Boys In the Band*, as Hank's wife stumbles into his love nest with Larry. The problem with Hopkins' version of this scene was the actor playing her husband, simply too dreary for us to care whom he loved. At that, as Hopkins was an Englishman writing about the English, he characterized the young boy friend—a shallow queen, by the way—with that insanely irritating English habit of calling everybody "love." *Find Your Way Home* lasted four months, presumably out of the public's interest in the theme, but even the grisly *Gilles de Rais* was better.

Another man giving up his marriage to live with a younger man in an English setting was Simon Gray's very acclaimed *Butley* (London 1971, New York 1972), complete with its star, Alan Bates. It was possibly the greatest role the actor ever had: of a university lecturer stalling various colleagues and students on the single day when his destructive, disorderly life is finally coming to a total end.

With his usual flair for separating normal people from eccentrics in his character writing, Gray created a huge and terrible protagonist, brilliant, witty, fascinating, and so full of some devilish misery that nothing delights him save making others unhappy. He keeps putting off his boss' phone calls—to summon Butley to a meeting at which he will be fired, we infer—while baiting his live-in and the latter's new boy friend and making trouble for a handsome young student for no reason other than sheer irresponsible malice.

Butley is all the same very funny, set in the office that Butley shares with his now exasperated lover, who, again, is just about to leave him. Everyone is. Butley's wife, even, is abandoning him for a bore of a guy: because anyone is better than the reckless Butley:

BUTLEY: Good God! Who would want to marry *her*?
HIS LIVE-IN: You did.
BUTLEY: That was before she'd been through the mill.

Gray piles on the entrances and exits of characters who, bit by bit, fill us in on the sinful chaos Butley has made of his life. At one point, Butley notes that the day's events are observing the classical unities:

BUTLEY: The use of messengers has been most skillful.

Interestingly, except for Butley's wife, more or less saying goodbye, all of the principals are gay. It's a rich mix of personality, too. Joey, Butley's incipient ex-lover, is smart but a bit of a flatterbox. His new partner, Reg, is from the North, provoking Butley into a viciously mocking tirade in Yorkshire dialect till Reg decks him with a blow to the stomach. Edna, a fellow academic, suddenly lets slip, rather touchingly, that she lost *her* (female) lover when the latter married a man.

Meanwhile, Butley lets fly with an observation on Stonewall culture (even if England didn't have a Stonewall per se) that is his most shocking statement of the evening. It seems that he is fed up with how common homosexuality has become now that all the "naughty thrills" have been legalized:

BUTLEY: The law, in making them safe, has made them drab.

Bizarre as that is, it typifies how some gays felt when they no longer had to bond ephemerally in bathrooms and alleys, no longer risked public exposure in a bar raid, no longer watched a bartender retrieve the glass they had been drinking from and smash it on the floor, a sign that they were not welcome. How warped does one's judgment have to be to miss bygone days of oppression? Or were these goons trolling before the internet gave the word its present meaning? Is *Butley* simply adding another outrage to his collection for the sport of it?

In any case, there were few drab gay characters in the theatre. Consider the 1971 revival of the twenties musical *No, No, Nanette*, part of a nostalgia cycle that brought back Ruby Keeler and Patsy Kelly from thirties Hollywood, supposedly under the direction of Busby Berkeley, though he turned out to be a drunken old foodledoo who could barely make it through the photo ops. (The show was ultimately put together by adapter and director Burt Shevelove and choreographer Donald Saddler with his assistants.)

No, No, Nanette was of course the opposite of drab, and while not a gay show per se it was certainly a gay production. The wild costume designs of Raoul Pène du Bois—especially the art nouveau sweaters for the boys in blazing primary colors—were a show in themselves, and the sight of Helen Gallagher in the dress of a thousand pleats for her torch spot, " 'Where Has My Hubby Gone?' Blues," was not the fashion statement hetero designers (if there be any) tend to make. Sometimes gay inheres not in characters and themes but rather in a look, an attitude, a kind of smartiboots worldview with a logic of its own. You *mussst* come over!

This *Nanette* also reminded everyone that if the chorus boys in musicals aren't gay as a rule then they might as well be. This was when "lightbulb" jokes were just starting to trend, as in:

Q: How many Jewish mothers does it take to replace a lightbulb?
A: Don't trouble about me, I'll just sit here all by myself in the dark.

The *Nanette* version was:

Q: How many straight Broadway chorus boys does it take to replace a lightbulb?
A: Both of them.

Another revival, of *Kismet*, in a black-cast revision called *Timbuktu!* (1978), added a new Big Lady to the list, Eartha Kitt. She had been prominent for over a generation, since her breakout debut in *New Faces Of 1952*. But only now did she really make it to top stardom, as she was difficult to cast except in exotic parts (such as *Batman*'s Catwoman) and was personally belligerent with everybody from co-stars to interviewers.

However, she was also courageous, and in 1968 she spoke against the Vietnam War and our soldiers being "sent off to be shot and maimed." This was at a White House luncheon hosted by First Lady Mrs. Johnson, and the enraged authorities compiled a dossier of scandals about Kitt's personal life, in an instance of cancel culture avant la lettre. Kitt was forced to seek work abroad, so *Timbuktu!* marked her return to American show biz.

She is of interest herein because her alluring stage presence seems to speak directly to gays with her trilling, elongated vowels and playfully overdone takes. Her entrance in *Timbuktu!* was a study in lazy insolence, as she prowled downstage, surveyed the auditorium of the Mark Hellinger Theatre, and, like a Roman grandee visiting the gladiators' quarters, asked, "Anyone new in town?" Later, when told that her (villainous) husband was dead and she was now a widow, she cried, "Aaaaa . . . wiiiiidoooow?" as she deftly fainted into a man's arms with her left hand fluttering outward and her right shielding her brow with vast delicacy. It stopped the show every time.

Speaking of musicals not precisely gay yet not precisely straight either, *Chicago* and *A Chorus Line* appeared back-to-back in 1975 as dueling high-maestro exhibitions of, respectively, Bob Fosse and Michael Bennett. Each show had a gay character, though *Chicago*'s prison Matron was never explicitly a lesbian, even if shyster lawyer Jerry Orbach called her "Butch" (and the *Chicago* movie accented the Matron's interest in young women). Orbach also called a tailor a "dumb fruit" when he accidentally stuck Orbach with a pin, but in fact *Chicago* was a pro-gay show in general, with a score by Kander and Ebb (though Ebb was never officially out) and a number of gay creatives, including both producers.

The gayest of all, as I've said, was Bob Fosse, straight but a major docent in the academy of fabulous in the way he moved his dancers, in the erotic character of his stagings, in his worship of the crazed deities of show biz— Delicia, Transvesto, Orgasmo. True, Fosse didn't focus on shirtless hunks in the Joshua Logan manner. Still, his chorus men gave off a whiff of homosocial welcome, and the women were physically intense—and Fosse didn't have Logan's casting luxury, because Fosse's choreography called for dancing expertise above all. Logan could hire a chorus of bodybuilders for *All American*'s aforementioned locker-room scene and to fill out their cheerleader jerseys when tossing a football in the aisles of the Winter Garden, and choreographer Danny Daniels had to work them into the dance numbers, like it or not. But Fosse needed the best dancers around.

It was a matter of housekeeping. A Fosse musical was first of all a talent show, one somewhat related to the glittery exhibition Zaza sings about in *La Cage Aux Folles*: "slightly 'forties' and a little bit New Wave"—but in an elevated temperature. The signifiers were everywhere, as when Jerry Orbach sang his ID number in *Chicago*, "All I Care About." The chorus girls, armed with huge feathered fans, moved around him at the end in a close-up cluster, and when they moved off, his trousers were gone.

Unlike Fosse, Michael Bennett was gay, though he bearded, marrying his dance avatar, Donna McKechnie. And he liked his musicals shiny as well as emotional, like a nutritious lollipop. Morever, *A Chorus Line* has an unmistakably gay principal in Paul, the dancer who suffers an excruciating injury during the audition and has the outstanding solo number. Yet it isn't sung, and the orchestra doesn't "soundtrack" the scene.

This is odd, because music is constantly playing in *A Chorus Line* even if no one is singing. It is almost never silent—except here, because gay itself had become so relevant that Paul's moment had to be highlighted, separated from the other confession solos like "At the Ballet" and "Dance: Ten, Looks: Three." They were generally merry or nostalgic: even McKechnie's "The Music and the Mirror," a plea for a job, is aggressive, not tragic.

Paul's solo is tragic. Elsewhere in the show the characters survive a disdainful acting teacher or navigate puberty, but Paul's story has no happy ending—even, as played by the first Paul, Sammy Williams, no possibility of one. A performer in a drag club, he finds his parents have suddenly shown up, and his father entrusts Paul to the stage manager. "Take care of my son," he says. And Paul adds, just before he breaks down, that his father had never called him that before.

It isn't really the script, by James Kirkwood and Nicholas Dante, that intensifies the scene, but Michael Bennett's genius for storytelling. In Paul's monologue, the locomotion of the show—the anxiously driving music and dance of it—goes absolutely still for a long while, thus jarring us into a different mode of attention. Up to this point, we have been attending a show about kids with kid problems. But Paul is a kid with gay problems.

The opposite of *A Chorus Line* in every way was the now forgotten *Sextet* (1974), in which two lovers (Robert Spencer, Harvey Evans) give a dinner to "meet the family"—Spencer's mother and her new boy friend and Spencer's old college roommate and his wife. The show makes an interesting sidelight in the theatre's exploration of the gay experience, here being the in-laws, more or less. However, *Sextet*'s book did not invent distinctive characters, so the Lawrence Hurwit–Lee Goldsmith score had little to amplify.

A Chorus Line, by contrast, offered some intriguing personalities, so Marvin Hamlisch and Edward Kleban had material to dig into even aside from the very theatrical air of shriving about the audition, for some shall be saved and some damned. Poor little *Sextet*, with its six humdrum characters (even the two gays were dull, which almost never happens) simply didn't take off as drama, and quietly joined the ranks of the modestly staged musical flops that had more or less become the rage (so to say) of the era.

Another small-scaled musical, this one on off-Broadway, was *Boy Meets Boy* (1975), though this one enjoyed a full chorus and many changes of set. A parody of old-style shows, it avoided the specific references of *The Boy Friend*'s tea-for-two musical comedy and *Little Mary Sunshine*'s operetta. Still, like them, *Boy Meets Boy* had a single author, Bill Solly (though he did have a cowriter for the book, Donald Ward) and a guiding principle to hang jokes and songs on a deliberately silly storyline.

The form works if the score is first-rate, but *Boy Meets Boy*'s isn't. And a fetching new talent in the heroine slot—Julie Andrews and Eileen Brennan in the two earlier titles—is very helpful. But of course *Boy Meets Boy* didn't have a heroine. The romance bonded a roguish American reporter (Joe Barrett) and an English wallflower (David Gallegly) who transforms in semi-Cinderella style into a looker.

It all took place in London and Paris at the time of Edward VIII's abdication, in 1936, and the piece might have sounded nifty on paper, but the book, though fast-moving, was witless and obviously the lame score was a problem. There was one cute bit, in the upbeat title song. Using the old paradigm of Boy meets girl, boy loses girl, boy gets girl, the chorus revised this to an equation fit for Stonewall, for now two males partner up in "a wonderful blend." Yes, Boy meets boy. Boy loses boy. "But Boy gets boy in the end!"

Revues were useful to microscope aspects of gay life. Too often, these were the most apparent events, such as meeting and parting. But Steve Sterner and Peter del Valle's *Lovers* (1975) did rove a bit, as in one sketch in which two leather boys want to hook up but each needs the other to make the first move. And one of the songs keened for the death of a boy friend—before anyone had heard of AIDS—in "You Came To Me As a Young Man," sung by Reathel Bean.

In Gay Company (1974) was even more inventive. A cast of four men and one woman, constantly changing costumes, dealt with, for instance, a quartet of Irish firefighters suspecting that one on the force is gay; or three men in tutus hymning the delights of the drag-queen ballet troupes; or the complaint of an undercover vice cop, tricked out in flashy wig, feather boa, short leather skirt, and fishnet stockings. Fred Silver's songs were at times quite clever, looking in on the urgings of a Jewish mother in "[You] Ought To Be Married." All right, so you're gay, couldn't you go through with it "just for show"? So don't sleep with her—"No one will know!" Later, in "Sondheim," she was now the frustrated girl friend, trapped in a Sondheim world. In a cunning spoken section, she pursued her lament using some thirty-five Sondheim song titles, including a few arcane cut numbers.

In Gay Company was attractive and pleasant, but one gay revue actually provoked a public bowwow over how gay art should behave. The piece in question was Al Carmines' *The Faggot* (1973), Carmines being an extremely prolific composer (and sometime lyricist) of off-Broadway shows who was as well an ordained minister at Judson Memorial Church in Washington Square, an Italian Renaissance building complete with a ten-story campanile. Carmines was also gay, of the phylum Merrily Facetious. He had fun with his shows and he hoped you would, too.

So first a bit of backstory. Carmines' musicals, from the early 1960s into the 1990s, treated everyone from Gertrude Stein to W. C. Fields. But his outstanding piece was *Promenade* (1969). In case anyone was wondering what happens when a gay man and a gay woman write a musical for the sheer mad fun of it, *Promenade* was the answer, for Carmines' librettist-lyricist, Maria Irene Fornes, was a playwright with an experimental bent and Carmines happily went along as she forged a path into this beguiling oddity, something like Theatre of the Absurd put on by opera singers who have just sampled some magic mushrooms.

The storyline? Basically, two charming convicts escape and encounter a host of bizarre people who burst into song about whatever occurs to them—"Unrequited Love," "Four [naked ladies]," "The Cigarette Song" (because the singer likes to parade down the street with a butt in one hand and a toothpick in the other: "Ah," she sings, "that's life!"). Carmines was highly eclectic in his music and never more so than in *Promenade*. His prelude suggests Nino Rota; "Chicken Is He" is ragtime; "The Moment Has Passed" bears a Kurt Weill overtone. In fact, Carmines' tunes somehow suggest an imitation of old forms even when he's inventing them.

Promenade wasn't just another off-Broadway musical. The cast included many Broadway veterans or soon-to-bes, such as Madeline Kahn, George S. Irving, Alice Playten, and Shannon Bolin (the wife in *Damn Yankees*). Eddie Sauter, long a major name in orchestration, laid out the arrangements, and the show even opened its namesake, the Promenade Theatre, on upper Broadway.

Clearly, Al Carmines was a hoot of a composer, so his gay revue, the just-mentioned *The Faggot*, would be very much on the merry side, combining present-day parish archetypes from queen to hustler with Great Homosexuals of History in a silly (or perhaps a *Promenade*-like) way. The tone was loving ridicule, as when Oscar Wilde (Carmines himself) told Gertrude Stein (Lee Guilliat), "No one is as pretentious as we are—that's why I love you."

Like it or not, *The Faggot* was all for fun. Yet this didn't stop the *Times'* Clive Barnes from theorizing that "Most homosexual shows . . . are either fiercely militant or atrociously maudlin," thereby ignoring most of the plays that had turned up in the wake of *The Boys In the Band*. Too, Barnes spoke of "the restless promiscuity" of gay, as if promiscuous straights were too rare to count.

It's not odd to find Barnes, one of the worst theatre critics in history, getting it wrong. But *The Faggot* had gay enemies, too. Political agitator Martin Duberman, also in the *Times*, laid *The Faggot* out to filth. "It's more than a failure," he said. "It's an affront." With its "tinkly tunes, perky chore-ography and cartoon realities," it "will help to perpetuate stereotypes that a serious movement [for gay rights] has been attempting to eradicate." As for Carmines' treatment of the historical figures, Gertrude Stein is made to sound "like Maria von Trapp." In all, Duberman much preferred Jonathan Katz's rival revue, *Coming Out!*, militant in its look at the history of oppression.

Carmines replied to Duberman, asserting more or less that gay culture is in the eye of the beholder and gay art need not strike policy positions every single time it is made. Given the tense struggles of the early Stonewall era, this was like bringing a tube of Pixy Stix to a gunfight, and here is where the grand *querelle* broke out, as readers wrote in to the *Times* on one side or the other, mainly against Carmines. Gay artists, it appeared, must be for the battle for right . . . or against it.

But isn't it sheer bullying to assail a slight musical revue with a "No time for comedy! Revolution for evah!" war cry? It wasn't as though Carmines' approach was prevalent, as many gay theatre writers were taking their characters into previously unmapped terrain—the American military, for instance, in David Rabe's *Streamers* (1976), in the little basement stage below Lincoln Center's Vivian Beaumont Theatre.

The title of *Streamers* refers to something rather grisly. It's slang that two oldish soldiers (Kenneth McMillan, Dolph Sweet) use for paratroopers whose chutes don't open after they've jumped, a metaphor perhaps for the gay soldier in a gay-hating environment. Peter Evans played a G.I. who unwisely risks being honest about himself, and in the end two of the soldiers were stabbed to death by a private (Dorian Harewood, in a coiled spring of a portrayal), reminding us that transparency is righteous only when effective.

Still, transparency is what many writers (both gay and straight) wanted to work with. James Kirkwood's *P.S. Your Cat Is Dead!* (1975) was a real novelty: a gay burglar (Tony Musante) seduces his lovelorn straight victim (Keir Dullea) while being tied up over the kitchen sink for most of the evening. And Albert Innaurato's off-Broadway *Gemini* (1976) sited the familiar trope of the gay crush on a straight friend in a most exotic landscape—the working-class row houses of South Philadelphia.

Innaurato colored his palette with a number of eccentrics, and *Gemini*'s television commercial featuring them, a staple on local networks, attracted a huge public that seldom attended the theatre. Apparently, they were fascinated by the characters' antics at the festive table. "Take human bites!" was the ardent plea of the mother (Jessica James) of an overweight loser, and another of Innaurato's people declared, "I'm not hungry, I'll just pick" as she scarfed up spaghetti from someone else's plate. It was the same wonderful shock of recognition that excited New York's juvenile gang members in the 1840s at unusually realistic plays presenting characters like themselves. No, it wasn't Shakespeare, but it was *my life*!

Far more artful than the Kirkwood or Innaurato but, again, rewarding the audience with figures they might have known personally was Susan Miller's *Confessions Of a Female Disorder* (produced regionally, 1973), a look at a young woman's vacillating approach to her sexuality. Whom is she attracted to? And why? At the Eugene O'Neill Festival in Connecticut, Swoosie Kurtz played the heroine, named Ronnie, married to Lenny Baker and involved also with Ben Masters but most impressed by Beverly Bentley, who tells her—as others do, constantly—"You don't exactly confront the issues."

But what if you don't know what the issues are? Ronnie doesn't want to understand them. She needs to feel them, reminding us that perhaps women are more intuitive and conceptual about sex where men are physical and definitive. Just as Lanford Wilson "enlarged" *The Madness Of Lady Bright* with the

Boy and Girl used in various ways, Miller gave *Confessions* little choruses of
Lettermen (the boys) and Cheerleaders (the girls), prototypes of the people
who relate strongly to normative beliefs. They know how they react to everything even before they meet up with it, while Ronnie lives in a state of permanent discovery. In Act Two, the boys and girls become Cocktail Party Guests,
now older yet still sure of themselves no matter what happens, as witness
Nancy, a doctor's wife:

NANCY: He let me work while he was going to school. It was really generous of
    him. He's making $85,000 a year now. We're divorced.

A writer, Ronnie closes the show in the company of these women, walking
around them and watching their doings. "It is an exploration," Miller explains,
"an unearthing, a transference." Then one of the women hits a single key on
Ronnie's typewriter. The others freeze in place as Ronnie gently touches the
woman, a stranger. A friend. She continues typing, and we wonder if now
Ronnie will confront the issues, as she seems to have someone to share them
with. And that's the end of the play.

There appeared to be no limit to these experiments in gay playmaking. Martin
Sherman's *Bent* (1979) opened with a surprise, on two gay partners in bathrobes
nursing hangovers after a night of revelry. They have taken a trick home, and
from the way they speak, these two could be circuit riders of New York's gay
scene. Even when one reminds the other that he "called [the trick] your own little
storm trooper," this could still be playful gay banter. Then the trick appeared,
for a slow, cocky tour of the stage completely nude, frontal and backal—yes, on
Broadway in 1979, very early for such a blatant skin exhibition.

By this time, something seemed off about the scene. Where and when was
this taking place? Because suddenly two men charged into the apartment,
and they really were Nazi storm troopers. As the two partners fled, the Nazis
shot the trick; one slit his throat. And while the audience gasped in horror, a
sign came down from the flies:

BERLIN—
1934

Blackout.

Bent was almost as filled with gay characters as *The Boys In the Band*.
Besides the two young men who opened the show (Richard Gere, David

Marshall Grant) and the trick (James Remar), there was Gere's Uncle Freddie (George Hall, superb in a one-scene role), and Gere's comrade in Dachau (David Dukes). There was even a drag queen who came down on a trapeze when the "Berlin—1934" sign appeared, though he said he was just, as a later porn-world phrase put it, "gay for pay."

Interestingly, even after his and Grant's frantic escape from their apartment, Gere laughed off his uncle's warning about how dangerous life will be for gays under Nazi rule:

UNCLE FREDDIE: They can arrest you for having fluff thoughts.
GERE: (*laughing*) Oh, Uncle Freddie.
UNCLE FREDDIE: It's not funny.
GERE: It is.

Yet virtually all the gay characters have been killed by the play's end.

Perhaps the playwright intended *Bent* as a cautionary tale: gay hatred is not a laughing matter. Gere ends up at hard labor in a concentration camp, moving stones from here to there and back with scarcely any rest. Dukes works near him—don't talk or the guards will kill you—yet the two manage to have virtual sex in the third most arresting scene, as they stand downstage facing the public, never touching or even glancing at each other. A sample:

DUKES: Kissing your eyes.
GERE: Hot.
DUKES: Kissing your lips.
GERE: Yes.
DUKES: Mouth.
GERE: Yes.
DUKES: Inside your mouth . . .

Eventually, an S.S. captain orders Dukes to throw his prisoner's cap at the electrified fence upstage. As the cap hits it, sparks fly. Now the captain orders Dukes to retrieve the cap and thus be electrocuted. Slowly, he walks toward the fence till, suddenly, he runs screaming at the captain and is shot dead.

It's the play's second most arresting scene, and it is followed by Gere's suicide, wearing Dukes' jacket, at the same fence, as the electric sparks become a glare that subsumes the playing area and, the stage directions demand, "blinds the audience."

Nevertheless, the *most* arresting scene, in the original New York production, was the trick's entrance at the beginning, for James Remar was not only nude but an outrageously beautiful blond boy insolently oozing across the deck, moving from stage right down to the apron, across to stage left, and up for his exit, meanwhile modeling the most perfect bottom in the Western world. On the night I saw the show, the audience went so still for this that we could make out the lyrics of the opening number of the Hoop-Dee-Doo Musical Revue Dinner Theatre in Kissimmee, Florida.

A story goes with this, though it was gossip and probably not true. The two storm troopers were of course standing in the wings at this point waiting for their cue to enter, and knowing what was happening onstage infuriated one of them. His colleague, so Nordic-looking that he was a go-to for roles of this kind, was live and let live about it. But the other actor blustered about having played Shakespeare and Ibsen; he knew Kazan; worked with the Lunts. "But all they care about is a sexy boy!"

Yes, it's funny how that works. *Bent* played 241 performances, a succès d'estime. It had already been seen in London at the Royal Court with Ian McKellen, also in 1979, so *Bent* is another of the English imports opening a gay conversation in these years (though playwright Sherman is American). Another example, this one wholly British, was the Lindsay Kemp company, visiting New York in the 1974–1975 season, first on Broadway for *Flowers*, a wordless pageant somewhat after Jean Genet, and then, off Broadway, in a revision of Oscar Wilde's *Salome*.

Lindsay Kemp was one of those figures who does not adapt to the prevailing behavioral codes. Of his national service in the Royal Air Force, he said, in numerous interviews, "I never marched, I danced." Kemp's art was a combination of dance and mime, extremely presentational with some extraordinary stage pictures and adopting the minimalist tempo introduced by opera director Wieland Wagner and later developed by Robert Wilson among others. Kemp's troupe usually favored the all-male casting of the very early Stonewall-era off-Broadway attractions we have spoken of, and he emphasized the young and svelte. Still, Kemp's style demanded near-cultists, ready to follow their leader into heretofore undiscovered areas of dramatic art.

Too bold for Broadway, *Flowers* ran only 24 performances. Yet Kemp kept important company—he was David Bowie's mentor and lover—and he was, like it or not, a visionary. True, his habit of playing only women's roles in rococo outfits made it easy for detractors to dismiss his work as arty drag entertainment. Then, too, *Flowers*, which was entirely mimed, was hard to follow even for readers of Genet. Nevertheless, one is reminded of a prominent movie historian at a screening of *The Matrix*, whispering to his young son, "I don't know what's happening."

To which his son replied, "Just watch it, Dad."

That is: the experience is sensual, magical, instinctual, primitive—not logical. At least *Salome*, based on a familiar tale, was easier to grasp, and it did have dialogue (though Wilde's original text was filleted). *Salome*, too, died quickly, though for some it was an extraordinary experience. When the lights came up at the start, the public was greeted by six young men wearing almost nothing, their faces painted white and their lips incarnadine. For a long time, they held position in a kind of embodiment of the eighties American watchword "We're here, we're queer, get used to it." After a while, they began to move—very slowly, as always with Kemp—and after a while they got into dialogue scenes. Some of it was shouted, even screamed; and much of the action was highly physical. Thus, the Baptist appeared first as an angel with gigantic feathered wings that were ritually cut away to leave him groveling on the floor.

Salome's scenery was makeshift, a thrift-shop Judea. Even Herod's throne was anything but regal, and the only notable fixture was the staircase down which Kemp as Salome made a Grand Entrance, lento, adagio, his head wreathed in a gigantic circlet of feathers. For some of the cognoscenti, Kemp's *Salome* was supremely theatrical, but others found it perverse even in its music, everything from Mozart to electronic buzz. What was the point of this? they would ask. In the *New York Times*, Mel Gussow called Kemp's heroine "a display rather than a characterization"—but that was how Kemp's theatre operated. The Baptist (David Haughton, Kemp's lifelong partner) was less saint than savage, and Herod (David Meyer) sported a dunce cap for a crown. But the Baptist was bewitched and Herod was beautiful, and maybe that was the point of the spectacle.

Flowers and *Salome* marked a kind of land's end of gay art, liberated beyond description. But some straight writers were still working the old "gays are murderers" line, such as Ira Levin in *Deathtrap* (1978), in the moribund form of the mystery thriller with shocko twists. It's a cunning piece, and a public that had abandoned thrillers because the movies realized them more deftly flocked to *Deathtrap* for 1,793 performances.

As so often in the postwar thriller, there was a small cast: an older man, a playwright, well established but failing; his wife; a younger man, attractive and charming. The two men are plotting to kill off the wife, vulnerable because her tender constitution might be subject to a stroke if she can be scared out of her wits.

Now for the first big twist: when the wife leaves the stage, the older man turns to the younger, says, "Come to Papa," and plants a big wet one on the younger man's mouth.

In the movie version, with Michael Caine and Christopher Reeve. On stage, the two schemers never even touched except when they were busy killing each other.

No, the play with the gay kiss was Bob Barry's *Murder Among Friends*, which played for only a week, two seasons before *Deathtrap*. This one offered Jack Cassidy and Janet Leigh as the married couple, with the unknown Lewis Arndt as the young man, actor Cassidy's agent. The two star names could not save the show from blistering reviews—and *Deathtrap*, one of the biggest hits of its era, got a few assaults, too. But it's clever, and its twists are genuinely surprising.

Still, even without a kiss between *Deathtrap*'s two leads, the play does make it clear that there is an erotic liaison between older man (John Wood) and younger one (Victor Garber).[†] However, these two never *acted* like lovers. And as *Deathtrap* is made of deception piled on deception, is it possible that they aren't lovers at all? Is Wood faking it to entice gay Garber? Is Garber fooling Wood? Are either of these two gay at all? Was Ira Levin toying with yet another mystery tease, or using the new gay presence on Broadway to give his play street cred?

In any case, *Deathtrap* is certainly one more piece about a married man shedding his wife for another man (at least in a way), which complicates our understanding of how gay fits into the history of Broadway. All these (straight?) guys now lusting after handsome youths? Were they straight, then gay? Or is it opportunism rather than eros, as Wood needs Garber to rejuvenate Wood's career as a playwright?

And in Michael Cristofer's *The Box* (1977), it's because Laurence Luckinbill's ex-wife is one of those people too sarcastically intelligent for their own good, fascinating yet deflating, irritating. She can't help it, though the belligerent young man Luckinbill is now living with thinks everyone is guilty of his or her life. If she's irritating, he reasons, it's because she wants to irritate.

[†] Marian Seldes played the wife, and she felt so comfortable in the part that she supposedly played every single performance of the play's four-years-and-change run.

The Shadow Box is one of the most remarkable plays of its decade, because of its brilliant character writing. Everyone comes utterly alive on stage, which is ironic because Cristofer's three most important characters are terminally ill. The play is set on the grounds of a hospital where these three live in cottages in some kind of experimental program, and Cristofer gives us a narrator who patiently interviews these patients right there, under the worst pressure a human can face: the contemplation of his or her imminent mortality.

One is a man whose wife is terrified of entering the cottage, for to do so would seem to abet the work of death by accepting it. Another is an old woman whose anger sorely tests her caregiver daughter. And one is Luckinbill, doomed yet strangely buoyant in the company of the young man who has replaced Luckinbill's wife.

A transfer from Los Angeles' Mark Taper Forum, directed by Gordon Davidson, *The Shadow Box* was very well cast in general, but we are going to focus on Luckinbill's cottage—where, once again in this decade of roaming husbands, a straight has a boy friend instead of a wife.

However, he didn't leave her: she left him, because his methodical way of living wasn't speedy enough for her. She wanted him to come out of his intellectual gravity and "just dance for a few years." Just share her way of mocking everyone (including herself) with such charm that life becomes an entertainment.

Patricia Elliott played the ex-wife, with the same rueful elegance she brought to the Countess in *A Little Night Music* four years earlier. Her scenes with Luckinbill's new love (Mandy Patinkin, aged twenty-four) were a fiesta of dueling personalities. He couldn't stand her (though she rather liked him), and the public, too, would have been wary of her. Yet Luckinbill both was and wasn't:

LUCKINBILL: I've missed your foolishness.
ELLIOTT: You hated my foolishness.
LUCKINBILL: I never understood it.
ELLIOTT: Neither did I. But it was the only way. The only way I knew.

A few lines more and they embrace.

It's a superb but depressing play, which is why it ran 315 performances— good enough, but less than it deserved. Patinkin had the show's most unbearable line: "You keep thinking there must be some way out of this." And the evening closes with the principals facing the audience to utter snatches of thought: "This music." "This task." "This breath." Luckinbill took the final line: "This moment." And there they all stood, waiting, till the curtain fell.

If the 1960s was the decade preparing the way for a gay theatre, the 1970s pursued the advance by exploring the possibilities. Many of these involved bisexuality, and the musical *Chicago* even got a fast little joke out of it, in "The Cell Block Tango," a number for murderers recounting The Reasons Why. Though *Chicago's* book was cowritten by its lyricist, Fred Ebb, and its director, Bob Fosse, Ebb was having trouble concocting laugh lines for the song's spoken passages, and Fosse called in his hotshot writer friends, like Paddy Chayefsky, to spice up the gags. Thus, Mona killed her boyfriend, Alvin, because he was so very artistic. He'd go out nights hoping to find himself, and "on the way he found Ruth, Gladys, Rosemary:

MONA: And Irving.

On a grander scale, the 1970s saw also the formation of gay theatre collectives. The aforementioned revue *Lovers*, for instance, was presented by a group called The Other Side of Silence. The most prominent of the gay groups really wasn't gay, the Circle Repertory Company. Founded in 1969 by director Marshall W. Mason, playwright Lanford Wilson, and actors Rob Thirkield and Tanya Berezin, Circle Rep didn't stage gay plays; it staged plays. Still, Mason and Wilson were the Circle's guiding spirits, and both were out. We have seen how Wilson's *Fifth Of July* counted two gay characters among straights without treating the couple differently than it treated the others, creating a new kind of gay play, wherein gay men or women would be just more people.

Like many future prominent outfits, the Circle started very small, in a loft at Eighty-Third Street and Broadway. It was a storefront theatre, so to say, with poor acoustics; every line had an echo. But the rent was low. The lease was signed by an organization invented for the occasion, the Council For *International Recreation, Culture, and Lifelong Education*: the "Circle."

Fame arrived with an early hit that moved from the loft to the downtown Circle In the Square, *The Hot l Baltimore* (1973), written by Wilson and directed by Mason. The setting was intriguing, almost like something from the 1930s: the lobby of a rundown hotel about to be demolished and populated exclusively by "the usual unknowns," as Italians would phrase it: a random collection of tenants personally demolished by life.

Though plotless, the play was very entertaining, thanks to a personable cast. Wilson's title stems from the burned-out *e* in the hotel's outdoor sign.‡ The piece ran for years, won countless prizes, and even inspired a short-lived television series (1975) that—almost incredibly for the time—contained a gay male couple, probably the first in TV history. Still, the showy role belonged to Conchata Ferrell (from the stage cast), noted for her wonderfully earthy laugh.

Generally, the group avoided showy roles throughout its twenty-seven-year history; it really was an ensemble. By comparison, composer-lyricist Jerry Herman emphasized star shows, especially built around Big Ladies from Carol Channing to Angela Lansbury to Bernadette Peters and taking in as well parish favorites such as Betty Grable, Phyllis Diller, and Ann Miller. At that, the two original Big Ladies, Ethel Merman and Mary Martin, inherited the Biggest of the indicated roles, Dolly, Merman on Broadway and Martin abroad.

This is gay thinking, and Herman was gay, also artistically conservative. His last off-Broadway show before he went to The Street, the revue *Parade* (1960), opened with "Show Tune," whose refrain states (to music re-used for *Mame*'s "It's Today, "There's just no tune as exciting as a show tune," and while the cast sang the second chorus, the soubrette intoned the names of famous examples . . . almost entirely from the 1920s and 1930s: Herman Time.

So Herman, who spent some twenty-five years on Broadway, was aiming backward. His first uptown title, *Milk and Honey* (1961), was almost an operetta, but then Herman unleashed a series of Big Lady musical-comedy titles: *Hello, Dolly!* (1964), *Mame* (1966), *Dear World* (1969), all in the glitzy style that Herman loved. But he had to fight to get the *Dolly!* gig, for its producer, David Merrick, had seen *Milk and Honey* and typed Herman as too lyrical. As Herman would later explain it to everyone, Merrick was not wrong, for *Milk and Honey*, set in Israel, centered on middle-aged people in a soap-opera plot with a Rudolf Friml score, high notes and all. Instead of joy-spreading dancers in pastels, the chorus was kibbutz workers.

"No," quoth David Merrick to Jerry Herman. *Dolly!*, he explained, "is young and sparkling and up. *Very up.* There's no soap opera in it, just merriment and coincidence and then everyone gets married. Your show didn't even have a happy ending."

‡ Obviously, the play should be referred to by its subject's name: "The *Hotel Baltimore*." Wilson, however, always pronounced it as "The Hot El Baltimore."

How was Herman to tell Merrick that he wasn't an operetta guy, that Herman was gay and glitz was the style he was born into?

Ha—an idea! Herman asks to take the *Dolly!* script home just to . . . oh, I don't know . . ."

"Fine," says Merrick. "Here."

And with that Herman locks himself up for two days, reading and rereading Michael Stewart's very funny *Dolly!* script for a crazy and pretty show, and Herman writes four songs for it, grabs a singer, and goes back to Merrick to demonstrate just how *Dolly!* Herman really was.

"And," Herman would say, "David. Merrick. Sat. There. Absolutely. *Stunned.*" And that's how Jerry Herman got *Hello, Dolly!*.

The show's director, Gower Champion, gave the production a high-tech air of chic revelry, but it was Herman who created in the razzmatazz score a new kind of gay theatre—not in subject matter but in the sharp show-biz instincts that are arguably part of the gay birthright. The fidgety uproar in "Put On Your Sunday Clothes," as some of the principals look forward to leaving the suburb to seize the freedom of the city, is arguably a gay anticipation of coming out, of throwing off the cautions of conformity.

Then, too, Herman was writing songs for eccentric characters. Every one of the leads is more or less a crazy, and at least one of those eventually cast— Charles Nelson Reilly, in a key role—was a gay crazy, and the audience had to have known it.

Oddly, for the chief crazy, Dolly herself, Herman was writing for Ethel Merman, a very sturdy and grounded performer, for all her one-of-a-kind personality. Champion wanted Nanette Fabray, also grounded. It was only when both women said no that Carol Channing was brought in: another wild and self-dramatizing performer that gays feel comfortable with.

Then Herman took on *Mame*, the same only more so, as it revived the gay content of *Auntie Mame*. After these two consecutive smash hits, however, *Dear World* proved a bomb, vastly troubled in rehearsal, tryout, and a lengthy preview period in New York. The frantic tinkering even reached the playbill cover art, which ended up undergoing four different renditions.

Now, it is a truth universally acknowledged that a Big Lady production needs a high-maestro director, someone like Gower Champion, who knows how to excite the details while keeping the overall vision intact. Unfortunately, *Dear World's* producer, Alexander Cohen, handed *Dear World* over to Champion's assistant, Lucia Victor, who was immediately overwhelmed and left, succeeded by Peter Glenville and then Joe Layton. Ironically, so much work had been done by the time of the constantly postponed New York opening that the show, problematic from the start, was worse than ever.

That problem was incongruent agendas. *Dear World*'s source was Jean Giraudoux's *The Madwoman Of Chaillot*, and like all French playwrights Giraudoux has a very spotty history of drawing a public on Broadway. True, Audrey Hepburn as the mermaid in *Ondine* (1954) made a, yes, splash in her fishnet tights with algae accessories, and *The Madwoman Of Chaillot* was in fact a big hit in New York in 1948. But Giraudoux is gentille alouette, delicate above all, while Herman's style is grand and emphatic—the glitz, to repeat, of Big Broadway with those anthemic title songs and pointed novelties like "Bosom Buddies" and "The Man In the Moon [is a lady]."

Strange as this sounds, the Giraudoux might have worked as a musical with a score like that of *Promenade,* with Maria Irene Fornes' mischievous lyrics and Al Carmines' sportive tunes. Received opinion blamed *Dear World* for being overproduced, but, more pertinent, it was overwritten, with those Jerry Herman patented proclamation numbers that build Giraudoux's airy people into heroes.

Thus, *Dear World*'s central music was Angela Lansbury's ID number, in which her fear that money-grubbing elites will seize the world takes the form of a desperation waltz growing more intense by the measure. But that isn't Giraudoux. It's Rodgers and Hammerstein thinking, strong and straightforward but completely overpowering a woman who is sly and silly, and it threw the slender story off. *Dear World* lasted three months entirely on its advance, and it marked a crushing defeat for Broadway's outstanding gay (if technically closeted) composer-lyricist.[§]

At least *Mack & Mabel* (1974) brought Herman back with *Dolly!*'s Merrick, Champion, and Michael Stewart. For a twist, this was not a Big Lady show but a vehicle for Robert Preston, as silent-film director Mack Sennett, to play opposite a bright new face as the delicatessen-clerk waif Mabel Normand, whom Sennett plucks from obscurity to build into a movie star. Similarly, Herman's Mabel would be a nobody of such verve and charm that she, too, would punch out to fame.

Herman was enthralled at the prospect. After three shows driven by finagling women, he finally had a finagling man, a fresh scheme to work with.

[§] Stephen Sondheim was at the time known more as a lyricist (for *West Side Story* and *Gypsy*) than as a composer. His two words-and-music titles, *A Funny Thing Happened On the Way To the Forum* and *Anyone Can Whistle*, did not have a major impact back then. But *Company* was one year away.

And much as Herman loved star-centered show biz, the plan to Discover the Mabel was *Forty-Second Street* all over again. When Mabel first appears, delivering a deli order, the audience wouldn't burst into applause but instead be filled with anticipation and wonder. "I don't *want* it to be a Bette Midler or a Debbie Reynolds," Herman told Norma McLain Stoop in *After Dark* before rehearsals began. "That suddenly throws the show!" Instead, let the audience create Mabel's stardom, claim her as *their* innovation.

Meanwhile, Herman could explore his favorite form, joyful musical comedy, with its showgirls and rococo plotting. "Thirty men in the pit," he said, "and production numbers like 'Hundreds Of Girls' with a line of bathing beauties kicking—that thrills me more than anything!" Imagine the marquee: David Merrick presents Robert Preston in the Gower Champion production of a Jerry Herman Show . . . and introducing Miss ___ ___, in a title that already sounds like a smash hit: *Mack & Mabel*!

So who would she be? The buzz touted many a young woman of relatively unknown quality, but Champion decided on Penny Fuller, several times a Broadway replacement but now having created Eve in *Applause* (1970). She wasn't an unknown, obviously. But neither was she a star—and she had worthy dramatic resources, a rarity in ingenues.

However, Champion changed his mind. Mabel was now going to Marcia Rodd, another performer between unknown and star, and—interestingly—generally associated with straight acting jobs while possessing an excellent belt voice. She would be a real find.

Then Champion happened to hear a genuine newcomer in the Sammy Cahn song revue *Words and Music* in the late spring of 1974, just when *Mack & Mabel* was gearing up for rehearsals, a long tryout tour from California to D.C., and then the Broadway unveiling. Hundreds of Girls! Merrick and Champion! Silent-film antics, a novel element. The music man himself, beloved of millions! And the new Mabel . . . Miss Kelly Garrett!

And Champion fired her. Yes, she was a wonderful singer. But something was missing, it seemed. The character just wasn't there—and Michael Stewart's Mabel Normand was not your typical musical-comedy kid but a troubled soul as much resentful of Mack as dependent on him. She needed Mack; he needed movies. "I Won't Send Roses" was his anti-love song to Mabel, because he isn't emotionally available.

But didn't Preston's charm lie in his very giving personality as a performer? Mack limited him. And when Champion finally settled on a Mabel, it was no newbie but the relatively established Bernadette Peters. She was of course terrific in a tricky role, and she and Preston made a strikingly incongruous pair, he so blustery and she so wistful. The first stand of the tryout, in San Diego, went well among critics and public alike.

Unfortunately, as *Mack & Mabel* toured, problems begat more problems, and they were all the same problem: this wasn't a musical comedy but a psychologically moody musical play with a very dark second act. What happened to the chorus people singing and dancing all over the place? The men were mainly grips carrying props during set changes, and the women were mostly bathing beauties just hanging around. The acting support, such as Mack's cheerleader Lottie (Lisa Kirk) and production assistant Frank (Jerry Dodge), didn't have interesting roles, though Frank had a secret crush on Mabel to work with. But musical plays need imposing character interaction, like *Carousel* and *Follies*: showing us one-of-a-kind characters living more or less on the edge. As for the zany comedy of Mack Sennett's silents, this really called for car-and-train chases, houses falling apart, epic pie fights—all beyond what the stage could replicate.

Worst of all, Champion could fix a broken musical comedy, but not a musical play, because he preferred fast and breezy books and musical plays work on solid librettos. So Champion's fixes only antagonized the art, enfeebling the show's subplots. Mabel's involvement with the shady film director William Desmond Taylor (James Mitchell) lost all its development, and Frank's crush on Mabel vanished except for a mention—in passing!—when Jerry Dodge made his final exit.

By the time the production reached D.C., the first act was amusing enough but the second act was incoherent and depressing, not least when Mabel became a drug addict and died. What, in a Jerry Herman musical? This is like little Shirley Temple choking to death on a poisoned jujube. There was still enough quality in the show—along with a marvelous score—to keep the public sort of liking it while feeling it really wasn't very good. It is a cardinal rule that some shows—*Oedipus Rex*, for instance—do not have to be life-affirming. But a Jerry Herman musical is not one of those shows—and there's a famous story about this that takes in another gay leader on Broadway, Michael Bennett.

The tale takes us to *A Chorus Line*'s first public performances, when it was still downtown at the Public Theater. Near the show's end, when the auditioners were chosen or discarded, Bennett felt strongly that the showrunner's former sweetheart, Cassie (Donna McKechnie), must be turned down because she was overqualified for a chorus job. It seemed like a personal rejection, though: the ex-boy friend coldly spurning his erstwhile close companion. But Bennett was adamant. His former love was now a principal, too good for the ensemble. "Don't pop the head, Cassie!"

As it happened, Neil Simon had been called to these previews to sweeten the book with some one-liners, and his then wife, Marsha Mason, noticed that all through the show, the audience was utterly enthralled—yet at the end the applause was somewhat deflated. Because Cassie had fought and worked and played by the rules and had a number, "The Music and the Mirror," in which she pleaded for the job . . . and her ex was rejecting her:

BENNETT: That's life. That's what really happens.
MASON: But it's not good theatre. Let Cassie get the job and the public will be on its feet screaming for joy.

And there was this: *Follies*, which Bennett codirected, also ended in loserness. And *Follies* was not a smash.

MASON: Do you want what really happens or do you want a smash?

Well, that gave Bennett pause. So he changed the ending, Cassie was hired, and at the end the public was on its feet screaming for joy.

Gower Champion didn't have Marsha Mason advising him, and we can imagine Jerry Herman's despair at seeing his dream of a way *up*, way *happy* (except for a teeny bit of drug addiction and death) musical comedy sinking in a wave of Gower Champion's view of what really happens.

So *Mack & Mabel* failed, closing after 66 performances despite its star power and that "Don't miss it!" title. It has been revised, but it never works, and Herman was going to have to revert to his sphere of expertise, which was the entertainment musical, a gay kind of show. Even . . . a gay show: *La Cage Aux Folles* (1983). We can imagine his momentary hesitation:

JERRY HERMAN: But do I have to come out?
SOMEONE: Jerry, you've been out to everyone except your mother for twenty years.

Still, Herman belonged to the generation that held that an official coming out was unnecessary, because, one, it's nobody else's business what you like; and, two, smart folks know and don't care; and, three, Oh, you've been wondering? Take a wild guess.

Anyway, *La Cage* wasn't Herman's project at first. Allan Carr dreamed it up, for after the phenomenally successful movie *Grease* but the phenomenally embarrassing movie *Can't Stop the Music*, Carr was in a Broadway mood. And having seen Jean Poiret's play *La Cage Aux Folles* (The Cage of Crazies), a long-run hit in Paris, Carr thought it would make a great stage musical.

His plan was to move the setting from the French Riviera to New Orleans, thus Americanizing it while retaining a French patina: *The Queen Of Basin Street*. And Carr hired the best, with Mike Nichols to direct, Maury Yeston for the score, Jay Presson Allen for the book, and Tommy Tune to choreograph.

So far, so good—but this was the late 1970s: would Big Broadway be hospitable to a musical full of drag queens? Wasn't it just a bit too early, with mainstream America still absorbing the effects of Stonewall liberation? A neophyte in stage production, Carr secured Fritz Holt and Barry Brown as his production managers. After one look at the spendthrift contracts Carr had signed with his A-Team, Holt and Brown told him *Basin Street* could never pay off, and, impressed with their acumen, Carr made the pair his co-producers.

Whereupon they fired everyone and started looking for a less pricey crew—at that, a gay one. Arthur Laurents was the new director, Harvey Fierstein the new book writer. This is where Herman came into the picture, so well off from *Dolly!* and *Mame* that he didn't care about money; his motivation was the project itself. Its very gayness attracted him—the flair and confidence of the drag queen, for instance, which is a musical-comedy style, really. And wasn't this history? The First Couple were both men!

Rushing to the piano, Herman started noodling, seeking a riff for his first number—"I Am What I Am," the furious ID piece of not just a gay guy, not even just a gay guy who had set up a household with another guy and raised a son, but the anthem of a drag queen, whether Big Broadway was ready for it or not.

Harvey Fierstein's participation was entirely logical, as it was the 1980s and his *Torch Song Trilogy* had fledged him as a humorist with an interest in The Issues. With the setting moved back to the French Riviera, *La Cage Aux Folles* was taking shape as daring in content yet conventional in format: a merry musical comedy with passionately held sociopolitics.

More: its protagonist was a man, Albin, who turns into a Big Lady when on stage. Effeminate and pouty as himself, he undergoes a personality change as Zaza—and of course a physical one, as he explains in "A Little More Mascara": the transformation frees him rather as coming out frees the closeted gay.

The first Albin, George Hearn, is straight, but queer performers have taken up the part over the years, and a few have played as well Georges, Albin's partner, originated by Gene Barry. As written, the couple's personal dynamics require Albin to be minty and Georges to be more level-headed. It's the classic duo of the Abbott and Costello or *Odd Couple* kind. Yet Albin becomes very forceful in that ID number that launched Herman's composition of the score, which ended as the show's first-act finale.

Thus: Albin and Georges' son is to marry the daughter of a gay-hating politician, but Albin will be sidelined—hidden away, really—to keep the bigot from Finding Out. So Albin explodes in that "I Am What I Am"—and it's not the anthem of a drag queen, after all, is it? It's the credo of a citizen of a democracy who deserves the rights everyone else has. And Albin is so disgusted that his own people have connived at this outrage that at the song's end he hurled his dress wig into Georges' face and stormed right down the aisle of the Palace Theatre as, behind him, the curtain fell.

It's revolution, a first for the Big Lady format. Yet, I say again, this show's form and structure and attitude were absolutely conventional. For instance, there were the jokes about marriage, a staple of the musical since at least as far back as the 1920s. (There's even one in *Blossom Time*.) So, when Georges and his son are scheming to establish the boy's mother in the apartment for the visit from the prospective in-laws, Georges warns his son not to park her in the master bedroom:

JEAN-MICHEL: But how will it look if she doesn't sleep in your room?
GEORGES: Like any couple married twenty years.

There was even an out-of-story gag, forbidden in serious shows like *The King and I* but a guilty pleasure in the gleeful musical, wherein a character admits he or she is in a play. The one in *La Cage* came about because Gene Barry was all too aware that George Hearn had by far the showier role. Hearn drove the action, told the audience how to feel about what was happening, and got first billing despite Barry's having been a major television star with several hit series.

It was hurting Barry's approach to his part to the point that there was talk of replacing him, till director Laurents coached Barry in building up the emcee aspect of the character. Georges is, after all, the drag club's compère, the middle man between the "notorious and dangerous" Cagelles on stage and the public in the seats, and Laurents wanted more oomph and command from him, letting Georges almost sing his spiels. Don't just announce the acts—*perform* the announcements. Act as if your life were a musical comedy.

So Barry brightened his line deliveries, relishing and tantalizing, and one of his new gags was the out-of-story joke I mentioned above. It occurred at the top of the second act, set on the promenade of St. Tropez, where Barry was pepping Hearn up in the fine art of being manly.

"You must face up to your destiny," Barry urged him, as the orchestra began to intone music of purpose and heroism. "I am a man! I am strong!" And as the players in the Palace Theatre pit continued their encouragement in a tiny piece that actually had a name, "Mountain Build" (because Barry's simile was a mountain that repels you till you show that mountain who is the master of the real estate). When the orchestra rose to the peak of a thrilling crescendo, Barry cried: *"I will climb back up that mountain!"*

And then he cut off the orchestra with a wave of his hand.

It's a throwaway joke, a bonne bouche of a little moment, but it helped affirm Barry's presence in the storyline even as he reminded the public that it was seeing not reality but a contrived entertainment.

On the other hand, the show was very, very well contrived. With its elaborate scene plot (designed by David Mitchell) in an age of far too many cheap unit sets, and its excellent choreography (by Scott Salmon), *La Cage Aux Folles* was, I repeat, a revival of what musical comedy was like in its Golden Age: clever and imaginative. Early on, Arthur Laurents feared that investors would shy away from a piece so richly gay, yet the show's capitalization enabled spendthrift visuals, as in its first moments, a view of a few St. Tropez buildings that moved individually around the stage before revealing the key edifice, the drag club. It was a wonderful effect, technically so complex that, during the first tryout performances, it stubbornly refused to cooperate. Then, one night, it worked perfectly and never failed thereafter.

There was as well a marvelous cinematic touch when, during "A Little More Mascara," the very stage appeared to move to house right in order to capture activity in the backstage area of the club (on the left). Actually, this effect had been pioneered by Jo Mielziner for Rodgers and Hammerstein's *Me and Juliet* exactly thirty years before. But the fact that so much time had passed before it was tried a second time, here in *La Cage*, proves how tricky (and, by the way, expensive) this display really is.

The costumes (by Theoni V. Aldredge) might seem a simple matter, as drag queens often favor an overdressed, anything-goes style, as the genre's founding fathers Julian Eltinge and Bert Savoy did. However, the demands of the First Number, "We Are What We Are," led Aldredge to run up a *series* of outfits, one atop another. Thus, a sort of colonnade came down from the flies after the dancers' opening routine, to ascend bearing the Cagelles' gowns, leaving them in lounge suits to enable a dizzy tap break. These, too, came off, with one energetic tug (and the clothes were then tossed into the orchestra pit), leaving the dancers to finish the number in sailor suits. All of this had to be planned with exquisite technical nuance to work not only without a hitch but precisely in time with the music.

Aldredge's work continued in the curtain calls, when the drag ensemble divested themselves of their onstage outfits to stow them in a cart traveling from stage right to stage left. Thus we finally got to see the chorus boys as they are in life . . . and two of them were women, one last surprising touch in a highly surprising show.

One thing about *La Cage Aux Folles* was not surprising: the score. It is one of Herman's best, but then they are all his best, because after the operetta-ish *Milk and Honey* they all sound alike, barring the odd novelty piece here and there, such as *The Grand Tour*'s very situation-based "Wedding Conversation." Herman's homogenization of oeuvre lies mainly in the music, extremely consistent over the years in melodic shape and harmony. There is none of the range we hear in Richard Rodgers, for example, who within just a few years leaps from the folkish "Blow High, Blow Low" to the jazzy "Honey Bun."

Nevertheless, the *Cage Aux Folles* score hits all the key points, even if Georges never gets an ID number of his own. But then, as we know, it was Albin and his crusade for acceptance that first fired up Herman's interest. Albin is the show's master; Georges is staff. Still, the big ballad is his—and it gave Herman an interesting problem. First, love songs are all clichés, and, second, this was a love song about two seniors, a delicate vexation as the musical formally favors youth above all.

But if you can write about gay for Big Broadway, you might as well obliterate another of The Street's little phobias, namely age. Thus Herman created, very cleverly, "Song On the Sand," and he got around the love cliché by making it not a love song but a song *about* a love song, some old tune one half-remembers. So instead of the worn-out amatory phrases, Georges sings "La da da da" a lot, stepping neatly around the platitudes. And the sinuous melody really does the job, rising to a passionate final line on "And I'm young and in love," a tremendous opportunity for the strong singers who took over the role in New York after Gene Barry. In particular, Keith Michell (who also starred in the Australian production, opposite Jon Ewing) went utterly opera in the last A strain.

Oddly, Herman's love of Golden Age music got him into trouble at the 1984 Tony Awards show, when he won for the *Cage* score against (among others) Stephen Sondheim, up for *Sunday In the Park With George*. With Tony in hand, Herman claimed it as proof that there was still support for "the simple, hummable show tune"—as opposed to Sondheim's more sophisticated style? In fact, it was rock that Herman was objecting to, not Sondheim, but his words were ambiguous, leaving people to draw their own conclusions about what he meant.

To put it another way, though, *La Cage* is typical gay art: wild and fabulous and—especially—different. And of course it has drag queens in it. As we've seen, the entire movement of gay culture coming to Broadway started with drag queens. And rock is typical straight art, which partly explains why gay songwriters flock to theatre writing and everyone else starts with a rock band in his parents' garage.

So it worked well that the original plan for Allan Carr's *Cage* musical replaced Mike Nichols, Jay Presson Allen, and Maury Yeston with Arthur Laurents, Harvey Fierstein, and Jerry Herman (even if Laurents was not a gifted director and Allen was a sharp and worldly writer), because this show really is The Gay Musical. Yes, it's about liberation, but it also takes that gay romance seriously, and "Song On the Sand" seizes the final curtain, as if to make sure that everyone in the audience Gets It, as Georges and Albin reprise the tune and start waltzing while the buildings we saw moving around at the very beginning of the show reappear to dance along with the two lovers, a beguiling symmetry. "Little slivers of moonlight float down on them," the published text informs us. And I'm young and in love.

However, "Song On the Sand" was not the first gay love song in the musical's history. Three months earlier, Charles Strouse and Alan Jay Lerner's *Dance a Little Closer,* based on and updated from Robert E. Sherwood's 1936 end-of-days play *Idiot's Delight,* offered two gay men (Brent Barrett, Jeff Keller) ice skating on a little strip of instafreeze or whatever it was as they sang "Why Can't the World Go and Leave Us Alone?" An irritated waltz that is more a lament than a statement of affection, it nonetheless gave music to a gay pair in love—and later, as the cast believes that the world is headed for nuclear war, the two men asked a cleric if he would agree to marry them.

Given that in 1983 marriage equality was not yet even a controversy, this was very advanced thinking from Lerner. He and Strouse got a big ensemble number out of it, "I Don't Know," as the show's principals discussed it over an anxious pulsing beat in the orchestra. "How can loving ever really be a sin?" the reverend wondered, though he feared that offering marriage vows to two of the same gender stood beyond the authority of his office.

At length, the show's heroine (Liz Robertson) capped the scene with the sympathetic "Anyone Who Loves," so we know the show was on the right side. And Lerner gave the issue full weight, as his gay pair were solemn figures rather than the mischievous Emory kind. Yet the scene felt a bit feeble in the context of the plot, as the world was more or less about to end that very night. At that, the show itself ended that night, closing after its opening performance.

Meanwhile, what may have been the most historic coming-out in theatre history belonged to The Master, who pretended to write a play about Somerset Maugham while really writing about himself. Noël Coward had never faked being straight. Still, even if everyone "knows" you're gay, it somehow doesn't count until you personally make proclamation. And Coward had finally got his knighthood, long delayed (so everyone thought) because of his sexuality. Thus, he had nothing to lose and now was the time, for he was aging at a pace, tired and ailing badly, with but one last act in him.

Of course, he proclaimed in his own way, starring in his own piece about an acerbic old writer confronting a former lover, a woman who has come to get his permission to quote from his love letters to her for her forthcoming autobiography. Conflict: he refuses.

Coward called it *A Song At Twilight* and planned to play it in London for his usual three months. Then, to spice up the event, Coward added a second evening of two one-acts to alternate as a unit with *A Song,* all three works using the same three leads in quite diverse roles and taking place in a single set, the sitting room of a hotel in Switzerland (where Coward himself was now living). To add to the fun, the same actor would play the hotel's floor waiter in all three pieces—"a startlingly handsome young man," Coward directed, because this wasn't to be one of those hetero things by Arthur Miller, stodgy but Good For You.

Banding the trio of titles together as *Suite In Three Keys*, Coward felt he was too weak to stage as well as star, and his producer, Binkie Beaumont, decided to try a relative newcomer, Vivian Matalon, summoning him to appear at once without telling Matalon what it was about or who would be there.

Of course the plan was to give Coward a chance to audition his potential director, and Matalon himself told the tale to Coward biographer Philip Hoare: Matalon walks in and finds himself face to face with the only man in the theatre who could fairly be called a legend. Even as Beaumont is making the introduction, Matalon cries out, "Oh, God!" And Coward responds with "Yes, quite right."

The shows were a hit, and they even got great reviews after so many years in which the critics savaged Coward with gleeful taunts. Now they loved him—had he lost his touch? No, there was one sour note ("Coward's return very tedious"—*The Sun*), "which convinced me," he wrote in his journal, "that I hadn't entirely slipped."

Such a success had to be taken to New York, though Coward's London co-stars, Lilli Palmer and Irene Worth, were replaced by Anne Baxter and Jessica Tandy; the latter's husband, Hume Cronyn, played the Coward roles. Vivian Matalon again directed, but the pair of evenings was reduced to just *A Song At Twilight* and one of the one-acts in a single bill as *Noël Coward In Two Keys* (1974).

And we're really interested now, as a New York stand has more impact on our topic. Coward's work had been playing New York since the 1920s, yet only here—fifty years later—did he feel it . . . let's just say "timely" . . . to sign his work as a gay man. Because when, in *A Song At Twilight*, the Coward role refuses to let Anne Baxter use his letters to her, she responds with a shocko Act One curtain. It seems she has other letters of his—letters to a man from years before. Better conflict:

CARLOTTA: He was the only true love of your life. (*As she exits*) Good night, Hugo. Sleep well.

Of course, it could still be Maugham, though "Hugo" suggests an analogue to "Noël." (Maugham's Christian name was William.) Some years before, Coward told Hunter Davies in *The Sunday Times*, "One's real inside self is a private place. . . . It is no one else's business." Yet would a straight writer have chosen this particular story as his farewell to art, as if making a deathbed confession? Anne Baxter's very spirited Carlotta got another key line, in Act Two, when crusty old Hugo tries to dismiss his early homosexual "tendencies":

CARLOTTA: (*calmly*) Tendencies in the past! What nonsense! You've been a homosexual all your life and you know it.

Well, there it is, and the gains that gay assimilation had been making since the Stonewall Rebellion were clearly following the example of black assimilation, from Bert Williams and Ethel Waters taking part in otherwise white shows on to strong black participation thereafter.

The theatre has always been the place where Americans have conversations about acceptance and opportunity, and Coward had a right and need to join it.

7

The 1980s

Well, Yes, Actually, Yes, I Have

Scenario: The protagonist needs to write a play in three weeks. It was supposed to be *Salammbô*, but three weeks is too short to capture "the splendor of the ancient world. The battle scenes. For that, we need at least four weeks."

The playwright sets to work, but the cleaning lady arrives and starts the vacuum cleaner. A United Parcel hunk, an Asian dragon lady in a slit skirt (she's the cook), and then a would-be songwriter named Ima Poussy (pronounced poo-*see*) all blunder in, distracting the writer. When the United Parcel man returns with flowers, Poussy forges a card; now they're from him. But his music is "asinine," and he's so irritating that everyone calls him "Pussy." He replies, "Poo-*see*! Ima Poo-*see*!" and the playwright's assistant snaps back, "I'll say you are."

And so it goes throughout the play, with constant interruptions from all manner of eccentrics, including a stage mother's little girl who sings "Ol' Man River" while gargling and a Generalisimo [*sic*] who demands a rendezvous with the playwright (a man, but he'll be in drag) and who says, "I keel heen" at the slightest suggestion of a rival. At one point, the assistant bursts in with "They printed your home address by mistake in the trade papers, and we're being deluged with vaudeville acts hoping for an audition!"

What kind of play could the writer possibly create with all this distraction? "Why don't you just write about all the . . . interruptions that happen?" his assistant suggests. Yes! As the next interloper butts in, the playwright is madly typing away at last.

Or try this scenario: Dumas' *La Dame Aux Camélias* with a man as Marguerite, his chest hair showing above his fake bosom. Despite a campy atmosphere, the script follows Dumas closely. But there are tweaks. Thus, when serving tea, Marguerite asks, "Sugar?" and then proceeds to slip the cubes into the cup. First one, a second, a third . . . until the thirteenth, when she clearly wonders if she's overdoing it and blithely terminates the operation.

Now, what of *this* scenario? A hotel is filled with, again, eccentrics, but this time many are folks we're familiar with, from Norma Desmond and Lupe Velez to Svengali and Trilby to God and the Devil. They all race around in the manner of classic farce, interacting, attacking, and crazing up the place. A ballerina named Birdshitskaya commits suicide by throwing herself off the hotel roof . . . over and over, in a running gag. Meanwhile, there are lines and tropes drawn from Hollywood and elsewhere. At one point, Norma Desmond says she has changed her name. Oh, has she gotten married?:

NORMA: No, it took more than one man to change my name to . . . Shanghai Lily.

(This is Marlene Dietrich's famous line in von Sternberg's *Shanghai Express*.) Here's another one: as the show nears its conclusion, the characters start to commit suicide. Birdshitskaya performs The Dying Swan. A certain Drago misquotes *King Lear* with "Like flies and wanton boys are we to the gods" as he, too, passes away. The hotel bellhop is inspired to take up this latest fad, first screaming, "Call for Philip Morris!" like the boy in the old cigarette commercials. But some don't kill themselves. Instead, they are—so the stage directions demand—"thrown into the flames . . . by perfumed slaves with oiled bodies."

Remember *Salammbô*? This one claims the most florid scenario of all as a kind of spectacle of the wild and raunchy, taking in one ungendered character who is topless and weighs something like five hundred pounds. Too, there is a troupe of bodybuilders oozing about the stage. Billed as "an erotic tragedy freely adapted from the novel by Gustave Flaubert," *Salammbô* was like a tiny version of the extravagant stagings of tales of antiquity in New York's biggest theatres—the Manhattan Opera House, the Century, the Hippodrome. Much of *Salammbô*'s action was so bizarre that a newcomer to the art could not have been certain whether the show was a send-up or just out of its mind.

But there were few newcomers at these shows, respectively *How To Write a Play* (1984), *Camille* (1973), *Big Hotel* (1966), and of course *Salammbô* (1985), because they played to a devoted following of the Ridiculous Theatrical Company, founded in 1967 and run by Charles Ludlam. Here was an actor-manager of actor-managers, for he not only directed and starred in his plays but wrote them. Even that micro-supervisor Eva Le Gallienne mostly acted in shows written by others, and Moss Hart seldom acted, at that only regionally, away from the critical eye of the cultural capital.

No, Ludlam was the complete auteur-organizer, at that of a style uniquely his own that was to prove extremely influential in the comic wing of experimental theatre: fantastical, wildly eclectic, rambling rather than centered, and above all imbued with campy mischief. Further, Ludlam had a base of operations (from 1978 on) in the Sheridan Square Playhouse in Greenwich Village. The Ridiculous Theatrical Company is often cited as off-off-Broadway, but the Playhouse was an off-Broadway venue—the home, for instance, of the long-running 1959 revival of Jerome Kern's *Leave It To Jane*, typifying off-Broadway's quondam love of restaging old Broadway musicals, something the radical off-off world seldom got to.

Ludlam also maintained a faithful troupe of players habilitated in their chief's style, a way of delivering lines at once facetious and sincere and recalling Martin Balsam's view of Audrey Hepburn in the *Breakfast At Tiffany*'s movie, that she's a phony but "a *real* phony."

Thus, Ludlam's Marguerite Gauthier *believed* in the *Camille* tale of thwarted love capped by death even as he knew that the antique ringlets of his wig militate against the traditional suspension of disbelief. To enjoy Ludlam, one had to disbelieve while believing, fashioning an art of real phonies and giving his career the longevity of genuine creativity. Ludlam's partner, Everett Quinton; Lola Pashalinski; Bill Vehr; and Black-Eyed Susan led the corps so faithfully that it's hard to imagine other actors in their roles, though Ludlam's plays are done all over the place, especially in colleges.

Looking at some of Ludlam's twenty-nine titles—*Turds In Hell, Eunuchs Of the Forbidden City, Conquest Of the Universe or When Queens Collide, Galas* (on the life of Maria Callas), *A Christmas Carol* (from Dickens), *Der Ring Gott Farblonjet* (Wagner's *Ring* enacted in pidgen German), *The Enchanted Pig* (billed as "A fairy tale for the disenchanted" and a cross between *Beauty and the Beast* and *King Lear*)—one marvels at the diversity of genres. Ludlam's style was consistent throughout his reign, but he loved playing around with form. *How To Write a Play* merrily unfolds in real time in an ordinary room while *Der Ring Gott Farblonjet* starts, as Wagner does, "in the depths of the Rhine" and ends there but only after some forty years have passed and the world has ended.

So two things above all bond Ludlum's works: that air of guilty-pleasure camp that is arguably unique to gay writers, and a love of travesty that finds expression in spoofs of art high and low but also in the figure of the drag queen. (One of the various meanings of "travesty" is cross-dressing.)

As for Ludlam's inspiration, the answer is puppets. Born in 1943, Ludlam was of that wonderful post-toddler age just when television appeared in middle–class homes, and weekdays brought early evening kiddy shows centered on puppets. "As a child," Ludlam was to write, "I was very withdrawn. I never liked other children. I never liked games. Animated cartoons and puppets shaped my life."

Young Charles had his own puppet theatre; he also staged plays in the backyard with neighborhood kids. Much later, one of them wrote to him after seeing the Ridiculous Theatrical crew in action, saying, "I can't believe you're still doing the same thing you were doing when you were seven years old."

The television puppet shows are a key to understanding Ludlam's mode of drama, for his plays share a love of anarchy and confusion that recalls the often improvisatory nature of early TV. Most of them used human hosts—Buffalo Bob Smith of *The Howdy Doody Show*, for instance. But *Lucky Pup* had no humans, which emphasized its magical nature, especially when it started to feature its most charismatic figure, Foodini the Great. Dogged by his not entirely helpful assistant, Pinhead, Foodini was a wizard forever dreaming up mad schemes. Eerie and self-absorbed, he even moved bizarrely, gliding along as if walking on air. Though he and Pinhead were hand puppets, they were animated with the nuances of marionettes, almost as if endowed with occult powers.

In a way, Ludlam recreated the atmosphere of Foodini in his shows, adding to it a kind of war of wizards, each trying to dominate the stage. So *Big Hotel* plays as a series of spoofs governed by rival divas. One minute the bellhop is quoting Macbeth:

BELLHOP: Help ho! Help ho! Sleep! They do murther sleep!

and the next the desk clerk is thrilling the audience with an aside while on the phone with:

DESK CLERK: The madly chic Norma Desmond!

Big Hotel is Ludlam's most typical work, but his most famous one is *The Mystery Of Irma Vep* (1984). It is also the unique title in Ludlam's output, a melodrama reviving the Victorian "quick change" genre: two actors (originally Ludlam and Quinton) played eight characters. So one watches fascinated as the two herald the arrival of someone else, one of them makes an exit, then suddenly reappears as that third party in a completely different outfit (and, often, gender) and attitude. Exhausting for the actors and exciting for the audience, *Irma Vep* pursues its "strange doings on a haunted English heath" plot with scarcely any rest periods, camp that rises to a work of serious art in its own demented integrity.

The Ridiculous Theatrical Company continued to play Ludlam's repertory even after his death, in 1987. Meanwhile, a kind of heir to the style appeared in Charles Busch, who also works with a mustered troupe and plays the leads in drag. *Vampire Lesbians Of Sodom* (1984), an hour of campy Hollywood shtick, started in a club called the Limbo Lounge but, on moving to the Provincetown Playhouse, it racked up a five-year run despite a lame (though energetic) rehash of the available clichés:

HANDSOME MOVIE STAR: Surely you're not Baby Kelly Ambrose, the hatchet-wielding vaudeville child star.
CREEPY BUTLER: (*Breaks into a time-step and swings an imaginary hatchet*) I did them all in after a milk-fund benefit in Kokomo.

It may be that *Vampire Lesbians* was so successful because straight audiences adopted it as an entry point in their exploration of gay theatre. But Busch was ambitious, tackling evening-length works with less camp and more substance. Now the costuming was more reality-based and the dialogue more everyday than flaming. Yet Busch was still in transition, finally giving the Manhattan Theatre Club a somewhat mainstream event, *The Tale Of the Allergist's Wife* (2000), the first show that Busch wrote with no role for himself or for his veterans. A Broadway-level grouping of Linda Lavin, Michele Lee, and Tony Roberts led the five-person cast, and the show indeed went to Broadway, gaining a Best Play Tony nomination and running 777 performances.

Oddly, from post-Ludlam camp, Busch had moved into Broadway postwar bourgeois comedy style (typified by Neil Simon) in this look at a marriage (Lavin, Roberts) irritated by a mother-in-law (Shirl Bernheim) given to confessions about her difficulties with her biological plumbing. Trouble begins (as they say in *TV Guide*) when the married couple takes in a daffy houseguest (Lee) who in a running gag has apparently been everywhere and done everything with any celebrity you name.

What vexes Lee's hosts is the way she completely takes over their lives, using their apartment as the headquarters of her gadabout existence.

Busch says he wrote the play for Linda Lavin and felt fulfilled at the table reading: "Everything I hoped [the character] would be was there."

True, Lavin has long been a favorite of gay writers because she is so protean, someone different each time out. She's imaginative, another trait of gay art, from Cole Porter to Tennessee Williams to Charles Ludlam. Randomly watching television reruns, one might spot Lavin in a dramatic show as a by-the-book bureaucrat without a shred of compassion; change the channel and she's guesting on *Rhoda* as a hoity-toity ex-schoolmate.

Even so, it is Michele Lee who drives *The Allergist's Wife*. Busch slipped in a touch of mystery—even surrealism—at the end of Act One, when it suddenly appears that no one but Lavin has had access to Lee, leading the others to accuse Lavin of having created an imaginary friend. True, *we've* seen Lee ourselves. But no one in the play has met Lee except Lavin. Moreover, Lee is implausible to begin with, supposedly connected to the elite class yet technically homeless. Then Busch plays an ace: even the building's doorman says he has never seen her. So Lee *is* a phantom!

But Lee breezes in in front of everybody, apologizing for her lateness:

LEE: I had this [Yiddish expletive] Indian cabdriver who took me all the way
    across the river.

And the first-act curtain falls, to the audience's amused astonishment.

It's a very funny play, an absolute breakaway from Busch's former parish la-di-da. This is middle-class humor with zing, as witness Roberts' reply when the mother-in-law says a female neighbor came on to her:

ROBERTS: Rivkie Dubow was a lesbian? She had six grandchildren and wore
    a hair net.

Actually, Rivkie no more than kissed the mother-in-law, on impulse. Nevertheless, at the end of the second act, Busch treats Lavin and Roberts to some genuine bisex, at Lee's seductive direction. "I feel like I'm in the middle of a Playboy spread," Roberts tells the two women, as Busch demands "the nocturnal revels begin."

Yet this erotic surprise is a relatively minor event in the continuity. In the end, *The Tale Of the Allergist's Wife* is a gay play (by its authorship) that isn't gay and scarcely touches on the bisex. This is queer playwriting in the age after *The Boys In the Band*, when both gay writers and gay characters got integrated into the general run of theatre production. So Richard Greenberg's *Eastern Standard* (1988) might, in the 1970s, have been about how artist Peter Frechette has a thing for big, gorgeous Kevin Conroy, who doesn't respond: a scenario, as I've said, basic to gay storytelling. In their big scene, Frechette accuses Conroy of deliberately causing him pain. "You tantalize!" he cries. Conroy's admirers are "just mirrors for you to see yourself in."

But that's not what's happening:

FRECHETTE: You're a monster.
CONROY: *Listen, I'm sick!*

And in the 1980s, he didn't have to say of what. It was a formidable scene because it confounded not only Frechette's expectations but the public's as well. Comparably, Greenberg opened *Eastern Standard* by playing the same restaurant scene over and over from different angles, to introduce his characters step by step.

Further, the play wasn't about Frechette and Conroy, but rather about a social set—theirs—adopting an enraged bag lady (Anne Meara, perfect casting) who eventually sneaks off with their valuables. In other words, *Eastern Standard* dealt with class issues among yuppies, not about a particular problem in gay life.

So gay was simply fitting in, and even straight writers availed themselves of the opportunity to widen their scope. On off-Broadway at the Provincetown Playhouse, the ever-bold David Mamet unveiled his boldest work yet, the sordid *Edmond* (1983), in which an average sort of man (Colin Stinton) more or less loses contact with the average world and travels through twenty-three short scenes set in a New York populated exclusively by cheats and crooks. The play was presented in a slightly uninterested way, as if by performers without commitment, suggesting a comic-book cover drained of color. Even more puzzling was the anti-hero himself, experimenting with racial animosity so dire one wondered if Mamet was trying to provoke his audience, as at the controversial *Oleanna* (1992).

So where does gay fit into all of this? It doesn't until the end, when Edmond, interrogated in a murder case, is asked if he is guilty or innocent:

EDMOND: I don't care.

Tried, convicted, and incarcerated, Edmond cells with a man who rapes him. Later, Edmond kisses him goodnight on the lips and the play is over.

Prison rape is notoriously often about a display of power rather than sexuality. Notoriously. Still, there it was: Mr. Average in a highly offbeat situation. More and more, gay was becoming an element of dramaturgy, a piece of a rich world rather than a thing-in-itself.

Biographical plays might have brought gay figures back in a genuinely gay setting, as *Oscar Wilde* did way back in the 1930s. But Sheldon Rosen's *Ned and Jack* (1981) dealt with playwright Ned Sheldon (John Vickery), historically thought to be in love with Jack, the charismatically fabulous John Barrymore (Peter Michael Goetz). Rosen showed them spending a single night together in alternately merry and moody chat, before both lives took terrible turns—Sheldon's in a mysterious paralysis (out of fear of Barrymore's rejection?) and Barrymore's into alcoholic deterioration. There must be a valid scenario in the gay and the straight locked in bromance that dare not speak its name, but Rosen never got to it. At that, the play ran but 1 performance.

A more potent (and more or less out) figure than Ned Sheldon was blues singer Ma Rainey—*the* blues singer, as far as Ma was concerned: the founding stylist. This was the twenties entry in August Wilson's decade-by-decade epic of black American life, *Ma Rainey's Black Bottom* (1984), like *Ned and Jack* occurring in real time as Ma and her entourage of girl friend and nephew show up for a Chicago recording date. This is impeded by Ma's insistence that her stuttering nephew announce the number on the disc and her refusal to sing without a Coke. There are a number of technical hitches as well. And then, suddenly, there is fatal violence among her sidemen.

Critics thought the murder erupted out of nowhere, a problem we'll revisit with Terrence McNally's *The Lisbon Traviata*. But it is Wilson's theory that abuse by those in power can cause those on the bottom to strike out helplessly even against their own kind.

Wilson researched commercial recording protocols in 1927; and we saw Ma (Theresa Merritt; Whoopi Goldberg in the 2003 revival) actually trying a number of recording takes, a lively realistic touch for a straight play. However, Wilson erred in showing both Ma and her irritating little nephew mouthing off at a white cop who wants to arrest them because of an auto accident they apparently caused and tried to run from. If anyone black had dared to speak to a white cop in twenties Chicago as aggressively as Ma and the nephew do here—regardless of who is in the right—both would have been taken into custody very intensely, and not, as here, let off (albeit after a bribe from the record producer). The entire scene is simply unbelievable.

Another flaw, this in Lloyd Richards' staging, was actor Charles S. Dutton, so intricately mannered as an ambitious trumpeter, all tics and grins and rocking motions in his chair, that he didn't match the naturalism of the other players. At that, it didn't match Dutton's quietly seething inmate onscreen in the *Aliens* sequel set on the prison planet. Dutton got the notices, but his showy portrayal threw the production off. And the nephew, Scott Davenport-Richards (the director's son), was execrable, one of the ten or twelve worst actors I've ever seen on Broadway.

What worked in *Ma Rainey's Black Bottom* was the rest of the cast, especially Theresa Merritt's Ma. Physically grand and glamorously kitted out even for a simple recording session, Merritt recalled the classic lesbian partnership of the older, heavier woman and the slender young chick. But note that the latter, Dussie Mae (Aleta Mitchell), is only along for the ride and clearly looking for a better-paying opportunity, most likely with a man.

As written, Wilson's Ma is an actress' dream part, very fully delineated and loaded with great lines. Like most if not all of the black women singers of the day, from Ethel Waters to Bessie Smith, Wilson's Ma knows exactly what she wants from music—in repertory, accompaniment, and overall style—and she views her prima donna behavior as tactics, political acts to remind one and all of who is most crucial to the making of money in the music world.

So she is the one in control—not the cop, not her manager, not even the producer representing her record label. Here, Wilson tells us, is a lesbian who knows how to run her world, despite going up against straight men because:

MA: As soon as they get my voice down on their recording machines, then it's
      just like if I'd be some whore and they roll over and put their pants on. . . .
      If you colored and can make them some money then you all right with
      them. Otherwise you just a dog in the alley.

Dussie Mae also understands how influence works. The trumpeter tries to hook up with her on the sly, telling her how he's going to make it big on what was known as the "black time" (the infrastructure of black show business) with his own band:

LEVEE: Can I introduce my red rooster to your brown hen?

DUSSIE MAE: You get your band then we'll see if that rooster know how
to crow.

The Ma–Dussie Mae relationship fascinates because it's so open yet doesn't
arouse comment from the other characters. They take it for granted that a
successful artist—again, a moneymaker—has rights others do not. And,
once again, the gay presence here is simply one more realistic detail of the
narrative.

Yet another real-life showbiz lesbian got a bio show, this one a full-
fledged musical, and it's our old friend Tallulah Bankhead, impersonated by
parish favorite Helen Gallagher and with music (to Mae Richard's lyrics) by
New York's least persuasive heterosexual, Arthur Siegel.

So *Tallulah* (1983) was something of a gay festival, even if Siegel's standing
in the coterie was one of those riddles wrapped in mystery inside an enigma.
Straight as a goose, one might say. A composer steeped in the Golden Age
Broadway songbook (his sheet-music collection, including unpublished
numbers in manuscript, was one of the nation's largest), Siegel contributed
to the great tradition with most of the best songs in the revues *New Faces Of
1952* and *New Faces Of 1956*. He also sang (in skinny tone but with authority)
at the keyboard. I once heard him cabareting in New York's Citicorps atrium
at lunchtime.

Siegel had long nursed ambitions to compose book shows for Broadway,
but *Tallulah*, which began on off-off, then moved to the West Side Arts
Center, was the closest he got to The Street as the sole composer of a work.
Tony Lang's book for *Tallulah* took the form of a chronological look at what
our primary gay/bi favorite did and how she felt about it. Five handsome
chorus boys mostly in tuxes, with Russell Nype as Tallulah's U.S. senator father and Joel Craig as John Barrymore and then as Tallulah's only husband,
John Emery, assisted. But casting really boiled down to Gallagher, the only
one with a part. And if the lyrics varied from clever to obvious, Siegel's music
called up a vanished era just as the very mention of Bankhead's name does—
and her show truly presented her as her gay fans knew her.

Thus, *Tallulah* opened with a voice introducing the star, and she
appeared . . . impersonated by one of those chorus boys in drag. Then another,
then another, and they all checked in with the inevitable "Dahlings!" till
Gallagher herself took over. She used the Tallulah voice and accent only now
and then, to avoid caricature, and in all the show was an ideal vehicle for her
as she uttered many lines that were either Famous Tallulah Sayings or should

have been. For example, on Tallulah's love of the New York Giants: "I would have followed them to the ends of the earth. Well, I did go to the Bronx." This led to "Don't Ever Book a Trip On the IRT," a spoof of Tallulah's well-known ID as someone unfamiliar with the instruments of everyday living. What, no dining car?

The show was generally fast and funny and did touch on Tallulah's bisexual escapades in "If Only He Were a Woman." Maybe it was all too funny, too fast, for the show cut Siegel's one deeply felt ballad, "The Right One Will Ask Me To Dance." It was the same old story: no one wanted anything from Bankhead but camp and posing, as we know from the way her "fans" hooted at her City Center *Streetcar Named Desire*. However, the show did talk about this, too, in an arresting finale. Singing "I'm the Woman You Wanted," Gallagher reminded us that Tallulah ended—against her will—as a vulgar imitation of herself.

From the energetically thematic *Ma Rainey's Black Bottom* and the pleasantly superficial *Tallulah*, we come to a third piece on a historical figure, Jay Presson Allen's *Tru* (1989). A one-hander, it offered Robert Morse as Truman Capote on two consecutive nights at Christmas, trying to get over the despair of his life, when his "swans" (the elegant wives of rich and powerful men) closed the iron door after he published gossip about them.

Like *Tallulah's* authors, Allen used many of her subject's actual utterances in her text, and her own inventions matched Capote's so well that one couldn't tell them apart, as when Morse said no one is truly rich "who cannot summon up fifty million in hard currency." Who created that one—Capote or Allen?

The author not only wrote but directed, and she proved a capable stylist. Still, the evening's asset was Morse, a Capote to the life in Karen Haney's replica make-up job, dancing about, laughing after almost every statement, singing snatches of Cole Porter, smoking a joint, actively addressing the audience, and, late in the continuity, smashing his fist through a painting of the young and happy Capote, everyone's darling, paying no price. It was a moment of terrifying rage, truly startling because there was no ramp-up. It just happened, very suddenly, and the public froze in astonishment. So it's not a comedy?

Tru was important if only because of its subject, one of our great gay celebrities, never closeted. "I've always been right out there," he said at one point. True enough. Yet we're impatient for plays that really delve into gay life, in both basic or unusual ways—the "I love you except when I don't" boy friend, say; or the gay bashers who wreck your life; or the unaccepting mother. Even the child you adopt.

So how about Harvey Fierstein's *Torch Song Trilogy,* a gathering of one-acts first unveiled separately at La MaMa: *The International Stud* (1978), *Fugue In a Nursery* (1979), and *Widows and Children First!* (1979)? The complete evening (1981) eventually moved to one of Broadway's small houses, the Little Theatre (now the Hayes), in 1982. Except for Fierstein's own portrayal of Arnold Beckoff, the cast changed from gig to gig, but his support at the Little included Court Miller (as Ed, Arnold's boy friend who turned out to be a confused bisexual), Paul Joynt (as Alan, Arnold's later lover and live-in, killed by bat-swinging teens), Fisher Stevens (as David, the cocky young runaway Arnold adopts as a single parent), Diane Tarleton (as Laurel, Arnold's rival for Ed), and Estelle Getty (Arnold's homophobic mother, later the tart-tongued senior of television's *The Golden Girls*).

Torch Song Trilogy is a long show, as it really is an agglomeration of three stylistically different and quite autonomous plays. For example, *Stud* offers Arnold and Ed (plus Arnold's confidant, Murray, unseen and unheard but a "telephone presence"). There is also some wholly unnecessary punctuation from a torch singer, as if the piece were embarrassed to offer so tidy a cast in a saga that will prove to be very messy, like life. But then *Fugue*, set on a gigantic bed, brings in Laurel and Alan and is structured, as its title suggests, to develop verbal and physical tropes, as when each of the two couples speaks alone, one on one but in intricately interposed dialogue, two on two; or when Ed seduces Alan, all bisexual confusion giving way to the confidence of a hard-on. But then the third play is frantically comical to the point of farce, as a visit from Arnold's mother turns Arnold's household (of him, his ward, and a "Now I really am gay . . . I think" Ed) topsy-turvy. In fact, the playing of this last third of the bill proved so amusing that the public's laughter sometimes obscured the actors' next lines, for too many stage waits for the laughs would have made the running time unsupportably long.

Throughout, author Fierstein upholds the lingua franca of the northeast urban gay, referencing Bette Davis, Blanche DuBois, and Katharine Hepburn's "calla lilies" speech in the *Stage Door* film. But we get some more universal bits, in the Neil Simon mold:

LAUREL: If you can't enter a house of God, where do you pray?
ARNOLD: Bloomingdale's.

or:

ED: Don't you think I could make a convincing homosexual?
DAVID: You could make this convincing homosexual.

Common sense tells us that three so very diverse pieces shouldn't adhere easily. But Fierstein's portrayal, consistent from start to finish, bonded them so neatly it is hard to imagine anyone else in the role, so touching but also sarcastic and passionate in combat with his mother, a monster who is nosy about everything, judgmental about everyone, and has no redeeming feature whatsoever. She's stupid, bigoted, and vicious. She even asserts that favorite hetero fantasy that gay is a choice:

ARNOLD: Ma, David is gay. . . . He came that way.
MRS. BECKOFF: No one comes that way.

True, Estelle Getty and replacement Chevi Colton presented that character most ably, seeking to locate the humanity amid the anger. Anne Bancroft, in the movie version, found another way: Mrs. Beckoff is inhuman, so there's nothing amid the anger worth playing. This is a woman living in a state of rage; the message—almost—is that hetero life is unstable while gay life is steady: which explains why Ed is unreliable even to himself until he throws in his lot with his gay side.

And let us note that Bancroft was at her most intense when she tells her son that his love for the murdered Alan is not comparable to the love of two heteros:

MRS. BECKOFF: So you felt bad. Maybe you cried a little. But what would you
    know about what I went through [when I was widowed]?

Arnold replies at white heat, ending with:

ARNOLD: You had it easy, Ma. You lost your husband in a nice clean hos-
    pital, I lost mine . . . on the street . . . killed by a bunch of kids with base-
    ball bats.

Whereupon his mother "has fled the room," though in the movie the scene occurs in the cemetery where Arnold's father is buried, way out on Long

Island, and Bancroft "flees" in their limo, stranding Arnold forty miles from his apartment.

What kind of relationship is this, anyway? Why does Arnold continue to know her—or are we allowed even to ask? Does Fierstein observe an unwritten law in which one retains such people in one's life no matter how they behave? But how would at least some (if not many) people feel if Arnold closed the iron door on that bitch?

But I digress with pleasantry. Let's move on to William Finn's "Marvin" Trilogy, which offers the musical complement to Fierstein's trio, on domestic issues but now in the age of AIDS. Like the Arnold plays, these came to light separately (at Playwrights Horizons, at the time untried in musicals) throughout the era: *In Trousers* (1979), *March Of the Falsettos* (1981), and *Falsettoland* (1990). Essentially, Marvin realizes he's gay, leaves his wife and child for a man named Whizzer while his wife, Trina, takes up with Marvin's quack psychiatrist, Mendel. Finally, Whizzer dies in the hospital.

Then *In Trousers* more or less fell off the cliff when the latter two titles seemed to bind, treating as they did another gay concept new to the musical, the extended non-biological family. So the second and third shows were combined into one evening as *Falsettos*, an irritatingly confusing title because of its resemblance to the titles of its constituent parts; only the aficionado who has nothing better to do can keep these three "falsetto" things straight.

But now we do have a "mostly gay" group of merry villagers: Marvin and Whizzer; Trina and the quack; Marvin and Trina's son, Jason; and a female couple, a lively pairing of doctor and caterer. "Look look look look look," the doctor happily carols as they enter, "it's a lesbian from next door." Later, in "Something Bad Is Happening," she takes an ominous tone, ushering The Disease into the musical.

Ostensibly, *Falsettos*' action moves toward Jason's bar mitzvah, but this becomes something of a maguffin once illness overcomes Whizzer. Finn specializes in eccentric characters, and this allows him to create songs on unexploited topics–"Four Jews In a Room Bitching" is *Falsettos*' opening, and "My Father's a Homo" and "Everybody Tells Jason To See a Psychiatrist" are other typical titles, more redolent of life than of what usually gets sung in musicals. But then, what's usual about extended families and a First Couple comprising two men, especially in a chamber piece with scarcely any visuals except a hospital bed? In director (and co-scenarist, with Finn) James Lapine's visuals, there's nothing to see except people.

Finn loves making music so much that he often composes operas rather than musicals, mercurial and conversational rather than aria-based, with an emphasis on rhymes, even odd ones. If a character uses, say, "oceanic," Finn will yearn to match it with "satanic." Further, he loves wordless placeholders such as "la la la" and "bum bum," and some of his lines burst out of their own scan, as if the lyrics had become so used to the story they started writing the score themselves.

Some have compared Finn to Sondheim, but they don't have much in common. Yes, both are gay composer-lyricists with offbeat subjects, but they don't sound at all alike. Perhaps their meeting point is that the best singing actors enjoy playing in their shows, because there's so much there in them. Thus, while Finn's musicals tend to emerge in non-Broadway or Broadway-adjacent venues, they always attract on-Broadway talent, as with the Marvin and Whizzer of Michael Rupert and Stephen Bogardus—each as impulsive as Finn's music is—or the two ensemble casts of *A New Brain* (1998; revised 2015), yet another wild ride of a show.

This one is autobiographical, as Finn himself underwent very serious surgery for an interior malformation that might have killed him. Typically, Finn's personal surrogate (Malcolm Gets; revival Jonathan Groff) was basic and personable while almost everyone else was an oddball—a tyrannical mother; an only partially devoted boy friend; an obnoxious boss, the host of a children's television show as the froglike Mr. Bungee; an eerie (though eventually quite capable) doctor; a homeless woman whose request for "change" means not coins but an alteration in the way the world works.

Both *New Brain* productions utilized an open stage with slight furnishings—another hospital bed, a bookcase in the hero's apartment, and so on. It may be that director James Lapine advised Finn on storytelling, as both productions were billed with "Book by William Finn and James Lapine" though of course through-sung shows like this one don't have books.

Can we pause? The book in a musical is the spoken dialogue between the songs, just as the score is the music between the dialogue scenes. The book and score have been combining intricately for a long time now, but they are nevertheless two different things. Except for the odd spoken line during or between the numbers, through-sung musicals don't have "books" any more than *Parsifal* or *Aida* has a book. Such works have only music and lyrics. Now, they do have a treatment, scenario, plot—whatever term one prefers. But they don't have spoken dialogue and therefore do not have a book.

Yet the credit for a book was so constant during the musical's history that it has led people who don't know what "book" means to assume that, somehow or other, *every musical has a book*. Thus, the Tony folk could give *Cats*—a dance revue made of a succession of musical numbers with no talking at all—the award for Best Book of a Musical, because of this erroneous belief that *every musical has a book*. Really, as long as we're assigning fake book credits to shows without books, why stop there? By this way of thinking, everything on the planet earth has a book—the Parthenon, English muffin pizza, my Aunt Agnes.

This relates to the topic at hand because it strikes me as typical hetero thinking about the musical: thinking from the outside, never quite "getting it." Indeed, James Lapine's work as a director exemplifies this in his drab stage pictures and refusal to program the grand dramatic moments that we think of as "theatrical." Thus, when "movement director" Randolyn Zinn suggested that Lapine let the figures in the painting in *Sunday In the Park With George* celebrate a climactic moment by bowing to the painter—their creator—Lapine made it so slight a gesture—perfunctory, really—that one scarcely noticed it.

This raises an old question once more: why are so many gay men so enthusiastic about musicals? And here's the answer:

Nobody knows.

There are theories. Mine is that young gaylings, realizing that society is weighted against them, need an angle: and musicals make you smart. They're written mostly by brilliant people, and listening to cast albums makes you smarter than your years, better able to defend yourself in a partly hostile world.

A New Brain, then, is one of those "makes you smarter" pieces, with its clever lyrics and complex character relationships based on antagonism. For instance, protagonist Gordon hates his aforementioned employer, Mr. Bungee (Chip Zien; revival Dan Fogler), who appears in a semi-frog costume on a scooter. Though he is actually "present" in the action only once, he haunts the show in concept-musical fashion, psychologically rather than physically there. And Mr. Bungee doesn't think too much of his songwriter, Gordon, because his writing is sophisticated. Gordon wants to make art; Mr. Bungee wants to please children.

There is antagonism as well with Gordon's mother (Penny Fuller; Ana Gasteyer), who throws all his books out while he is in the hospital. She's nothing like the gay-hating Mrs. Beckoff of *Torch Song Trilogy*, yet everyone does seem to have some beef with Gordon. Even his lover, Roger (Christopher Innvar; Aaron Lazar) sings "I'd Rather Be Sailing," accenting his need for solitude, even in romance.

But then, Gordon, too, has his sharp edges. When he has to write Mr. Bungee a Yes Song (including, for instance, Yes, I will do my homework and other good-boy concepts), Gordon comes up with a No Song (featuring what to do when an unknown adult invites you into his car). As so often in *A New Brain*, the other characters are shamelessly having a grand time supplying backup for the number, till Mr. Bungee orders them to stop and they (and the orchestra) die out like a balloon losing its air—again, pure concept-musical thinking, as Mr. Bungee isn't supposed to be aware that he's a character in a musical.

The *New Brain* revisal improved everything, making Gordon much younger, with none of his ambitions yet realized. His father, only spoken of in the original, was now a functioning character (Bradley Dean) with an opera-level baritone. He doubled as the doctor and had the show's funniest line, a reference to *Fun Home* (which we haven't got to yet) so incongruous that it brought the house down. It needed to, for Finn's at times bleak worldview can add dark weight to his stories. At the end of *A New Brain*'s "A Really Lousy Day In the Universe," the Homeless Lady (Mary Testa; Rema Webb) says, "They all are."

Yet another "true-life adventure" show was David Henry Hwang's *M. Butterfly* (1988), drawn from an espionage case that became notorious in 1986, when French diplomat Bernard Boursicot was convicted of sharing state secrets with the Communist Chinese. Boursicot was taken in by a honey trap, as they're called: an attractive woman expresses erotic interest in a man not adept in the courtship arts. His self-esteem thus elevated, he can be played into betraying his country. What interested Hwang was that the "honey" was not a woman but a man—and the hetero Boursicot never knew he was cohabiting with a professional cross-dresser. That is, his partner was not a transsexual but an actor who played women on stage.

Well, as· everyone said at the time, *Wut*? But the spy was clever and Boursicot a willing stooge inclined simply to lie there and let the sex happen. And Hwang saw a theme herein, as a typical Westerner misapprehends the East. Here's Hwang's character, Song Liling, Hwang's version of Boursicot's Chinese agent:

SONG: The West thinks of itself as masculine—big guns, big industry, big money. So the East is feminine—weak, delicate, poor. . . . The West believes the East, deep down, *wants* to be dominated—because a woman can't think for herself.

As Hwang's title tells us, he was using not only the Boursicot headlines but the *Madame Butterfly* tale, a much-adapted short story most famous as Puccini's opera: an American Naval lieutenant "marries" and then abandons a (Japanese in this case, not Chinese) naive young girl who kills herself in despair. However, while Puccini's Westerner uses Butterfly, Hwang's Westerner *is used* by the "woman," whom he does seem to love. Thus, it is he who becomes the play's Butterfly. And he is the one who ends in suicide.

Is this a gay play at all? Two men are having at least some sort of sex, and that much is gay. But both are hetero, one engaging in what he thinks is anal intercourse with a woman and the other enduring the liaison, in fealty to his Communist bosses. Meanwhile, in his version of *Madame Butterfly's* Navy man who loves and leaves, Hwang's Boursicot (here called Gallimard, and created on Broadway by John Lithgow) suddenly ghosts Song (B. D. Wong). He does this "wickedly," he says. Because this classic nerd says he "felt for the first time . . . the absolute power of man."

So Hwang really has two themes to gnaw on, not only the West's ignorance of the East but the male's ignorance of women. This enriches the work, and the production, directed by John Dexter, was visually rich as well, employing inset scenes of Chinese opera. Add to this Hwang's letting his characters address the audience directly, and *M. Butterfly* became, in the modern style, meta-theatre. Further, some Puccini was heard, along with new music by Lucia Hwong, adding to the feeling that *M. Butterfly* was the straight-play version of a concept musical.*

Speaking of musicals, the 1980s saw the high prime of another gay director-choreographer, Tommy Tune, in *Nine* (1982), *My One and Only* (1983), and *Grand Hotel* (1989), three extraordinary stagings. *Nine*, from Fellini's movie 8½, boiled that phantasmagoria down to its protagonist (Raul Julia) and his women in a festival of Big Ladies, from sexy (Anita Morris) to authoritarian

---

* Almost everyone pronounces the title as "Em Butterfly," but that makes no sense. What is "Em" supposed to mean? And of course "M." is the standard abbreviation for "Monsieur." In fact, Hwang first called his play *Monsieur Butterfly*, but his wife thought that "too obvious" (as Hwang explains in his Afterword to the published script). She suggested *M. Butterfly* as "more mysterious and ambiguous." And of course Hwang's tale is made of mystery and ambiguity; it's a perfect fit. So, boys and girls: Stop saying "Em."

(Liliane Montevecchi) to austere (Karen Akers). *Grand Hotel*, with a largely gay cast, had as well a few gay characters. Akers was now the personal assistant of Montevecchi's star ballerina (the Garbo part, in the old talkie), not just Montevecchi's employee but ultra-devoted and self-sacrificing: an unrequited lover. In her short hair and mannish suit, Akers anticipated the two of them retiring together in "Villa On a Hill," a lovely ballad that was nothing less than a lesbian love song. And one scene, between the Baron (David Carroll) and his Chauffeur (Ben George), began in what seemed like the moment just after sex, as the Chauffeur was buttoning up his uniform top. (In the Boston tryout, Carroll briefly tried playing the scene discreetly nude.)

It's worth comparing Tune with Michael Bennett, as both fashioned high-style shows rich in the flamboyance and glamour that gay show biz lives on. And Tune had worked for Bennett, most prominently playing an apparently gay dancer in *Seesaw* (1973). However, Bennett bearded, as I've said, supposedly because an industry honcho told him he'd never make it in Hollywood as an out gay. And Bennett was ambitious.

He was competitive, too, so when Tune's *Nine* won the Best Musical and Best Director Tonys over Bennett's *Dreamgirls*, Bennett became one of those frenemies that show biz specializes in: congratulating you on your smash hit while hiding the voodoo doll and pins behind the back.

Still, Tune and Bennett together dominated the age in musicals, though of course the topmost name of the high maestros, active since the 1990s was Stephen Sondheim, also gay, though apparently everybody knew it before he did.

Yet didn't his lyrics lack the defining trait of gay songwriters, saucy snark? Cole Porter, we know, reveled in it, and we've enjoyed an example of it from Lorenz Hart as well. Here's another, in *On Your Toes'* "Too Good For the Average Man," on the perks and glitches in the lives of the elite. There's plastic surgery on one hand, dipsomania on the other. And of course psychiatrists "are all the whirl," even if a man might end in "waking up to find that he's a girl."

Sondheim avoids that kind of thing, because it characterizes the author rather than a character. A Sondheim snark will be something like *Company*'s three girl friends on Robert's strange approach-avoidance attitude with "I could understand a person if a person was a fag." It was exactly how hip girl friends of 1970 might have phrased it, though Sondheim later rewrote the line to soothe parish feelings. And he did produce two gay principals in the final version of his last piece, *Road Show* (1999).

Now, in the 1980s, is when Sondheim wrote what may prove to be his most popular title as composer and lyricist, *Into the Woods*. Further, now is when

Sondheim truly ruled: this is the Age Of Sondheim, whereas earlier he was controversial, argued rather than admired. Yet we must admit he made his most potent history developing the concept musical with producer-director Harold Prince in the 1970s, a series of five classic titles including what is arguably the gayest best musical of all time, *Follies* (1971).[†]

Yet what's gay about it? It tells of two middle-aged couples attending a reunion. The wife of one couple and the husband of the other couple want to be together, even though she's now depressed and bitter and he's exhausted and nihilistic. Well, so far, so good—but he wants her only if they can be twenty-two again. So *Follies* is filled with their personal flashbacks, not to remember but rather to relive, rejuvenated. Yet in the end nothing happens, and the couples leave with their own spouses.

It's a very hetero story—but it plays against show-biz flashbacks set out in the electricity that gays respond to, the vignettes of music and dance on old Broadway. And now *Follies* is about more than those two couples. It tells how our ever-evolving entertainment mirrors American life. Thus, *Follies* becomes the show of shows: a musical about the performing life, the truth and lies of life, the myth of the musical.

So Sondheim's work takes in gay (in a way) musicals, but he has no *Cage Aux Folles*. *Into the Woods*, even with its huge complement of principals, hasn't a whiff of gay in it. Yet Sondheim does have *Company* (1970), the first of his concept shows, boasting a protagonist who both is and isn't gay, Robert. Some might call him closeted or bisexual. He isn't. What he is is Anthony Perkins, who *was* gay, though he "ex-gayed" himself under coercion by a destructive psychologist, bearding in marriage and even siring children, which gives Perkins one of the most confusing IDs in thespian history.

Company is confusing, too, because it questions the most essential trope in the American musical—the happy ending of Boy Gets Girl. *Company* asks, what if it isn't happy? More confusion: *Company*'s bookwriter, George Furth, modeled Robert on Perkins, as he and Sondheim and Prince and maybe even Michael Bennett (responsible for "musical staging") expected Perkins to play Robert in the finished show. Indeed, Perkins appeared in *Company*'s first advance ads, but then abruptly dropped out.

[†] We've had this term "concept musical" a few times already, but this is the appropriate place to define it. Everyone uses it in his own way, so it has lost its meaning, which was, originally, the meta-theatrical work that comments on its storyline as it unfolds. *Allegro* (1947) and *Love Life* (1948) launched the form, taken up again by *Cabaret* (1966) and the Sondheim–Prince shows.

It was logical casting, though, as Perkins had sung very personably as the star of Frank Loesser's *Greenwillow* (1960). He had even played in a Sondheim piece, the television musical *Evening Primrose* (1966), in a *Twilight Zone* kind of story, most fitting for the actor who was to spend his life trying to live down *Psycho*.

That doesn't mean that Robert is a homicidal mama's boy, though Sondheim's shows in general are quite fantastical, with ghosts, cannibalism, a painting come to life, fairy-tale magic, even a host of presidential assassins appealing to a hesitant Lee Harvey Oswald to go ahead and make their day.

But then, Sondheim's art transgresses to reach thematic density beyond the scope of most musicals. The German poet and Dramatist Friedrich Schiller is instructive here, in his breaking poetry (meaning also theatre) into "naive" and "sentimental" art. Naive art is created impulsively, a first draft, instinctive and emotional. Sentimental (really "thoughtful") art is created by plan, to develop a viewpoint. Some samples:

Naive symphonist: Schubert.
Sentimental symphonist: Mahler.
Naive comic strip: *Peanuts*.
Sentimental comic strip: *Krazy Kat*.
Naive blasphemy: "Judas Priest!"
Sentimental blasphemy: Madonna's cone bra.

Now: if *Company* had been conceived as an example of Schiller's naive art, it would be any old musical comedy about this guy and his friends and his dates. It's a lot of fun, and then he gets married.

But *Company* is sentimental, building its hero around a pre-existing Robert—gay Anthony Perkins—even though Robert is supposed to be straight. And the show is not only sentimental but errant, because Robert is straight in the play but gay in real life. This may be why George Furth wrote in a little bisexual bit for Robert and one of his company, Peter. In the *Oxford Handbook Of Sondheim Studies*, Scott F. Stoddart revealed that this scenelet, interpolated into the Sam Mendes Donmar Warehouse staging, in 1995, was actually written for the original production but deleted "right before the play opened." In it, Peter asks if Robert ever had "a homosexual experience." Flustered, Robert stalls. Then:

ROBERT: Well, yes, actually, yes, I have.

So word is out, it seems. Yet I don't believe many theatregoers think Robert's statement means anything. Is he recalling a conclusive mating, the works—or did he just stand there while someone gave head? Because that's not much gayer than, say, Sylvester Stallone playing pinball in an arcade on the Jersey shore wearing a hat he borrowed from Ernest Borgnine. Robert's avoidance of marriage isn't sexual: he's afraid of giving up his privacy, his independence. Then, rather suddenly, he seems about to at the show's end. He has been naive all evening and now gets sentimental.

Isn't that a flaw? Why does he change his mind? Dean Jones, the Robert who rehearsed and opened *Company* but left four weeks after the New York premiere, was expert enough to fill in Robert's lacunae with his own nervous aplomb, and the show played very, very well in the Prince and Bennett (and set designer Boris Aronson) production. Jones even managed to pacify the confusions of the Frankenrole that Furth made while grafting Robert onto Anthony Perkins. But what are these confusions exactly? In other words, is Robert bisexual? Or even was Anthony Perkins bisexual? The very word hides in mystery, because everyone defines it differently. To some any engagement with one's own gender, however slight, is bi. Others require physical or emotional involvement. Here's yet another view: a hetero star of gay porn films in the 1990s, a big blond boy of fabulous beauty, was doing it only "for the money." Then his girl friend came home early from work and surprised him in bed having cheat sex . . . with a man. Thus, bi extends from perfunctory contact to full immersion.

Robert isn't bisexual. Nor is he gay. Nor straight. What Robert is is the musical's unfinished symphony: an underwritten role filled with missing pieces because he was based on a neurotic who actually underwent the hateful fraud of gay "conversion therapy" two years after *Company* opened. What's Robert's sexuality? *Fear.*

Here's another question: as Dean Jones left so early in *Company*'s run; did his replacement somehow clarify Robert's sexuality? And here's the answer: no. Because it was Larry Kert; a good singer but a no more than functional actor. (He was also gay, though that's irrelevant in terms of acting.) Some say he grew into a valid Robert during the run, but I saw one of his last performances, and he was the same insipid narcissist he always played. Offstage, Kert was constantly telling everyone it was "time I had my own show," that he was ready to be "up there with the biggies." Yes, he talked like that. For years, he nourished a dream of coming to Broadway playing Al Jolson, another narcissist, but Kert may not have realized that *Company* offered him the role of a lifetime, because the show's story suspense lies in waiting to see if something can break the No Trespassers sign on Robert's soul.

Maybe the solution to the *Company* question would be to make Robert openly bi. Why not let a man play the flight attendant whom Robert beds, in the most sexual of Robert's "dates," so we can see him living on both sides?[‡] And the show's finale could be staged showing Robert relating to both a man and a woman.

Company needs definition. As it stands, it's a tease. To refashion the famous pitch for a Kathleen Turner–Nicolas Cage film of 1986, Robert got married . . . or will he?

‡ In fact, this finally happened, in a *Company* revision that reversed the genders. Robert was Roberta—so the show was still about hetero mating habits after all, and that cannot enlighten us any more than the confused original does.

8

The 1990s and 2000s

They're Taking Over

Terrence McNally was gay and a playwright, also Edward Albee's romantic partner during Albee's most influential period, in the early 1960s. McNally was cute, too, which adds to the fun. He was as well prolific, writing not only many play and movie scripts but also librettos for over half a dozen musicals (and some operas). And in the long view of it, most of his output is either openly or subtly gay.

Openly: *Corpus Christi* (1998), a look at the first set of disciples when Christianity was a Jewish heresy, supposed that they were all queer. An offering by Manhattan Theatre Club (with which McNally was enjoying a fruitful relationship), the play provoked the anger of religion purists and even death threats. Fearing violence at performances, MTC canceled the production, outraging the theatre community; Athol Fugard threatened to withdraw his work from its stages, and MTC relented. McNally declared himself surprised at the furor; he said he thought he was writing a piece about some nice Jewish boys.

That was openly. These were subtly: *Lips Together, Teeth Apart* (1991) has a small cast, all straight. Yet they're out on Fire Island in a house where a gay man died of AIDS, and on either side are (unseen) gay guys partying. *Master Class* (1995) boasts of a Big Lady protagonist from the world of opera, Maria Callas, an established goddess of opera-buff gay men. *The Full Monty* (2000), though apparently about hetero men turning stripper out of unemployment, allows two of them to recall a youth devoted to the cast album of *The Sound Of Music*. How many straight boys are devoted to Broadway cast albums? Later, at a funeral, one of the two moves to stand with the other so feelingly that we realize that they have more than show music in common.

So Terrence McNally is a thoroughgoing gay playwright, though he himself rejected the term. As he viewed it, he was gay and a playwright, the two not necessarily congruent. "I still remember the relief and pride I felt," he wrote in his *Selected Works: A Memoir In Plays*, "when Jane Chambers' *Last*

Summer At Bluefish Cove was reviewed as a play about lesbians and not as a lesbian play."

Yet what distinction is he drawing? If it's gay, then it's gay; it is what it is. What are you defending yourself from when you insist that "a play about lesbians" isn't "a lesbian play"? This semantic finesse is what V. S. Naipaul calls "a university idea," here meaning the intellectual's equivalent of calculating how many angels can dance on the head of a pin. McNally and others who feel as he did can call their work whatever they like, but it seems futile and bogus to try to de-gay a career so imbued with gay lifestyles and gay attitudes that McNally deserves consideration among Tennessee Williams, Edward Albee, and other gay dramatists who forged new paths for the theatre to take.

Even so, McNally made a somewhat absurd Broadway debut, in 1963, as the adaptor of Giles Cooper's translation of Dumas' *The Lady Of the Camellias*, directed and with scenery by Franco Zeffirelli, with Susan Strasberg in the role Garbo filmed. Strasberg's Armand was John Steele (understudied, by the way, by Frederick Combs, later of *The Boys In the Band*) and the costumes were by Marcel Escoffier and Pierre Cardin, the music by Ned Rorem. It was if nothing else sumptuous, but it was nothing else, and it bombed so conclusively that it ended Strasberg's Broadway career (though she continued to work in the movies and television) and, more pertinent to us, so embarrassed McNally that he suppressed mention of it.

It ran two weeks—but so did McNally's next Broadway title, *And Things That Go Bump In the Night* (1965), a horror thriller suggesting the collaboration of Edward Albee and the Scary Clown Monster. The reviews stood among the worst of all time, mainly because an unmistakable homoerotic aura enveloped the proceedings, and this was an era in which most of Broadway's critics seemed determined to stamp out gay activity in the theatre by disincentivizing it with notices so vicious that gay writers would self-censor simply to survive.

So McNally couldn't pursue a policy of Talking About It . . . yet. Still, he was writing on the far edge of respectability, and of course *The Ritz*, ten years after *Things*, could be seen as a defiance of the professional bigots of the press. Then, ten years after *The Ritz*, McNally made his first serious examination of gay life, in *The Lisbon Traviata* (1985; revised 1989).

A four-hander with an all-male cast, this work compares the intensity of the opera buff to the fire of love, its need and anger. They are the same, McNally suggests, bringing out the demon in the "fan" whose will is thwarted.

Whether the loved one is music or another man, the hunger is extraordinary, even dangerous.

The play's title refers to a newly discovered radio transmission of one of Maria Callas' many live *Traviata*s, which Anthony Heald owns and Nathan Lane is insanely eager to hear—to own and call it his. These two occupy most of a long first act talking about almost nothing but opera in insider's terms, a daring move by McNally: how niche should a play be? But the second act turns us toward the more universal topic of romance, as Heald's lover (Dan Butler) is leaving him for someone less complicated and driven (John Slattery); in the end Heald stabs Butler to keep him from going. And note that McNally specifically makes this real-life murder analogous to murders in *Tosca* and *Carmen*, carefully forewarning us that what happens in opera doesn't necessarily stay in opera. Butler is bleeding to death in Heald's arms as the play ends.

There was much public consternation about this finale. It seemed to some a non sequitur, especially after the play's abundant humor, as witness Heald's joke about where he had hidden erotic photos of Butler and himself:

HEALD: The last place anybody would look. On the bookshelf behind *The Story Of Civilization* by Will and Ariel Durant.

Then, too, McNally craftily switched tone, from a comedy in Act One centering on Lane to a more serious piece in Act Two centered on Heald, growing as he does in barely suppressed rage as he tries to prevent Butler from slipping out of his life. *The Lisbon Traviata* is really two plays conjoined, one running right after the other, so the murder isn't supposed to match the humor in the first act—that's from another work, so to say.

Even so, McNally felt pressured into altering the ending, allowing Butler to walk out on Heald. In this version, the latter closes the evening by himself, soundlessly "singing" along with a Callas recording, his mouth outlining a cry of despair.

At first, this was final *Lisbon Traviata*. But in *Murder Most Queer*, Jordan Schildkrout theorizes that this new, murder-less finale marked a revival of an old homophobic tradition wherein the straight audience watches in smug satisfaction as the gay man kills himself. Thus, Schildkrout writes, "The hostile queen turns his rage and self-loathing inward rather than outward, becoming impotent and silent, unloved, dying as surely as Violetta [in *La Traviata*]." The play became the *New York Traviata*, and, Schildkrout adds, "The gay victim is more palatable than the gay perpetrator."

Yes. And McNally may have felt so, too, for he once again altered the last scene, restoring the murder for an absolutely guaranteed final *Lisbon Traviata*. Perhaps on second view, some of the public will notice how the play slyly counters the first act's merry passion with the second's more determined passion—how Heald's character in effect becomes "operatic" in his actions, actively rather than passively gay.

Kiss Of the Spider Woman (1993), a musical version of Manuel Puig's novel, with a Kander and Ebb score, gave librettist McNally a chance to ennoble another traditional gay victim in the person of an effeminate lover of exotic movies (Brent Carver). Serving time in a Latin American prison for a sex offense, Carver is in a cell with his opposite, a leftist agitator (Anthony Crivello), as fierce and dominating as Carver is gentle and huffy.

As the show proceeds, the two men almost exchange roles, as Crivello reveals a tender side and Carver rises to heroism. But what really excites the show is the title role, Carver's movie idol (Chita Rivera) and the central figure in the cinema recaps and dream visions that spice up the Kander and Ebb score.

One of the most thoroughly rewritten musicals of all time, *Kiss Of the Spider Woman* started as a fully-staged workshop on a college campus in the New York suburb of Purchase, where it suffered from far too much of the movie scenes. They were all terrible, anyway, and the Spider Woman was written as a soft role, rather lamely alluring.

Instead, the part needed reimagining as a Big Lady, tempestuous, erotic, even eerie. When Rivera was invited to "spring in" (as they put it in German theatre) for a revision in London with Broadway to follow, Rivera was baffled by how short her role seemed to be in the script. But then, McNally had little to give her: the Spider Woman, called Aurora, was in effect a phantom conjured up by Carver's escapist worship. She was not just a movie star but a gay man's dream of a diva, existing entirely in the world of song and dance. Aurora isn't in the script: she's too fabulous for earthbound boilerplate. She dwells on the planet Show Biz.

It's a strange way to run a musical, for the top-billed star, Rivera, isn't really in the story at all, making *Spider Woman* something like a theatre piece entirely by Kander and Ebb. It is as well a harrowing experience, making Carver's flights of fancy our only release from the machinery of the police state grinding against the prisoners.

Kander and Ebb are known for having maintained the saucy and hummable musical, as opposed to the dark shows such as *Sweeney Todd* or

American Psycho. Yet Kander has long dealt with dark topics—Nazism, rape, even (with a new partner after Ebb's death) the kidnaping of a teenaged boy by a sexual predator, coming up in our last chapter.

Kiss Of the Spider Woman does manage to retain a taste of the glamour of old-time musical comedy, as in a vision of Rivera in a man's white double-breasted tailcoat suit with slouch hat, lounging against a wall while enjoying a cigarette. And despite all that Carver's character was up against, the actor was charming even as a loser, a window dresser for a department store, the gayest job imaginable. It created his ID number, "Dressing Them Up," the melody syncopated to underline his quirky personality. It's proud music as well, because he knows he's great at his job—but it provokes an enraged outburst from Crivello, the virile straight disgusted by a preening faggot.

This is a heavy concept for a musical, and while Carver was physically drawn to Crivello and Crivello schemed to exploit that for his own purposes, *Spider Woman* was treating a controversial theme, that of (some) gay men's attraction to trade. In the end, whom did Carver worship more—the diva or the dangerous man?

And exactly how honest was gay theatre to be? Back in the saddle in his own (that is, non-musical) plays, McNally thought to create a *Boys In the Band* fit for the very much more open post-Stonewall age, in *Love! Valour! Compassion!* (1994), on three successive summer holiday weekends among a tight-knit circle of friends.

Already, we see a major difference with Mart Crowley's group. *His* boys don't all know one another, an outsider (the "Is he or isn't he?" Alan) lurks among them, and for that matter an outsider controls the gathering. It's Michael, often mistaken to be an intimate of all the guests but (as we noted many pages ago) a near-stranger to most of them.

There are some newcomers in *Love! Valour! Compassion!* (hereafter *LVC*), yet the atmosphere suggests community, a gay world that has had a few decades of freedom in which to sort out its lifestyles, while back in Crowley's play survival is too topsy-turvy to admit of community. Rather, McNally wants to examine truly deep friendships, the place where people know you so well there's no point in having secrets. Then, too, while *Boys* has a few showy parts, *LVC* is more evenly derived.

In fact, *LVC* has no protagonist. It has an alpha male, Gregory, a dancer and choreographer successful enough to own the weekend getaway the play takes place in. Nevertheless, McNally has written a few important roles here. The audience immediately notices Buzz (Nathan Lane's part), as he is that favorite gay character the musical-comedy buff, constantly referencing the major titles as he whisks his way through life. Buzz has the funniest lines, too, as in this merry little spoof of straights' complaint that the once-invisible gay world had become cultural wallpaper:

BUZZ: I was in the bank yesterday. [Straights] were everywhere. Writing checks, making deposits. . . . It was disgusting. They're taking over. No one wants to talk about it, but it's true.

One other role could be called exhibitional—two, actually, as John Glover played identical twins, one malign and one saintly. It's a Tony-baiting gig, and indeed Glover won one despite the saintly brother's lack of personal spark and the malign brother's really rather minor vexations. Lane, whose performance did win other awards, should have got that Tony if only for a shocking outburst late in the show when the typically festive Buzz gave way to an impassioned tirade about AIDS, marrying his love of musicals with his outrage at . . . well, trying to survive the disease without health insurance. Even the sad musicals, he cries, end happily, as "the actors get up off the floor, the audience puts on their coats, and everybody goes home feeling better." Because the music makes it lovely—*The King and I, West Side Story.* Music is hope—and it's infuriating:

BUZZ: I want to see a *Sound Of Music* where the entire von Trapp family dies in an authentic Alpine avalanche.

or:

BUZZ: A *Kiss Me, Kate* where she's got a big cold sore on her mouth.

He's even mad at his friends who aren't sick, and the way the anger came pouring out of Lane was a slap of reality in a, yes, realistic but all the same somewhat fanciful play.

In fact, another difference between *Boys* and *LVC* is McNally's use of what we might call "concept-musical time and space," in which actors can address the audience or appear on stage together when the plotline has them in separate locations. Sometimes, several scenes of different natures are interspersed with one another, and the cast even ended the evening by telling the public what was going to happen to their characters after the play was over.

Most interesting is the dramatis personae, quite unusual next to Crowley's. Just having a prominent choreographer is a twist, especially as he is middle-aged and his boy friend is in his early twenties and blind. Yet McNally's crew blends better than Crowley's, what with Larry's all but existential defiance of Hank's jealousy, Emory's shrill harlequinade, Cowboy's status as a lost-and-found chew toy, and so on.

But the most important difference between the two plays lies in the difference between the eras in which they first appeared. *The Boys In the Band* is, for all its dramatic vitality, a museum piece, because gay life isn't like that anymore. In particular, the internalized homophobia that Michael suffers from is rare nowadays. *Love! Valour! Compassion!* will age with finesse, not least because of McNally's free use of modernistic theatrical conceits, enchanting next to Crowley's absolute naturalism.

Is this McNally's best play? It doesn't need reviving to be with us, as, like *Boys*, it got an authentic filming, almost as faithfully cast with its stage people as *Boys* was. And it has that piquant moment when the characters perform a bit from Tchaikofsky's *Swan Lake* attired as ballet girls, a touch of cross-dressing that puts the show in tune with our present-day tolerance of gender liberalism. It would be impossible to imagine Michael, Hank, Bernard, Harold, and the rest of the Boys toe-dancing in tutus.

Meanwhile, even works that didn't take close-up shots of gay culture routinely stocked their character inventory with gay men and women. The attitude was something like "Life is more interesting when gays are around." So Faith Prince played a lesbian in the plot-heavy whodunit musical *Nick & Nora* (1991), and an imposter posing as Sidney Poitier's son was caught with a hustler he had brought to the apartment of the Manhattan family he was conning in John Guare's *Six Degrees Of Separation* (1990).

The very popular through-sung *Rent* (1996), a retelling of Puccini's *La Bohème* set in New York's East Village, offered two gay couples, male and female. However, these were not token gays, as the setting, Manhattan's center of experimental living, virtually demanded it. Comparably, *Spring Awakening* (2006), a musical after Frank Wedekind's play about youngsters on the edge of sexual self-realization, also included from the original a young man caught between liking and lusting after a fellow male student.

On the other hand, *Tommy* (1993), a clever staging of The Who's innovative double album song cycle, had to touch on sex crime, as "Fiddle About" treated Uncle Ernie's taking advantage of the helpless "deaf, dumb and blind" hero when he was still very young. It's shocking even for The Who, a group that made shocking a feature of their art, though of course the scene had been known to the culture since the original LPs (1969) and the Ken Russell film (1975). Still, while Russell showed us Ernie (physically brutish with a missing front tooth and a Hallowe'en grin), the nephew he defiled was played by Roger Daltrey, clearly a grown-up presence at the age of thirty-one.

However, the stage musical's director, Des McAnuff, let the episode play out with a child, though here Uncle Ernie was natty in a suit and did at least look guilty and ashamed. The vignette began on a couch even as Ernie sang, "Down with the bedclothes, up with your nightshirt," but the set then revolved to an actual bed. Both performers remained clothed and the movements were stylized rather than realistic, yet there was no doubt that Ernie was interfering with his nephew.

Almost as louche is Joseph Moncure March's verse novella of 1928, *The Wild Party*, and because its copyright had lapsed,* two separate musical versions of it appeared in 2000, one on off-Broadway by Andrew Lippa and the other on Broadway by Michael John LaChiusa (collaborating on the book with George C. Wolfe). The authors differed on the disposition of March's characters, but Lippa took Madelaine True right off the page, sexy and slithery, a charismatic predator whose mouth is cruel and whose eyes are green: "heavy-lidded; pouched; obscene." Further, March is blunt about her sexuality, for if "women adored her," it was "less often, a man: and the more fool he—she was Lesbian."

Accordingly, Lippa gave Madelaine "An Old-Fashioned Love Story," a comic national anthem for gay women, the music moving from stealthy in the verse to intense yet jovial in the refrain. This lady makes her plan, then celebrates a women's world, for she is no integrationist. She wants a cosmos free of men, who would only upset the girls and crab Madelaine's act. Alix Korey made the most of the spot, relishing Lippa's amusing off-accents in "*love sto*ry" with a sly whimsy while envisioning a utopia in which "girls are girls and boys stay out to sea."

LaChiusa's *Wild Party* emphasized gay men in the black d'Armano brothers. They sing at the keyboard as in March, though the poem pictures them as shrill queens and LaChiusa made them sleeker and musically artful, socially observant in "Uptown" and seductive in a haunting ballad, "Taboo."

---

* The old law, covering works up to 1978, demanded an unnecessary and impedient requirement that copyright holders execute a renewal to be timed punctiliously or ownership be forfeit. What on earth was the point of that? The new law grants ownership for the creator's life plus seventy years.

One of the brothers enjoyed a unique gay moment when a woman guest arrived with a hunk of a trophy date. Dressed to kill in black tie, he smoothed his way across the stage while one d'Armano looked right at the audience with a "Did you *see that number?*" expression on his face.

LaChiusa retained Madelaine's lesbian sexuality without featuring her as strongly as Lippa did. But LaChiusa did emphasize March's bisexual, Jackie, the wildest of the guests, with a backstory both sleazy and ritzy. "His hips were jaunty," March explains, "and his gestures too dextrous." As for his tastes: "He was ambisextrous"—a coining so luscious LaChiusa preserved it in Jackie's breathless ID number, "Breezin' Through Another Day." Lippa portrayed his Jackie as a mute sweetheart (Lawrence Keigwin) who dances around the apartment after the other guests have passed out from revelry fatigue. LaChiusa, on the other hand, made his Jackie (Marc Kudisch) not only garrulous but dangerous, at one point sniffing cocaine and then forcing himself on one of the women in "More," which precipitates a riot.

By the 1990s, musicals were becoming very comfortable with gay emancipation, as in the contentless revue *Naked Boys Singing* (1999), "corrected," one might say, by Howard Crabtree's revues *Whoop-Dee-Doo!* (1995) and *When Pigs Fly* (1997), which for one thing had costumes.

In fact, elaborate clothing was Crabtree's focus; *When Pigs Fly* was especially rich in wild get-ups. One of the all-male casts—the show's hunk, David Pevsner—appeared as a centaur, shirtless and with all of that biological real estate behind him. He couldn't figure out why other guys thought he was, as his solo put it, "Not All Man."

Much of *When Pigs Fly*'s score, by Dick Gallagher and Mark Waldrop, was pastiche—a close-harmony quartet for "You've Got To Stay In the Game"; a Fosse vamp with snapping fingers for "Light In the Loafers"; ukulele and steel guitar for "Hawaiian Wedding Day," when "Even sourpuss Aunt Connie will finally get a lei."

The show's aim was to silly around with gay topics, and as if to disarm criticism of the kind that scorned Al Carmines' *The Faggot* a few pages ago for its lack of political zeal, late in *When Pigs Fly*'s continuity came "Laughing Matters," a gentle piece with a key line, "Human spirits need to be leavened by some levity."

Indeed, it does seem as though there is always a lot of politics but never enough good comedy, especially the unique kind in a show that can't readily be categorized. And that would be *Avenue Q* (2003), like so many modern titles an off-Broadway original that moved to The Street (and enjoyed a colossal run). Jeff Whitty's book took us to outer-borough New York, where a mixture of humans and pleasant monsters live in harmony, much as do the inhabitants of television's *Sesame Street*, *Avenue Q's* apparent inspiration.

Thus, as in the PBS children's show, the score (by Robert Lopez and Jeff Marx) taught lessons in fair and sensible living. On TV, the songs related to kids' activities, such as learning to share or master the art of forgiveness. *Avenue Q's* songs treated adult themes—"The Internet Is For Porn," "What Do You Do With a B.A. In English?," "I Wish I Could Go Back To College," even the delights of "Schadenfreude."

The music is catchy and the lyrics are clever, but there was an extra layer of fun in the use of hand puppets—again, as on *Sesame Street*. A game cast animated them superbly, not least in a gay subplot, for one of the characters is closeted. Imagine, a closeted puppet! It took him the entire show to come out, but we knew he would, as *Avenue Q* was above all buoyant. Typically, the neighborhood super was Gary Coleman—the "Whatchu talkin' 'bout, Willis?" Gary Coleman—and "he" was played by a woman, Natalie Venetia Belcon.

Avenue Q was not a spoof but a new show in its own right, using the tropes of childhood to create an above all youthful work. But *Johnny Guitar* (2004) was an out-and-out spoof, at that a campy version of a movie that is already campy, Nicholas Ray's western of the same name. Beloved of gays for its "when divas collide" feud between Joan Crawford and Mercedes McCambridge, *Johnny Guitar* the movie is loaded with anger, as all the men engage in hard-on contests and McCambridge's Emma seems to want to score Crawford or at least kill her. Further, the film came out of Poverty Row's Republic Pictures, which even had a campy photography, in Trucolor By Consolidated.

How does one camp camp? The stage show's songwriters, Martin Silvestri and Joel Higgins (the former actor, and the only one in history to call the formidable George Abbott "George") and its bookwriter, Nicholas van Hoogstraten, decided to musicalize *Johnny Guitar* as it was, camp for camp.

True, heroine Judy McLane made no attempt to replicate Crawford's elocution-school Trudiction, and hero Steve Blanchard, a go-to Lancelot and Gaston in the regions, didn't goof on the title role, filmed by Sterling Hayden. And there was a bit of out-of-style tomfoolery when a little back-up chorus in the title number brandished their pistols and one of them got shot and dropped dead while the others went on (nervously) singing. Still,

Johnny Guitar's fun inhered in simply doing the movie's overwrought fifties dialogue:

JOHNNY: How many men have you forgotten?
VIENNA: As many women as you've remembered.

What on earth does that bit of Trustichomythia (by Consolidated) even mean?

No matter: it's always amusing to revisit anything as (gayly) crazy as *Johnny Guitar: The Film*, and, lo, Ann Crumb, famous for having been more or less run over by Maria Björnson's huge sliding screens in Andrew Lloyd Webber's *Aspects Of Love*, made a superb Return in Mercedes McCambridge's part. The Silvestri–Higgins score is quite tuneful in the tumbleweed manner, and, as an inside joke, most of the numbers come right out of the movie script, as in "A Smoke and a Good Cup O' Coffee" and "Tell Me a Lie" ("Lie To Me" in the film). Most important, the cast were all fine singers. So while the stage show couldn't do justice to a story filled with the outdoors, it made a dandy CD.

And the show isn't gay just because of its camp and parody. McCambridge's Emma, all holstered up for killin' over her skirt, is a maybe-lesbian—and, for that matter, Joan Crawford was one of Golden Age Hollywood's great phallic women; only Clark Gable outdrew her, so to say.

So *Johnny Guitar: The Movie* has a kind of queer reputation. But *The Color Purple* isn't generally thought of as gay, though its heroine, Celie, has a passionate affair with a woman, and the *Color Purple* musical (2005) let its Celie, LaChanze, hold true to the character in Alice Walker's novel.

The musical's billing credits as source material both the novel and its movie version, all three set in a village in Georgia over the course of forty years. Librettist Marsha Norman had a lot of story to juggle, obviously, and there are many principals. Yet the score, by Brenda Russell, Allee Willis, and Stephen Bray (and very imaginatively orchestrated by Jonathan Tunick), amply differentiates character. Further, this isn't just a story: it's a saga, embedded in a culture that obeys its own unique laws. If sophisticated societies treat women better, primitive societies—like Celie's—treat them worse. So when the very worldly and casually independent Shug Avery (Elizabeth Withers-Mendes) comes into Celie's life, Celie is struck by this virtual grandee's glamour—but also her kindness. "God is inside you and everyone else," Shug tells Celie, unknowingly referencing what Quakers call "The Inner Light."

And while Celie's father and her husband, Mister, call Celie "ugly," Shug's love song to her is "[You are] Too Beautiful For Words."

No doubt psychological gratitude is an established basis for love: feeling, perhaps for the first time, wanted, one needs to so to say marry that want. However, the *Color Purple* novel makes it clear that Celie is drawn to Shug sensually, physically. Writing to God as she habitually does, Celie tells us, in her unique brand of the language, "First time I got the full sight of Shug Avery long black body with it black plum nipples . . . I thought I had turned into a man. I wash her body, it feel like I'm praying."

And note that the last sentence in this quotation appears verbatim in the show, when Celie sings "Dear God—Shug." Here is another first for our book—a gay woman's very blunt assertion of her erotic ID in a serious musical. (That is, not counting the facetious "Old-Fashioned Love Story" in the Andrew Lippa *Wild Party*.)

Celie and Shug have a number of songs together, and their duetto d'amore, "What About Love?," is outstanding, so gently passionate one can almost hear them caressing each other. As the clarinet starts the cue-in, Shug tells Celie, "No one ever loved me like you," one of the great lesbian lines. "Damn, girl." And when Shug takes stage at a honky-tonk, her specialty is a hot-jazz item set to a shuffle beat, "Push Da Button," another of those pieces of the old school, using dog whistles to invoke sex. Although a great deal more than romance occurs in this very eventful tale (its driveline is how Celie is finally reunited with her long-lost sister), still the Celie–Shug Avery subplot is an important addition to our inventory of gay themes on Broadway.

Another aspect of gay life is the crush a gay man or woman may have on a straight, a trope we've already clocked more than once. Stephen Flaherty and Lynn Ahrens' *A Man Of No Importance* (2002), with a book by Terrence McNally, deals with Alfie (Roger Rees), a ticket-taker on a Dublin bus, closeted yet unmistakably gay in his obsession with the theatre.

Albert Finney played the role in the 1994 film: a shy man who becomes vivacious around his amateur theatre group or with people he knows. They include Rees' vocational colleague, Robbie the bus driver (Steven Pasquale), a high-energy devastato whose shameless confidence reminds us of Thomas Mann's division of humanity into introverts (like Alfie) and Robbie's kind, so merry and outgoing that they "fall down in the dance," high on their own clumsiness.

A Man Of No Importance closes in on this notion in Robbie's ID number, "The Streets Of Dublin," telling of the folk he consorts with, uncultured, all

rough and ready. Stephen Flaherty is always at his best when he has an eth-
nicity to musicalize, and "The Streets Of Dublin" has a driving sort of Irish
lilt that authenticates this tale of a gay man so closed up that he needs Oscar
Wilde, founder of the line—Wilde in person—to advise him.

Bringing us even closer to home is the very moving *Yank!*, which played
New York in 2010 after numerous regional productions and revisions. This
one tells of an American soldier (Bobby Steggert) in World War II, too awkward and sensitive for the testosterone-rich environment of uniformed society. Somehow, he connects with a protective and even loving guy in his
outfit (Ivan Hernandez), embodying a gay daydream fantasy: the stalwart
hero who fancies you, of course platonically.

But *Yank!* offers a twist: the crush, called Mitch (even his name is strong),
secretly requites the affection of his admirer, Stu. Yet more: it seems there is
an underground of gay men and women in the Army, an entire subculture
thriving in its occult way even under the paranoid surveillance of zealous gay
haters.

Thus, at one point, we meet the General's secretary, Louise (Nancy
Anderson, playing all of *Yank!*'s women's roles), who in "Get It, Got it, Good"
confesses that her language is rough because "It puts men at ease." Still, she
doesn't give too much away: "My shes become hes." Yet when the General
asks her to tender a list of suspected queers, she straight-out tells him her
name would head the list. How did she dare? "He needs me and he knows it."

Further, Stu works for *Yank*, one of the Army's publications, more personable than the officially respectable *Stars and Stripes*. And working on *Yank*
with Stu is Artie (Jeffry Denman), a photographer whose ID number, "Click,"
reveals the dos and don'ts of the gay Army. "Clicking" isn't just what a camera
does; it's sex. Amusingly, the photographer's vocal slips into a dance break
without concluding, letting the two duet in movement.

It's a clever show, *Yank!*, but also a sweet and sorrowful one, because word
man David Zellnik and composer Joseph Zellnik (his brother) build their
plot around a journal that a narrator, S. (also played by Bobby Steggert), has
found in a junk shop. It's Stu's story in his own words, and as he reveals that he
and Mitch are actually planning to move to Mitch's home town to live openly
as partners, we start to worry about these two. They sing of this dream in "A
Couple Of Regular Guys," and . . . *really*? Who besides the aforementioned
Louise is going to accept gay men as "regular" in the 1940s?

So this is an impossible romance, a dark piece on the oppression of gays by
the military. True, much of the score has a period charm, with some of that

mellow forties sound, especially in the main ballad, Mitch's "Rememb'ring You." Like "The Day After Tomorrow," the pastiche wartime ballad Lionel Bart ran up for *Blitz!*, "Rememb'ring You" suggests real-life music from long ago, a soldier's love poem to his girl when we first encounter it. Yet it is also the very last thing we hear from *Yank!*, as the lights fade on the narrator, and now of course the song bears an entirely different meaning. S. informs us that Mitch died young, of acute alcoholism, and no one seems to know what happened to Stu.

As S. continues his wrap-up, we reflect on how different this topic is today, when marriage equality is the law of the land and gay men and women can— "Wait," he says, this is my favorite part of the song." And there's Mitch's voice singing the last phrases of "Rememb'ring You," as the trumpet soars upward to the tonic chord and the lights fade on one of the saddest tales in the history of the musical.

This was also an era of "problem plays," the old-time genre in which The Theme is a social controversy that the principals discuss, a favorite form for George Bernard Shaw among others. Jonathan Tolins' *The Twilight Of the Golds* (1993) looks in on a close-knit family: David (Raphael Sbarge), his aged parents, his sister, and her husband. The last two are expecting, new technology tells them the baby will be gay, and they decide to abort the fetus.

However, David, gay himself, argues that this is in effect an attempt to murder *him*: to express that straight world's long-held dream of finally moving the gay thing off the stage. Parting company with it. Exterminating it.

Indeed, right from the start of the play, there are hints that the Golds are not as close as they like to think they are. David's partner never appears, because he thinks the brother-in-law is "homophobic"—but doesn't he mean that they all are but the brother-in-law especially so? Near the start of the second act, David's father tells him what he has bottled up for years:

WALTER: I think you're sick and diseased and if there were a cure, I'd want you cured.

But would you want David killed? Like the aborted fetus?

The scene is unusually powerful because Broadway's Walter was David Groh, the actor whose ID depended entirely on his having been Valerie Harper's husband on *Rhoda*, a spinoff of *The Mary Tyler Moore Show*. These were all beloved characters, so hearing this rejection from former good guy Joe Gerard was unnerving.

So was a later scene in which David, an opera buff, recounts the plot of Wagner's *Ring* operas to his sister, emphasizing that the *Ring*'s hero is abnormally conceived, just as, in a way, gays are. Siegfried grows up to be something like a superhero version of Christ, so David is describing the born-artist valence of gay people in a near-religious way. This explains the play's title, for Siegfried's death in the last *Ring* opera, *Twilight Of the Gods*, brings on the end of the world, corrupted by power. As the gods must pass on, so must the heterosexist Gold family.

Tolins is drawn to the problem play in the gay milieu. His comedy *The Last Sunday In June* (2003), set among New York Pride paradegoers (including the by now almost requisite Beautiful Male, shirtless in the summer heat), discusses the place of the physically unattractive man in gay culture. *Last Sunday* satirizes gay culture even as it blueprints it, but *Twilight* is in deadly earnest, for David decides to cut himself off from his family and will not forgive them despite their entreaties. This act of independence must have outraged the New York critics, who whaled on the piece. Perhaps they identified with the rejected father, who—according to hetero culture—must always rule.

Douglas Carter Beane's *The Little Dog Laughed* (2006) is less a problem play than a spoof of the showbiz-media complex. Still, it presents a problem that the cast of four then discuss. And that problem is: how to handle a movie star on the rise (Tom Everett Scott) who decides he's gay and threatens to come out, which will destroy the economic foundation he rests upon.

Narrating the action while driving it is his agent (Julie White, who won the Tony). Her attitude is something like "gay schmay, stardom and its rewards are what matters in life." Beane voices her with the fast-spoken coastal urban observational sarcasm we associate especially with gay men. Here she is imitating "show business professionals" ordering lunch:

THE AGENT: Yes, I want the Cobb salad and could you make sure that the chicken and the bacon are not touching and I want no egg, but bonus avocado and on the side extra-virgin olive oil and seven lemons.

It's a very funny role, surefire with audiences. But more: with the often unfocused movie star, the drifting hustler he picks up (a very young Johnny Galecki), and the hustler's compliant girlfriend (Ari Graynor) dithering around, it is the agent who must herd the other three into a solution, besides keeping the public attuned to the show's pacing, which slows whenever the two men are alone together but hastens at all other times. So, midway in the continuity:

THE AGENT: Let's take a fifteen-minute break [for the intermission] and we'll sort this all out on our return.

Yet even more: the agent controls the perspective, to keep us from falling into the other characters' fuzzy dreams about who they are or can be. The movie star is the worst; he never seems to realize what is at stake for him—for anyone who plays chicken with the establishment. The agent must constantly pull him out of the clouds:

THE ACTOR: I have to think of myself this once.
THE AGENT: You're a movie star, you think of yourself constantly.

Complicating the agent's job is the unusual mix of characters, as these are not stereotypes: the hustler went to prep school, while his girl friend is much more savvy than the old cliché Pollyannas, or gold diggers, or professional victims. She's quite able to hold her own while negotiating her role in all this—for she's pregnant and the hustler is the father. So now what?

Note that Beane isn't offering a political pep talk. The problem isn't gays' fear of Hollywood homophobia. The problem is *Hollywood homophobia*, and smart folk, such as the agent, have to devise workarounds in order to prosper despite it. So the play's ending is rather surprising: the girl friend marries the movie star, giving her some security and him a cover. And the hustler is left to go on drifting, which he may actually be content to do—the actor playing him can select his nuances. "My life is beginning," he suggests, and the agent closes the show with "We fade to black, the credits roll. The ending."

And here's another comedy: Paul Rudnick's *Jeffrey* (1993) dealt with AIDS amid the fun, specifically the title character's depression and fear of death. It's a gloomy topic, obviously, but Rudnick's impish wit lifted its spirit. Are gay men obsessed with sex? No:

JEFFREY: All *human beings* are obsessed with sex. All gay men are obsessed with opera.

And, really, it's absurd to compare the two:

JEFFREY: Because you can have good sex.

In a way, *Jeffrey* played as a romantic comedy with vexations, as the title character (John Michael Higgins) was attracted to yet anxious about Steve (Tom Hewitt), who is HIV-positive. The credo of the age was Silence=Death, but to Jeffrey sex=death A very small cast except for Higgins played multiple roles, but *Jeffrey*'s main support was the long-term couple of older, blasé Sterling (Edward Hibbert) and younger, uninformed Darius (Bryan Batt), who dances in *Cats* and thinks nothing of going around town in his costume. It saves time. Jeffrey likens this pair to Martha Stewart and Ann Miller, and, as they say, Darius should turn in his gay card when he replies to this with:

DARIUS: Who's Martha Stewart?

and for heaven's sake even:

DARIUS: Who's Ann Miller?

Everyone in Jeffrey's life urges him to seize the moment, AIDS or no AIDS. But then Darius dies.

And let that usher us into a group of AIDS plays, starting with "the" two in 1985, often compared: William M. Hoffman's *As Is*, from the Circle Rep; and Larry Kramer's *The Normal Heart*, at the Public Theater. Hoffman (co-author of the aforementioned *Cornbury*, that play about the cross-dressing governor of New Amsterdam) proposed something of an AIDS primer. For starters, the published text was dedicated to the memory of thirty-seven who died (including Charles Ludlam and, incidentally, a math teacher at my high school, the Locust Valley Friends Academy).

The action of *As Is* centered on a couple (Jonathan Hadary, Jonathan Hogan) treading the delicate and terrible path of disease, as one of them is infected. But Hoffman surrounds them with the so to say News of the Epidemic, such as thinking someone you know suddenly got taller (because he lost forty-five pounds); or reviewing the dark humor of the AIDS jokes, as when your doctor diagnoses you, you say you want a second opinion, and he adds, "Okay, you're ugly, too"; or a look at men working an AIDS hotline, with the usual hate caller.

Nevertheless, the central couple dominated the continuity, a major difference between *As Is* and *The Normal Heart*, because the latter's comparable couple is viewed against the struggles of Larry Kramer's alter ego, Ned Weeks (Brad Davis, succeeded by Joel Grey), who takes on a completely uninterested establishment virtually singlehanded. Like The Who's little hero Tommy, those in power are seen as deaf, dumb, and blind as AIDS takes root, whereas other epidemics—Legionnaires Disease, for example—got relentless press coverage and government attempts to conquer the afflictions.

As Is and *The Normal Heart* did, however, have much in common. Both were set in New York and played on a largely open stage. But *The Normal Heart*'s set bore on its back wall the facts of the case—the figures for New York's and San Francisco's AIDS budgets, the former's at $75,000 and the latter's at $16,000,000. Too, a key piece of data told how the American Jewish Committee tried to get the U.S. to help the Jews of Europe during the Nazi period. The Committee made nice to government operatives who blithely did nothing through the entire era, right up to the end of the war. Nothing, nothing, nothing. That's what you get with nice.

And *The Normal Heart*'s premise is that, when gay is concerned, the government is a wedge of haters. You don't make nice. You scream and publicize, exposing and vilifying and ridiculing, forcing them to act out of embarrassment. So *As Is* was a methodical and trim piece while *The Normal Heart* was passionate, suspenseful, despairing, and enraged every minute. In part autobiographical, it could be seen as Kramer's attempt to exorcize his demons. "Weakness terrifies me," Ned admits, and gays fighting impedient officials must not be weak. He thinks gays must pester, accuse, threaten. Of course, then officials won't like you.

But nothing else will work—or so this wild ride of a play tells us. Perhaps the casting of the trim and handsome Brad Davis as Ned was an attempt to make nice to the audience; a looks-and-charm star can soothe the irritation of the pestering. And Ned at least was a leader, if the only one in the pack:

NED: I thought I was starting with . . . Ralph Naders and Green Berets, and the first instant they have to take a stand on a political issue and fight . . . they turn into a bunch of nurses' aides.

Despite the atmosphere of history being enacted, *The Normal Heart* has its emotional issue as well. Thus, the first act ends when Ned's lover, Felix (D. W. Moffett), pulls off one of his socks to reveal a purple spot on his foot.

So the storytelling is suspenseful even though the audience foresees the outcome. This was not unlike the usage in Ancient Greece, when theatregoers took their seats already knowing a play's plot line—King Oedipus, the House of Atreus, the cult of Bacchus, and so on—but eager to see how the playwright will spin it.

And Kramer had an arresting take. As he saw it, the history has a villain in Ed Koch, New York's mayor at the time. The most blatant closet case in the city's annals, Koch feared that showing any amity with gay matters would out him. With some covert gays, it's an open secret. With Koch, it was an open banner headline. So whom was he fooling, except himself?

Of all the AIDS plays of the period, the outstanding title is Tony Kushner's *Angels In America*, subtitled "A Fantasia On National Themes" (Los Angeles 1992; New York 1993). One meaning of "fantasia" (as per Webster 3) gives us a work "in which the author's fancy roves unrestricted," and *Angels* really maps around, with its many short scenes moving from New York apartments and offices to the animated diorama of the Visitors Center in the Mormon Temple on Sixty-Fifth Street and Columbus Avenue to hospital rooms. It's almost as if a sharp and somewhat offbeat theatre troupe was improvising its way through the narrative.

One reason for all this activity is the play's intermingling of throughlines; we are hardly used to one location before the scenery bustles off to enlarge our perspective with a different sort of place entirely. But another reason is the play's rather grandiose figures. They need a lot of real estate in which to expand, and the result is a two-evening sit, *Millennium Approaches* and *Perestroika.*[†]

The leads are actor magnets, with extremely meaty roles. These are Prior Walter (Stephen Spinella), an AIDS patient whom the primary angel recruits as a prophet; Joe Pitt (David Marshall Grant), the closeted Mormon whose nightly walks (i.e., cruising) and general lack of spousal need drive his wife, Harper (Marcia Gay Harden), crazy; the real-life Roy Cohn (Ron Leibman); and that central angel herself (Ellen McLaughlin).

There are other fine acting parts as well, but three roles above all strike me as the best, especially Roy Cohn. Another AIDS patient, he blatantly threatens to destroy his doctor, named Henry—whom he has been seeing for nearly thirty years—if the doctor dares to call Cohn a homosexual. *Angels'*

[†] The "reconstruction" of Russian political and economic life in the 1980s.

Cohn isn't evil opportunistically or, like Shakespeare's Iago, congenitally. Rather, Cohn chooses evil, because he knows what it's for and likes how it works. Evil is power:

COHN: Homosexuals are not men who sleep with other men. Homosexuals are men who in fifteen years of trying cannot pass a pissant anti-discrimination bill through City Council.

Cohn is so powerful that there is no one he cannot bend to his will. He can place a phone call and in less than five minutes he will be speaking to . . . Guess, Henry:

THE DOCTOR: The president.
COHN: Even better. His wife.

Thus, *Angels* puts the indomitable Cohn at the first disadvantage of his life: he can't power-broker his way out of AIDS. True, he can commandeer his own private stock of AZT, defying experimental protocols, because—once again—he can terrorize the right party into submission. Still, as he discovers in a tremendous death scene, he can't browbeat AIDS.

Another excellent character is Harper, the wife of closeted Joe Pitt, who is busily engaged in one of the most laborious coming-outs in the history of the closet. Whimsical and clever, Harper is exactly the sort of woman a by-the-book Mormon would choose as his beard. She won't, he thinks, harry him when he seems sexually aloof. She will be companionable, uncomplaining, a good sport.

However, as Mike Tyson once said, Everybody's got a plan till they get punched in the mouth, and the Harper–Joe relationship gives us a much richer look at the mésalliance a gay man creates with a straight woman than other plays have presented, even compared with the one in *The Shadow Box*. Oddly, despite enduring a breakdown, Harper is still smart and charming. Because *Angels In America* is above all fantastical, she meets Prior Walter in a dream, and later he runs into her at the Mormon Visitors Center. Both find it odd: have they met before? No, really? And what's he doing here, anyway?:

PRIOR: I'm an angelologist.

Okay, that's weird, Harper thinks. But she's game:

HARPER: Angelology. The field work must be rigorous. You'd have to drop dead before you saw your first specimen.

Prior is yet a third superb role, as the character whose peregrinations hold the sprawling narrative together. On yet another wacky meeting with Harper, this time in heaven (yes, that heaven), Prior can say, in honesty, "I'm here on business." The constant use of fantasy amid very naturalistic scenes spices the continuity. There's science fiction—or perhaps more truly spiritual manifestation—mixed in with heavy naturalism, such as the conversation I quoted between Roy Cohn and his doctor or the various fights we witness between Prior and his partner, Louis (Joe Mantello).

So there really are angels in America, and Prior Walter is visited by ghosts of his ancestors in period dress, and Roy Cohn is haunted by Ethel Rosenberg (Kathleen Chalfont), whom he prosecuted for passing nuclear secrets to the Soviets. It is as if the very planet were spinning out of balance, opening unstable relationships between space and time.

Yet this drastic pageant is almost a comedy. Audiences are uneasy about laughing because they have been told that this is Major Work, but many of the lines are funny. When Prior and Harper meet in their mutual dream:

HARPER: I'm a Mormon.
PRIOR: I'm a homosexual.
HARPER: In my church we don't believe in homosexuals.
PRIOR: In my church we don't believe in Mormons.

Nevertheless, this is an epic, and epics aren't comic, as a rule. And the work really opens up in the most panoramic sense after *Millennium Approaches* yields to *Perestroika*. That is when this fantasia of a play must start to fulfil its many throughlines, sorting through its principals to see whose story this is. With Roy Cohn dead, Prior and Harper are the last people we see, tossing their partners out of their lives. Harper has the final lines, aboard a night flight bound for San Francisco. "Chase the moon across America," she says; it's almost a second subtitle for the entire work.

Yet the play's most memorable image is the Angel's crashing through the ceiling of Prior's apartment at the end of Part One. Each staging of *Angels* comes up with a different solution to the problem of animating this character; at Britain's National Theatre, a team of puppeteers dressed in black (to avoid pulling focus) worked the Angel's huge wings, moving along with the actress almost ergonomically to keep her presence volatile, unpredictable. The playwright says she must be "breathtaking, severe, scary, powerful, and magnificently American."

9

The Present

Mr. Albee Never Changes His Mind

By now, the possibilities for gay theatre are boundless. Big Broadway can star drag queens, as in *Priscilla, Queen Of the Desert* (2011) and *Kinky Boots* (2013), both from foreign movies. So *La Cage Aux Folles* wasn't a one-off. *On a Clear Day You Can See Forever* returned in 2011 in a revision that melded the original's reincarnation-ESP theme (already a problem, as the two don't belong together) with transsexualism, losing the show's zany humor as well as much of its score. The set looked cheap, too. Back in 1965, *On a Clear Day* boasted a vivacious first half followed by the most crippling case of Second Act Trouble in history. But this new installment offered no cure.

We were hoping for a good, solid lesbian musical, and *The Prom* (2018), interestingly, was based on a real-life event wherein a Mississippi high-schooler wanted to attend the ball in drag with a date of her choice. In the musical, she was hindered till visiting Broadwayites interceded on her behalf. However, this hurdy-gurdy Hallmark Card of a show hid from view what really happened: with the ACLU fighting for the lesbian, the school allowed her to go to the prom as she wished but this prom was a fake: her schoolmates were enjoying the "real" prom elsewhere, organized in secret, leaving the lesbian and her date (and the unpopular students—because as long as we're drawing lines in the social contract, let's hurt the kids who aren't cool enough) alone in their exile. Conservative Mississippi was not the right place to pick a gay hill to die on, and in the end *The Prom* makes nice to an evil tale, for in real life the two gay women walked out soon after arriving, leaving those unpopular kids to go through life remembering how it felt to attend a losers' prom.

Yet we do have a first-rate lesbian musical—also based on real life—in *Fun Home* (2015), with book and lyrics by Lisa Kron and music by Jeanine Tesori. Closely following its source, Alison Bechdel's ingenious autobiographical "comic book," *Fun Home* gives us a dysfunctional family in a small Pennsylvania town, with a tyrannical father who forces his children to assist in his obsessive interior decoration.

This father, Bruce Bechdel, is an English teacher who doubles in the family business he inherited, a funeral home; he is also gay, and both fascinates and irritates young Alison. In a significant image in both novel and musical, she plays "airplane" with him: he lies on his back with his legs perpendicular to the floor to support his little daughter, who stretches out her arms as if flying. It is perhaps the only moment when any of the three Bechdel kids can feel truly close to their father, yet author Alison, dedicating her memoir to her mother and brothers only, says, "We did have a lot of fun, in spite of everything."

Arguably the most acclaimed graphic novel since Art Spiegelman's *Maus*, *Fun Home* is complex, a narrative crammed with activity. Most works have several throughlines (as in *My Fair Lady*: Henry Higgins' zealotry about language; Freddy's crush on Eliza; her father's reckless lifestyle) but only one driveline (the relationship of Higgins and Eliza). Yet *Fun Home* has two drivelines: the Bildung of Alison's personality and the twisted and ultimately tragic life of her father. Girl and man are both queer, but Alison blooms into her sexuality, catching up with it while she's in college, first shy about it then reveling in it. "I'm changing my major to Joan!" she sings, of her first love, reminding us that self-discovery can sometimes be the most exciting part of gay life.

Father Bruce, on the other hand, is glum when he isn't exploding with anger, and as a married man and a sort of pillar of the community (in this town of six hundred souls, when you die, Bruce buries you), he releases his sexual frustration in furtive side trips and even seductions of local boys. Artist Alison draws him almost never smiling, and Michael Cerveris' Bruce had the difficult task of letting us into his feelings while playing someone almost completely hidden.

But director Sam Gold had a very resourceful cast, not least in the three actresses playing Alison: in youth (Sydney Lucas), post adolescence (Emily Skeggs), and maturity (Beth Malone). This allowed the show to span many years in Alison's life, giving the piece the breadth of the novel—its intimacy, too, as *Fun Home* occupied the oval-in-the-round space of the Circle-In-the-Square. The characters were real enough to touch, which allowed the public to share for example Alison's joy when she let Joan the Wonderful into her life.

Still, to repeat: *Fun Home* was more than an Alison saga, as it treated also the tale of Alison's bond with her father, almost a separate issue. He's bossy and impatient and he keeps trying to "straighten" her out with long hair and cuddly fluffernutter frocks. But they know each other as no one else can, and as Tesori and Kron keep breaking into the songs with dialogue, the musical becomes something like a marriage counseling session for father and daughter.

Yet let it be said that the crucial music is pure song and pure Alison, in yet another possible lesbian national anthem, "Ring Of Keys." This solo for small Alison, important enough to have served as *Fun Home*'s promotional spot on the Tony Awards, stems from a scene in the novel when the girl is in a luncheonette with her father. They watch as a heavy set, butch delivery woman drops off an order. With her short hair, plaid work shirt, and detached professional expression the woman is unquestionably a sister. Bruce is scornful: "Is *that* what you want to look like?" Because he's all about the appearance of things while she cares about the soul of them. In an interesting detail, author Alison (remember, this is her memoir) draws the woman's key ring attached to her belt without emphasizing it—in an inset, say, or with an arrow pointing it out. And it's partially obscured by the diner counter. If one fails to study the panel, one might easily miss it.

Tesori and Kron didn't miss it: they made it the central number in the score. In the novel, Alison tells us in a caption, "I recognized [the delivery woman] with a surge of joy," and the musical gives us an exultant salute to this piquant symbol of a stranger living freely in a style she chooses for herself.

In other words, here is a woman without a father. A boss. A master. A *father*. Tesori sets the number's key line, "Oh, your ring of keys," with a five-note melisma on the first word, lending it an air of tumultuously benign discovery. The novel closes the episode with a shot of Alison and Bruce outside the luncheonette as he pulls her along while she looks back for more visual information "of the truck-driving bulldyke."

We get it: he's fed up with his daughter's growing awareness of her sexual orientation and she's buoyed up by it. And the musical wants us to see how crucial this moment is for Small Alison. "Do you feel my heart saying hi?" she sings. She believes she's the only one who understands how "beautiful" the woman is. No. Not beautiful: "handsome."

Yet as the girl grows up and becomes Medium Alison and then just Alison, complete at last, the father whom she loved and feared and needed and resented continues to haunt her. He ends as a suicide, for any of several reasons, and he clearly was a soul whose pleasures in life were overwhelmed by his frustrations. Novelist Bechdel ends with father and daughter in a swimming pool, she about to jump off the diving board into his arms. Then she does jump—and his face as he reaches up is impossible to read. But narrator Alison tells us, in the book's final line, "He was there to catch me when I leapt." The musical instead returns to the "airplane" game of Alison's youth, and "final" Alison recalls that sometimes "There was a rare moment of perfect balance when I soared above him."

Yet another straying gay husband turned up in Scott Frankel and Michael Korie's *Far From Heaven* (Williamstown 2012; New York 2013), from Todd Haynes' film recalling Douglas Sirk's fifties soap operas for Universal. The Sirk originals, though highly praised by cineastes, seem to other eyes to be dreary kitsch filled with stick-figure movie stars, but Haynes' film has real content in its tale of three out-of-the-ordinary people in a community that requires "ordinary" as requisite for survival.

The three dissenters are the gay husband (Steven Pasquale), the wife he will abandon (Kelli O'Hara), and a black man (Isaiah Johnson). Obviously, there is a problem if the husband is gay—but as the wife finds a kindred soul in the black man, the only person in town she can feel at ease with, there is another problem, as the setting is the racially segregated 1950s. I often summon up *The Captive* in these pages, as it seems to have founded a line of titles covering the gay wife or husband who strikes off on her or his own—Hank, say, in *The Boys In the Band*, for we learn nothing about the woman (and children) he left for Larry. The stories favor the walk-out.

But *Far From Heaven* centers on the abandoned wife, on her struggles with her straight-except-when-he-isn't husband and then with the society that turns on her simply for being friendly with a black. Even the other blacks in town don't like it, and we are far from heaven for certain.

Frankel and Korie are apparently drawn to women's stories, as in *Grey Gardens* (2006) and *War Paint* (2016). Still, as they tell of the wife's experience, their very characterful score—intricately orchestrated by Bruce Coughlin for twelve players on twenty-two pieces plus percussion and keyboards—expands to site all three principals as isolated in a world ruled by connections. So, in "Interesting," the townspeople mock a modern-art show. "A face with two noses," one man sings. "It sure isn't Grandma Moses." Yet Raymond and Cathy (the black man and the wife) admire a Miro, duetting imaginatively as they consider its abstractions.

It's a poetic moment, one that the poor husband never gets to. *His* important music has him trying to pretend that gay is a germ that corrupts the system rather than the thing that he is. Somehow, Raymond and Cathy get a lot of sweet music, honest music. The husband is all bluster and fraud—and we knew it was on the way, as the show's prelude is an uncanny little tone poem simultaneously picturing the idyllic surface of life as well as the troublesome undertow lying in wait for anyone who won't float that life on lies.

Thus, on a Florida vacation to try to reignite the spark of their marriage, Pasquale and O'Hara hit a snag: the Beautiful Male, a young man in swimming trunks who conclusively breaks down Pasquale's attempt to ex-gay himself. But O'Hara doesn't therefore end up with Johnson, as if in a Gilbert and Sullivan finale. They can't even be platonic friends. It's the 1950s, and the "odd" couple must part.

So here's yet another Beautiful Male, elemental in gay theatre. Christopher Durang's comedy *Vanya and Sonia and Masha and Spike* (Princeton 2012; New York 2013) features one of the great ones in Spike (Billy Magnussen), the giddy, exhibitionistic boy toy of cinema star Masha (Sigourney Weaver), visiting her loser siblings Vanya (David Hyde Pierce) and Sonia (Kristine Nielsen). Masha supports them, and they're living in a house she owns but now intends to sell out from under them.

It sounds dire, but Durang's tone is lighter than air. His use of names out of Chekhof and the looming sale of property (as in *The Cherry Orchard*) suggest a spoof of the Russian playwright, and Durang is indeed a gleeful satirist. However, here he is amiable, merely using a few Chekhof references to give the piece a certain tang. In one set with only six characters (who face no major acting challenges), *Vanya and Sonia* is an easy stage and ergo has become very popular in the regions. But it isn't especially funny or interesting.

First of all, the two biggest roles—Masha's hapless siblings idling away their lives in a rustic retreat—have no content. (Chekhov's unhappy characters, by contrast, teem with personality.) Even the play's Sword Of Damocles—the threat of the house's being sold—melts away, as Weaver simply decides not to sell after all.

If anyone can enliven a dull role, it's Sigourney Weaver. Yet while her dialogue often runs to recounting her skylarking exploits among the fleshpots of Hollywood, everyone's favorite subject, the actual writing gives her very little to work with. Ironically, the dim-witted Spike is the only high-energy character, constantly getting out of his clothes, running around enjoying life (he has but to see a pond to dash off for a swim), and seldom comprehending anything that is said to him. It sounds easy, but it's tricky to ground what is essentially a caricature, and Billy Magnussen, offstage a playful, wry fellow, slid so smoothly into the role that he got a Tony nomination, unusual praise for a pin-up part.

Besides Spike's high-jinx, the play offers one moment when Durang had something genuine to share, a lengthy tirade from Vanya, provoked when Spike ignores the party to check his mobile. And Vanya thereupon loses it in railing against social media, the great disintegrator of the American community. Whatever happened, he asks, to everyone's tuning in to the Ozzie and Harriet television sitcom? No, it wasn't good, he admits. In fact, it was empty nothing. Still, it brought all Americans together.

Is *Vanya and Sonia* a gay play in any real sense? Well, its author is out; its male lead, Pierce, is out; his character, Vanya, is out; and a Beautiful Male is on hand, not only undraped but twerking. Compare this with a play everyone accepts as totally gay, Jonathan Tolins' *Buyer & Cellar* (2013): its author is out; its main character is out; and instead of a Beautiful Male it's Barbra Streisand on hand, which hits the gay jackpot.

Buyer's sole player, Michael Urie, took on numerous roles in this solo outing—the protagonist, hired to superintend Streisand's famous private mall of shops in her basement; the protagonist's confidant, also a gay man; a Streisand employee; Streisand's husband, James Brolin; and Streisand herself. Urie impersonated this crowd as a series of "types" defined vocally. Thus, his Streisand is less an imitation than an invention, albeit using the *uhm* noises and squinty head movements that "suggest" the diva. The idea was to present an idol who has stepped off her pedestal and gone human on us.

Essentially, Tolins gave Urie a chance to create a play out of his own thespian bravado, especially in an episode wherein Streisand wants to buy a doll in the doll shop and Urie's character extemporizes a wild backstory for the doll's history but then prices it so high that bargain-hunter Streisand may have to deny herself the doll that—in fact—she already owns.

It's wildly imaginative playwriting, especially when compared with Durang's dreary crew; we expect wit and daring from our comedy authors. So consider Douglas Carter Beane's *The Nance* (2013), a backstager set in New York's 1930s. This title has enough personality for three shows, as it reveals what happens to the folk who worked in burlesque as comics and strippers when the prudish Mayor Fiorello La Guardia banned the industry. On top of this, the lead comic—the title role, of one Chauncey Miles—was a gay man living in a gay-hating society that was, in its own way, eager to ban gay people.

Nathan Lane played Chauncey, which called for great reserves of comic technique and actory depths, for *The Nance* is at once a comedy and a tragedy; its protagonist is half-Pseudolus and half–Titus Andronicus. We are in a vastly different setting than in Beane's *The Little Dog Laughed*, and not only in tone. *The Little Dog* is basic in structure while *The Nance* is rangy, tilting back and forth between real life and the on- and offstage life of the burlesque house.

In fact, *The Nance* is really two stories intertwined, one on the plight of the burlesque troupe and the other on Chauncey's uneasy relationship with Ned (Jonny Orsini), an unworldly younger man Chauncey takes home one evening. He thinks he has landed that timeless gay icon the straight boy open to suggestion, but Orsini turns out to be as gay as Chauncey and thus not what the ever-straying Chauncey needs in his sex life. Ned seeks monogamy; Chauncey, like many performers, needs a set change at regular intervals:

NED: Sorry I didn't stay "trade" for you.

But it's part of a nance's style that he admires trade above all. Remember how ecstatic Danny Kaye was back in *Lady In the Dark* when movie star Victor Mature showed up for a photo session? It's that strange period belief that gays aren't real men:

CHAUNCEY: I don't want to be playing house with some nelly kid!*

The Nance enjoyed an elaborate production, as John Lee Beatty's scenic design, set on a revolve, showed us the burlesque house both on stage and in the wings as well as the other main location, Chauncey's apartment. There were other places on view, including the famous Forty-Sixth Street Automat, which recalls our discussion, many pages ago, of Polly's and other places the vice squad had its eye on, where just sitting at a table with another man could invite an arrest. Truly, *The Little Dog Laughed* was about how to survive in a society that tolerates gays up to a point. *The Nance* was about how to survive, period.

Yet Chauncey can't bring himself to submit when the authorities demand he give up the nance act. No, he *must* camp around, lisp, wave his arms, roll his eyes, skip and prance. Like it or not, his stereotypical Uncle

---

* The now retired "nelly" meant effeminate. The last time I heard it used was when Tennessee Williams, replacing an actor in his own *Small Craft Warnings* (1972), ad libbed on stage about his play's being evicted from its theatre by "nelly Coward"—a revue of Coward songs.

Tom ID is his art. It's not something he does opportunistically: it's what he *wants* to do.

But not out of a need to ridicule his own kind. Rather, the effeminate caricature—the "nelly" we just heard about—released something perhaps basic to the gay identity *in that age*. We've come a long distance from that position. The Stonewall Man crushed it; even *The Boys In the Band*, one year before the uprising, had but one flouncy character, the rampaging butterfly Emory. Still: is there a swish side to gay at all? And is Chauncey deriding the style or fondling it?

And note that Chauncey is completely different offstage, forceful and plain of movement. Swish is an act—because Chauncey is volatile, a man of moods. Beane dedicated *The Nance*'s published text to Nathan Lane because this actor can not only revive ancient burlesque modes but make us see how bizarre they are. We call nances effeminate, yet women aren't like them any more than most men are. Again, it's an act, something that belongs to gay yet doesn't quite truly represent it.

Chauncey knows that, yet he won't give the act up. In a weird way it's a symbol of liberty precisely because the authorities hate it. Swish scares and outrages them, because to the fascist mentality it's not an act. As Beatty's theatre structure revolves, burlesque comes alive for us in all its high-strung bawdry. It's no more erotic than the vocabulary of a child who heard the adults snickering and adopted a word or two, and we wonder precisely why this innocuous entertainment so threatened the establishment. And Beane shows us: it's because Chauncey is a Big Personality even on that little stage, independent and persuasive, an influencer. The ruling class wants its helots passive.

A rich play, *The Nance*. A surprise, even: so pre-Stonewall in its survey. It was bold of Beane to go there, but then what are we to make of a musical about a teenager (Brandon Flynn) abducted and imprisoned by a sexual predator (Jeffry Denman) with music by John Kander? Yes, that John Kander, writing with post-Ebb collaborator Greg Pierce. The show is *Kid Victory* (Arlington 2015; New York 2017), the title referring to the boy's user name in an online boat-racing game.

Kid engages with fellow racer Yachticus9, unaware that he is a pedophile. Kidnaping the boy, Yachticus holds him in isolation for eleven months, finally releasing him to return to his Kansas family and community, a religious society unaware that Kid is gay or even what gay predation entails. Led by Kid's mom (Karen Ziemba, dressed in mid-American plain far from her customary attire as a musical-comedy merrymaker), these smalltown souls are pure and naive. They have a concept of sin but can't process the concept of evil in any real sense.

And that's where the musical begins.

As I've already said, the John Kander we know from his long association with Fred Ebb merged show biz (his Liza Minnelli side, so to say) with dark elements, as if Bob Fosse and a serial killer wrote musicals together. So *Kid Victory* is not really a Kander breakaway, especially as some of the score brings a lightness of touch to a disturbing tale, with its unstable villain and town caretakers who don't understand what they're taking care of.

Kid—his name is actually Luke, securely sourced in Christian belief—gets along better with his madcap employer at a novelty shop than his family. Even a fellow gayling, who sings the show's brightest up-tune, "What's the Point [of people if you don't let them excite you?]," complete with the patented Kander vamp, doesn't ease Kid's readmission to his village surroundings. At that, Kid is the only character who doesn't sing, as if to say he can't belong at home, in a musical, anywhere.

Most interesting is Michael, the show's villain, seen in flashbacks, charismatic except when he's tightening his grip on Luke in fury. In the number "Vinland," Michael thrills Luke by imagining him as the hero of a Norse saga. Yet when Luke balks at one point, Michael scolds him with "You don't say no to me. Ever." Yet once Luke is free, Michael haunts his thoughts, and not entirely in a bad way.

We last saw Jeffry Denman as a very different gay character in *Yank!*, merrily explaining how gay gets along in the army. It treated the cute side of a serious topic. But *Kid Victory* shows us the serious side of a cute topic, that of the older mentor figure, not uncommon in gay life—Eva Le Gallienne as an acting coach, for example, with debuting ingenues. And note that these are not necessarily physical relationships. Often, there's a certain platonic idealism at their core, a pedagogical construction.

Still, it's a dangerous topic because it can be so easily misunderstood, especially when—for example—Luke finds himself more in tune with the evil Michael. Not with his power over Luke, of course. Rather, with Michael's sympathy for that part of Luke that his family and community don't comprehend.

Looking back, we say that gay theatre started with the simplest of jobs: to put gay men and women in view, liberated from Shadowland. But by this time, the gay play leads in the battle to force the public to deal with the contradictions and mysteries of human life.

And that brings us to the question of who is the Great American Gay Playwright. We know who the Great Playwright itself is—Eugene O'Neill. It's official, so don't argue. However, another office is open, that of the gay counterpart—or, alternatively, who was the most *influential* such? I believe it's Edward Albee, because his sudden arrival on the scene, in 1960, with *The Zoo Story,* followed by a few other off-Broadway one-acts and then, on The Street, *Who's Afraid Of Virginia Woolf?* (1962), registered a seismic shock that tore apart the cautions the America's theatre community had been respecting from the start.

It was that stupid "restraint" favored by all the little Fauntleroys and Pollyannas, that fear of alarming anyone with a bold approach. We remember how in *The Normal Heart* Larry Kramer taught us how piffling— how ineffective—restraint is. It's cowardice, it's self-censorship, it's Jeb! talk. Albee always said that he didn't care if the audience liked his work or not as long as they *engaged* with it. And isn't great theatre supposed to shake us up? "It's called," he would say, "playwrighting."

As a direct result of those first Albee shows, theatre writers—especially gay ones—could start blasting wide former borders of "good taste." All at once, the unthinkable was at hand. Ironically, Albee seldom touched on gay material. There are allusions to it here and there, and *Finding the Sun* (Colorado 1983; New York 1994) actually has gay lovers, though they also married women (in the thirties manner, like John Latouche and many others). And one Albee title from his all-important first period revolves around an intense gay romance, as we're about to see.

Still, it's not the sociological content of Albee that's gay as much as his style as a writer, his tone, his jokes, his unmissable gay persona, even if he was for a long time so closeted that his lover in those early Albee years, Terrence McNally, had to make himself scarce on opening nights and other social galas.

Albee's gay ID recalls to us that famous comment on jazz, that you may not be able to articulate the elements of this gayness, but you know them when you hear and see them. Certainly, New York's drama critics knew them, which is why some of them tried to hunt Albee from the stage relatively early on.

We'll have more about that in a bit, but for now, here's Albee: adopted in infancy because the vaudeville tycoon E. F. Albee, once one of the most powerful men in show biz, told his son and daughter-in-law that they'd better produce an Albee grandson to bear his name. And what E. F. wanted, E. F. got.

However, the baby, Edward Franklin Albee III, had a terrible time with his adopted parents, a vacant father and an imperious, intolerant mother. Young Edward rebelled and finally left home to odd-job in New York, taking in two years delivering telegrams for Western Union, which he loved. It was an adventure: he saw the city, he met real-life people instead of his parents' Society dolls, and he "liberated" a typewriter for writing plays.

The Zoo Story, Albee's first produced title (in Berlin, in German), comprised just two men on a bench in Central Park. Strangers. Peter's a well-meaning drone and Jerry's right out of the fifties "cool" handbook: wild, very verbal, imaginative. He was once a looker but now, in his thirties, he's somewhat soft and exhausted though still sexually charged (and often cast with a Beautiful Male). Jerry "befriends" Peter, promising to tell him about a bizarre event at the zoo. Then Jerry prods and pesters Peter, finally pulling out a knife, forcing it into Peter's hands, and impaling himself on it. We never do learn what happened at the zoo.

Albee's other one-acts were less strenuous but also startling, as in the quasi-Absurdist *The Sandbox* (1960) and *The American Dream* (1961), both featuring Daddy, Mommy, Grandma, and a Beautiful Male—in the former, a lifeguard in trunks who is also the Angel of Death; and in the latter, a "clean-cut, Midwest farm boy type, almost insultingly good-looking in a typical American way." These are the character's own words, though phrased as only a New York gay smarty would phrase it, and if anyone didn't know that Albee was queer before, he or she knew it now. Moreover, casting a hunk as the Angel of Death is a gay concept; we recall Tennessee Williams doing it in *The Milk Train Doesn't Stop Here Anymore* a few years *after* Albee. At that, *The Zoo Story*'s Jerry, at once attractive and needy, smart and penniless, and personable in an almost feral way, was a real-life New York gay type.

So these one-acts at the start of Albee's career were dead giveaways to even moderately worldly straights that a gay playwright with apparently no artistic boundaries was on the rise. However, those who would have played gatekeeper and blocked his passage were perforce disarmed by *Who's Afraid Of Virginia Woolf?* (1962), as its blazing theatricality swatted away all possible dissent. As the *Journal-American*'s John McClain put it, "This is a big one."

True, there were pans. Some of the reviewers attacked the play's validity as art, angrily aware that it was going to be a hit no matter what they said. Some simply resented the coarse language (though most of it had been toned down in rehearsals) and rufftuff behavior, as the eternally spatting George and Martha (Arthur Hill, Uta Hagen) toyed cruelly with their guests, Nick and Honey (George Grizzard, Melinda Dillon) in a drunken all-nighter.

Virginia Woolf has no flaws, though there is one knotty point: the whole thing was strangely plausible yet frankly preposterous. As would occur with other Albee plays, some asked, Is something else going on? Thus, a rumor sprang up that Albee was really writing about two male couples. However, as he often said in interviews, "If I had wanted to write about two male couples, I would have written about two male couples," reminding everyone that—I repeat—here was a writer without limits. The statement also underlines an essential characteristic of Albee's dramaturgy: unpredictability.

This was all the more noticeable as he began to be set alongside Arthur Miller, Tennessee Williams, and William Inge as the presiding postwar Broadway masters, because Albee had more in common with Eugene O'Neill in terms of the wide range of their ambitions and their sense of surprise. Miller and Inge have a dogged quality; you can tell where *Death Of a Salesman* and *Come Back, Little Sheba* are going fifteen minutes in. Williams is different because he's poetically boisterous, yet his best plays, all produced before Albee got to Broadway, were hobbled a bit by the cautions of the day, even if in *A Streetcar Named Desire* and *Cat On a Hot Tin Roof* Williams stormed across the red lines of "restraint."

Besides his unpredictability, Albee was also intent on showing how people aren't listening to anyone. Most of Albee's scripts are filled with "What?" or the equivalent—because his characters are wrapped up in themselves, cut off, disestablished, ever talking around or through one another. Are George and Martha locked in blitzkrieg because it's the only way to penetrate the human armor of deafness? Part of *Virginia Woolf*'s réclâme obtained in the public's fascinated horror at how these two claw away at each other—but Albee pointed out that theatre is naturally about conflict. Dramatic writing about happy families, he said, was "television," not art. In an interview with Stephen Bottoms, Albee even said, "George and Martha do love each other very much—they're trying to fix a greatly damaged marriage."

Still, *Virginia Woolf* can horrify the public—and fatigue the actors. Nancy Kelly, Martha on the national tour, likened it to "a torture chamber" in a radio spot with Studs Terkel. She felt drained after each performance, yet it was "exhilarating" as well, even as the two hosts turn their baleful attention to their two guests. Feeling his way through Nick, George Grizzard asked the director, Alan Schneider, why he doesn't simply collect his wife and walk out, to which Schneider replied, "Why doesn't Hamlet kill the king?"[†]

All his life, Albee got mixed reviews, but *Virginia Woolf*'s best ones were enough to send customers thronging the box office. In those days before on-line ticket buying, the most common way to nab good seats was at the theatre itself, and Broadway watchers were attuned to assessing the dimensions of the line on the sidewalk feeding the two box-office windows with their decks of little rectangular cardboard tickets. *Virginia Woolf* enjoyed quite a showing starting right after the reviews appeared, and those who waited too long to book seats had to make do with a "matinee cast," which also stood by in case of an indisposition at night. At one point in the show's 664-performance run, that prime exponent of mean-girl termagants Elaine Stritch took over in the day cast as Martha.

Further, George Grizzard (who, incidentally, was "quietly" gay, meaning he lived openly with a partner without making an issue of it) had been offered the chance to tackle Hamlet in the regions, and his contract allowed him to leave *Virginia Woolf* after three months to fulfill the Shakespearean engage-ment. At a Dramatists Guild panel on the show, Grizzard told how he ran into Billy Rose in Sardi's, Rose being the owner of the Billy Rose Theatre, where *Virgina Woolf* was playing. Rose took Grizzard's defection personally, and that time in Sardi's he pointed out how foolish it was to walk out on a smash.

It's also unfair to the public. "Fanny," quoth Rose, referring to his ex-wife Fanny Brice, "never left a play till everybody who wanted to see her in it" had done so.

"Billy, I am going to play Hamlet," Grizzard told him.

Rose countered with "Oh, you actors. Hamlet—it's like Hedy Lamarr blowing hot in your ear, right?"

Who's Afraid Of Virginia Woolf cost $42,000 and paid off in—I hope everyone's sitting down for this—three weeks. Now "Edward Albee" was the buzz-term of the season; he couldn't have been more prominent if he'd taken to striding down Broadway with a wyvern on his shoulder. Further defying the cautions and daring the unthinkable, he followed *Virginia Woolf* with arguably the gayest play to be seen on Broadway to that time, so lush and

---

[†] We've encountered this before, with *The Boys In the Band*: why didn't the abused guests just leave? There was a reason for that (the rain storm), and in *Virginia Woolf* it's because of college pol-itics: Martha's father is the president of the school, and an ambitious professor doesn't offend the president's daughter.

crafty that it made *The Green Bay Tree* and *Oscar Wilde* look like *The Sound Of Music: The Ballad Of the Sad Café* (1963).

Based on Carson McCullers' Southern Gothic novella, this show turned on bizarre doings in the general store-turned-café run by the Amazonian bootlegger Miss Amelia (Colleen Dewhurst). A childlike dwarf, Cousin Lymon (Michael Dunn), shows up claiming to be kin, and though ordinarily surly and antisocial, Miss Amelia takes a fancy to the newcomer and moves him into her house.

One of this work's strengths is its examination of the folkways of rural small-town life, especially its appetites and bigotries. So we see the villagers treat Cousin Lymon—the gay character, be it said—with scorn and suspicion. But they do love to hang out at the café. Then news breaks out that Marvin Macy has been paroled.

Who is this character that clearly infuriates Miss Amelia and whose name hushes up the townsfolk? Cousin Lymon is intrigued, but no one will answer his questions. "Tell me about Marvin Macy," he implores them. "Tell what he done!"

Michael Dunn, a resourceful actor with a fine gift for the petulant, the mischievous, the macabre (he was later the popular recurring villain Miguelito Loveless on the aforementioned homosocial television series *The Wild Wild West*), really drove this scene to the utmost. It was as if Cousin Lymon had already decided that the as yet unencountered Marvin Macy was a sexy, dangerous cowboy of a guy and Cousin Lymon was going to fall in love and run off with him after the two of them destroy Miss Amelia's life.

And that's exactly what happens in the play, so the Ministers of Public Morality (sometimes called "theatre critics") knew for certain that Albee was wild and free and that he was intent on bringing his gay devilry to Broadway unless he was banned from the place.

Nevertheless, the audience could get quite caught up in Albee's theatrical strokes, and *The Ballad Of the Sad Café* was full of them. Indeed, the Marvin Macy scene above ended with one: as Cousin Lymon fairly danced about the stage in frustration, Miss Amelia moved out of the café onto her porch and Cousin Lymon followed, asking for the hundredth time for the story of Marvin Macy.

And suddenly the two of them turned to look stage right . . . at Marvin Macy himself, for the actor, Lou Antonio, had simply materialized (actually slipping onstage during an especially riveting moment in the Amelia–Lymon conversation). As the audience stared in curiosity, Cousin Lymon started toward Marvin Macy as if enchanted, but:

MISS AMELIA: (*To Marvin Macy*) You clear outa here! You get on!

Marvin Macy laughed and sauntered off, and Cousin Lymon, now alone on stage, wailed in impotent wonder:

COUSIN LYMON: WHO IS MARVIN MACY!

Well, now: Marvin Macy was a criminal who loved Miss Amelia enough to reform and be worthy of her. She couldn't have cared less, but she married him, because that's how she was—in Albee, all the most interesting people are crazy. Marvin Macy even gave her an engagement ring, which she handled a bit, then gave back:

MISS AMELIA: It silver?
MARVIN MACY: Yep, it silver. Miss Amelia, will you . . .
MISS AMELIA: Bet it cost some.
MARVIN MACY: Miss Amelia, will you marry me?

Colleen Dewhurst thought it over for a long, long time, inscrutable. Then:

MISS AMELIA: Sure.

But when he tried to kiss her, she threatened to whack him, and finally just stalked out with a "G'night.‡

The marriage fails spectacularly. But why exactly? We never learn, because even though Albee used a Narrator, some parts of the story were missing, because that's how McCullers told it:

---

‡ In one of those tales that runs through the Broadway community in a day and recounted by Lou Antonio for Mel Gussow's Albee bio, at one performance Antonio lost his hold of the box with the ring and the circlet dropped and rolled off the stage. He couldn't continue the scene without it, because the way Dewhurst looked at it—assessing its value as merchandise, not as a token of love—was central to who Miss Amelia was. Staying in character, Antonio stomped downstage, looked daggers at the man in the front row who was nearest the ring, and told him, "Gimme the ring." The man did as told, but when Antonio turned around to continue the scene, he found Dewhurst flat on her back, hysterical with soundless laughter.

NARRATOR: What happened that wedding night of Miss Amelia and Marvin
Macy, no one will ever truly know . . .

Apparently, Miss Amelia hadn't counted on the sex part of marriage, and
was so outraged by it—too independent for it?—that she hated Marvin Macy
ever after.

Still, Albee's Narrator (Roscoe Lee Browne) was good company, delivering
his lines in easy-flowing standard English, which framed the dense dialect (a
sample: "Do Miss Amelia know Marvin Macy comin' back?") of the actual
characters in the story.

Albee claimed in several interviews that he had to invent all the talk himself as McCullers' original had "not a line of dialogue" or, elsewhere, "two
lines of dialogue." In fact, though the novella is heavily recounted in third-
person synopsis, McCullers did rely on a certain amount of conversation—
but then, Albee was something of a cut-up in interviews. It brought out his
playful side, hating to be pinned down to a single answer about anything.
And he loathed having to formulate a "creative" reply to those silly questions
interviewers simply *will* ask. Thus, at a Dramatists Guild Q & A with Terrence
McNally:

MCNALLY: Can you define the one-act form?
ALBEE: A one-act play is a play that is in one act.

The Ballad Of the Sad Café ran 123 performances, disappointing if only because of the three superb leading principals. I think what held it back was the
director, Alan Schneider. He was Albee's favorite such for the first Broadway
titles, because Schneider was text-faithful in the extreme and Albee was intense about seeing his scripts staged without any editing whatsoever.

So Schneider was a playwright's director—but not an actor's. Many
performers hated him, and he further had no visual sense. His productions
were dry and stolid, saved only because Albee controlled casting and held
out for the best, self-starters who would work around Schneider and draw
their characters out of themselves. Dewhurst and Antonio despised him, and
midway through rehearsals Dewhurst laid Schneider out to filth with such
penetrating contempt that the two never spoke again.

Typically, Schneider was at his most feeble in staging *Sad Café*'s climactic scene, a bare-knuckles battle between Miss Amelia and Marvin
Macy. Fights are all but impossible in the theatre; they never look real, and

Schneider was so befuddled by the challenge that he tried to choreograph it as if it were a ballet.

Luckily, Dewhurst's then husband, George C. Scott, worked privately with her and Antonio to naturalize the battle: two brutes, one determined to rid herself of this pernicious admirer and the other defending his outraged masculinity. It was virtually a fight to the death, Dewhurst in a loose-fitting rag of a dress and Antonio in nothing but denim shorts, the villagers looking on and Dunn following every move with the scrutiny of a lab scientist.

And when Dewhurst seemed to get the upper hand, walloping Antonio with blow after blow, Dunn suddenly leaped off the café counter onto Dewhurst's back, forcing her down to let Antonio seize control. At last, beaten for life, Dewhurst closed the café as Dunn and Antonio—as the Narrator told us—wrecked the café and took off for parts unknown. So boy got boy in the end.

Had Schneider been able to bring McCullers' weird and sorrowful tale to life on stage as Albee had done in his script, *The Ballad Of the Sad Café* would have been a hit. So, in a way (and still using Schneider), Albee chose in his next play to tackle The Gay Thing from another angle: an attractive boy is killed as a presentation to the deity in the form of a beautiful woman who fronts for an ectoplasmic whoknowswhat on the theme of Yes, God exists, but not in the form humans have invented.

This was *Tiny Alice* (1964). The notion of a human sacrifice being a beautiful youth—thus the "sacrifice" in the concept: his people must part with someone they treasure—is as old as time itself. And of course a comely stripling adds the Beautiful Male to the package.

But everything went wrong. The script was much, much too long and opaque; none of the actors had the vaguest idea what it meant, and Schneider of course was no help. Even Albee amused himself by urging them to find their own way through the text, without explaining any of it. Then, too, the casting of John Gielgud— sixty years old at the time—as the "boy" obscured the erotic nature of the rite at the story's center.

Yet it was hard for Albee to resist going with Gielgud, the first "classy" name to appear in his work—a Shakespearean Brit, no less. And he would certainly pronounce the text well. Albee was so eager to acquire Gielgud that when the actor, still thinking it over, asked what age his character was supposed to be, Albee (so says Mel Gussow) suggested fifty as target casting: close enough to Gielgud.

But a middle-aged sacrifice surely wasn't what Albee had had in mind when conceiving *Tiny Alice*, to be the third in Albee's line of too-cool-for-school Dangerous Broadway. It should have been Brad Pitt, new and unknown. A mystery, sweet and hot. "The sexual fires weren't quite right," Albee admitted in an absurd understatement to interviewer Stephen Bottoms, much later. "But I was grateful to have him." And, true enough, revivals tend to look for much younger men than Gielgud was.

One wonders what would have happened if a director like Elia Kazan had been in charge. Ah, but Kazan edited playwrights, and that was Albee's terror. Kazan would have demanded the overlong script be cut back and the subtext clarified: but the piece would have blazed.

There was one effective element: William Ritman's scenery. The play's action took place mainly in the library of Alice's mansion-*cum*-castle, and to perfect its symbolism as the center of the universe Albee demanded "a huge doll's house model of the building" to dominate the view. There were hints that the model contained a smaller model—an exact replica—that likewise contained a yet smaller model and so on, in the infinity of faith, or perhaps of science or mythology. The very world was here, and at one point a fire broke out in Alice's house and the audience could see a tiny fire raging inside the model—as if what happened in the play was happening in the cosmos.

That model might have been the inspiration for *Tiny Alice*. Albee tended to get an idea for a play and then ponder it for a year or so, visualizing, editing, constructing. But it seems that his starting point was always a coup de théâtre, something vivid, exciting. A visceral thrill to center the experience. One example would be George stalking into the *Virginia Woolf* living room with a rifle aimed at the back of Martha's head and, as Nick rises in consternation and Honey screams, George fires . . . and a little Chinese parasol comes out of the barrel. *The Ballad Of the Sad Café* had that moment when Marvin Macy suddenly appeared out of nowhere, like the hero of a saga.

Tiny Alice had a number of these, most impressively at the finale (for this work does play as something like an opera without music). A mortally wounded Gielgud, abandoned by the other characters to die alone, delivered an endless monologue. The actor begged for cuts, but Albee somehow didn't realize how foolish it was to delay the curtain when the show was obviously near its end and the audience ready for closure.

Long after *Tiny Alice* had ended its run, Albee did finally shorten this speech. But meanwhile he used the moment to create suspense out of the play's metaphysical ID, for while Gielgud was intoning his mad scene, the audience noticed a strange dark something in the model, moving through the structure as if stalking Gielgud. There was a sound effect, too: a heartbeat? Closer and closer it came, the heartbeat in a mad crescendo, till Gielgud cried out, "MY GOD, WHY HAST THOU FORSAKEN ME?," and some sort of shadowy gosh-knows-what moved into the room behind him. It wasn't anything physical, but it was *there*, and Gielgud died with his arms flung wide as if in crucifixion. The noise suddenly cut off, the lights faded, and when the stage had become absolutely dark, the curtain came down.

At 167 performances, *Tiny Alice* was only a bit more successful than *Sad Café*, but *Alice* had more talkabout than even *Virginia Woolf* had enjoyed. It was the mystery of the decade; if you didn't have your own theory on What It Meant, you were intellectually ruined.

In commercial terms, what Albee needed now was a solid hit, something so easily engaging that like *Virginia Woolf* it would slip past the critics to fascinate the public. But Albee would never compromise his art, and his next play was still quite gay, if in disguise, an adaptation of James Purdy's novel *Malcolm* (1966).

Here is another tale of sacrifice, that of an appealing teenage boy who falls in with a dodgy lot of parasites and is eventually killed by having too much sex. In the title role was ultra-blond Matthew Cowles, who was to spend most of his career as a soap-opera star, and the air of almost drooling predation that surrounded the youngster (not to mention the leather clone among the characters) told even the clueless that something very gay was holding court in the world of Albee.

The gay haters had already been circling him like buzzards, but he was by no means the first queer playwright to be clobbered because of what he was. In an interview with Charles Ruas for *Conversations With American Writers*, Gore Vidal pointed out that Tennessee Williams had this problem back when Albee was running around in a propeller beanie.

"The people who ran the *Times*," Vidal said, "did not like Tennessee or [gay life]."§ Brooks Atkinson was their theatre critic, and he was "just too big, they couldn't handle [i.e., "control"] him." But the unnamed theatre writer at *Time* magazine, Louis Kronenberger, "never gave [Williams] a good review; he attacked everything from *Glass Menagerie* on."**

§ The word Vidal used for what I phrased in brackets was "degeneracy."
** Yet as editor of the Burns Mantle *Best Plays* annuals, Kronenberger did include Williams' titles in his digest versions—and we recall Kronenberger finding space also for André Gide's *The Immoralist* some pages ago, perhaps the outest title of the 1950s.

And, says Vidal, "it was house policy at *Time* to attack Williams, because I asked [*Time*'s owner] Henry Luce." Vidal's father had roomed with Luce at Yale and gave Luce financial help in starting *Time*. So when Vidal and Luce were on the DC-NY shuttle, Vidal took the opportunity to point out that by harassing Williams *Time* made itself "look silly."

"Well, I don't like him," said Luce.

"Yes," Vidal replied, "but other people do."

A more generalized attack on gay theatre showed up after Brooks Atkinson retired, replaced by Howard Taubman. In 1963, the *Times* ran Taubman's catalogue raisonné on "how to scan the intimations and symbols of homosexuality in our theater." It was unmistakable that Taubman was taking Tennessee Williams and Albee as his models, discerning for example the "character whose proclivities are like a stallion's" (most obviously Stanley Kowalski but surely the Beautiful Male in general, physically robust and thus a reproach to the flaccid opinionati class) and "the hideous wife who makes a horror of the marriage relationship" (Albee had already set forth several of those, culminating of course in *Virginia Woolf*'s Martha).

In that same year, the *Times* let playwright Joseph Hayes take a crack at the gay-baiting, here singling out Williams and Albee by name. Hayes' argument centered on their negative outlook; words such as "wasteland," "cruelty," and "bitchiness" abounded.

Albee replied to this, also in the *Times*, pointing out that the greatest dramatists, from Aristophanes to Shaw, have been critical of their societies in order to enlighten them. This was an invulnerable rebuttal, for most important plays could be described as "negative." (Even that American folk classic *Our Town*, so often thought of as the equivalent of a Grandma Moses, is in fact a rather deflating experience on stage.)

It was too bad for the *Times* that it couldn't have found a stronger expositor than Hayes, who was—as Albee reminded the reader—an author of "escapist commercialism," known only for the thriller *The Desperate Hours* but also, just before this, the semi-success *Calculated Risk*.

Now a full-scale bowwow broke out, as readers wrote in on one side or the other. The crime novelist Evan Hunter (also widely known as Ed McBain) denounced Albee's "strident hair-pulling reply" while Hayes joined in to cite Albee's "hysterical, finger-clawing attack on me." What they really meant was a playground sing-song chorus of "Edward Albee is a fag, *ha ha* ha-*ha* ha!," and it was they who came off as vindictive queens.

There was yet more of this, notably from those icons of virility Philip Roth and Stanley Kaufmann, and though Tennessee Williams was still active, his plays were by now attracting much less attention than before, even closing after just a few days. So it was really Albee who had provoked the witch-hunters, emerging as the most controversial playwright in Broadway history. Of course, no one in the arts can be said to have truly arrived till he or she has been attacked by enraged mediocrities, and controversy often sells tickets.

Yet by 1966, Albee was struggling to maintain his artistic prestige. It was a terrible year for him, starting with that *Malcolm* adaptation, a genuine bomb of a failure, for James Purdy's novel is so niche in appeal that the show was bound to play into the hands of Albee's worst enemies. The atmosphere was so hostile that Albee's next original, *A Delicate Balance*, stuttered through a shortish run even though the usual mixed notices included some that were almost enthusiastic. Word of mouth may have been disappointing, though, as this is one of Albee's most talky plays, lacking the Sturm und Drang of *Virginia Woolf*, the exotic tang of *Sad Café*, and the intellectual breadth of *Tiny Alice*. True, *A Delicate Balance* won Albee his first Pulitzer Prize, but that can be an unreliable booster.

What would have saved the show was the Lunts—and, yes, Alfred and Lynn were willing to come out of retirement to play it. That would have been nothing less than historic, but they made it conditional on a London opening and a contract for but half a year, and Albee didn't accept conditions.[††] Not till the 1996 revival with George Grizzard, Rosemary Harris, and Elaine Stritch, directed by Gerald Gutierrez, did *A Delicate Balance* habilitate itself as one of Albee's best plays.

But that awful 1966 wasn't over yet, as Albee saw it out by trying a musical. *Holly Golightly*, from Truman Capote's novella *Breakfast At Tiffany's*, played Philadelphia and Boston tryouts without coming together properly, mainly because its librettist and director, Abe Burrows, wanted to please a public that treasured the charming Audrey Hepburn film while composer-lyricist Bob Merrill, starting work before he saw a script, wrote more in the style of Capote's rather bleak story. With David Merrick producing and Mary Tyler Moore and Richard Chamberlain in the leads, audiences were expecting a

[††] Some actors lose important work because of their conditions. Geraldine Page was the first to be offered Martha in *Virginia Woolf*, but she demanded that Actors Studio guru and professional egomaniac Lee Strasberg sit in on rehearsals. No comment.

smash. So this confused version—half Capote and half musical-comedy fun—greatly disappointed.

Then Merrick, who produced on the notion that Crazy Publicity creates hits, commissioned Albee to write a new book, to be put in when *Breakfast At Tiffany's* (as it was now called, with a new director, Joseph Anthony) started New York previews. But Albee's *Tiffany's* was even darker than Capote's: at one point, a butch female cop slugged Mary Tyler Moore in the stomach.

Albee claimed to have hewed closely to Capote, but he really seemed to be hewing close to Albee, and halfway through the first week of previews at the Majestic Theatre, Merrick abruptly terminated the show rather than subject the public to what he called "an excruciatingly boring evening." But we'll hear more from this title shortly, when it will be revived for the one and only time till its copyright lapses, in the year 2087.

We can date the end of Albee's first period to this time. It had been his era of greatest influence, when the diversity and the imagination of his work sparked the same in other writers. But his public deserted him in his second period. Even though *Seascape* (1975), a disquisition on evolution by two humans and two reptiles, won Albee his second Pulitzer, the show lasted only 65 performances.

Worse was to come, when three Broadway Albees in a row folded in just a few days each: *The Lady From Dubuque* (1980), *Lolita* (1981), and *The Man Who Had Three Arms* (1982). *Lolita*, from Nabokov's dangerous novel and in a production by people Albee mostly didn't know, was the worst experience of his career. His text was severely cut (there was enough for a two-evening presentation), and star Donald Sutherland altered his part, defying Albee to stop him.

The playwright's enemies were already writing his professional obituary, carefully interring Albee's stylistic quirks—the abstract, even interplanetary conversations delivered in suburban living rooms; the Absurdist view of life as a comedy of illusion; the nagging sexuality of everything. In fact, these form part of Albee's originality; they aren't glitches. Like O'Neill and Tennessee Williams, Albee wrote plays in his own fashion, and that is worth praising.

Nevertheless, in economic terms Albee's second period was one of failure and loss of reputation (though he pursued an active sub-career working with young writers at regional universities). Over ten years passed without a new Albee title on Broadway. But then came a third period, of reclamation, starting with *Three Tall Women*, which premiered like *The Zoo Story* in central Europe, this time in Vienna and in English (1992). In New York (1994) at the Promenade Theatre, the show won Albee his third Pulitzer and ran 582 performances, a hit. It also gave Albee a new producer partner, a can-do, no-nonsense lesbian named Elizabeth McCann.

More grandly, *Three Tall Women* revealed as never before what Albee had in common with Tennessee Williams: they both wrote great roles for great actors. The decent troupers of what Germans call the Stadttheater style— the resident journeyman companies far from the unique talents of the cultural capitals—always fail to spark these often detached works. With a few exceptions (*Virginia Woolf, The Ballad Of the Sad Café, Malcolm*) Albee's plays are based entirely on not story but the eventless dialogue of character interaction. Thus, *Three Tall Women* comprises just the title roles (and one silent young man), avatars of one character at different ages, called simply A. (The others are B and C.)

A is Albee's mother, Frankie (for Frances). In that interview with Terrence McNally, Albee says, "I have never written a character that is either auto-biographical or biographical and I have never limited a character to a real individual."

That was in 1985, long before he wrote *Three Tall Women*. Still, Albee's parents—the vacant father and self-absorbed mother—appear as cartoons in the one-acts *The Sandbox* and *The American Dream* (as does Albee's maternal grandmother) and then dominate *A Delicate Balance*.

True, they have been edited. Daddy in *The American Dream* is clearly emasculated by Mommy, but Reed Albee (the playwright's father) led a lively life whenever he was out of the house, hobnobbing with theatre people and dating showgirls. But those early studies of Frankie eventually gave rise to one of her son's most grateful roles, the A of *Three Tall Women*.

Some actors love to come off as wonderful—Gertrude Lawrence, for instance. They want to light up the stage with a personal radiance. But we remember Tallulah Bankhead going full-bore monster in *The Little Foxes*, so evil she's worse than the play's official bad guys. A is more that sort of part, and its creator, Myra Carter, gave a performance to rival Laurette Taylor in *The Glass Menagerie*, always the first stop on the tourist's itinerary of great acting triumphs. Carter wasn't anything like Frankie in real life—but she had her moments. When she went to Hollywood to appear on the television series *Frasier*, Albee told Mel Gussow, "She changed hotels six times on the first day, one of them because she didn't like the doorknobs in the room."

After young Edward walked out on his parents, he was cut off from Frankie for a generation. Then he made it up with her (his father had died), though he still had to put up with the homophobic cracks without which, she felt, no social occasion was complete. Her son would invite friends to meet her, but few enjoyed the event. In truth, her tactless, bossy grandeur appalled them. Well, that was Frankie. But was that A as well? Albee said, "People who have seen [A in] my play find her fascinating." And he adds, "Heavens, what have I done?"

Surviving a destructive mother typifies the artistic writer, as does too much drinking of the kind that makes one quarrelsome and nasty even to close friends. But later Albee mellowed, cultivating a wry outlook to replace his cantankerous past with sportive, elusive word games. It became his hobby to hide in plain sight, answering interviewers' questions with remarks that belonged to someone else. As Jesse Green wrote in *New York* magazine, "In his plays and in his public persona you most often glimpsed him dodging behind paradoxes and disappearing into syllogisms." And when Green interviewed Albee, the playwright asked to look at Green's handsome digital recorder. He held it for a bit, then put it down—and somehow he had disconnected the recording device and the entire conversation went into the ozone.

Albee also became more flexible about everything—except, as before, the sanctity of his dramatic texts, no tampering allowed. When a regional company tried staging *Virginia Woolf* with two male couples, Albee shot it down: because that isn't what he wrote.

Yet as his third period reclaimed his stature as America's greatest living playwright, he also became capable of seeing things from others' perspectives. When Ian Marshall Fisher, impresario of London's *Lost Musicals* series, planned a revival of *Holly Golightly,* the first tryout version of the *Breakfast At Tiffany's* musical, Fisher got permission from all the copyright owners and was days away from rehearsals for a sold-out run when the William Morris agency told him that, by the wording of the show's contracts, he needed Albee's permission as well, even though Albee worked on the *second* version of the musical only. And Albee did not grant permission. Fisher asked to send Albee a letter, but William Morris said no: "Mr. Albee never changes his mind."

Anne Kaufman, daughter of playwright George S. Kaufman, knew both Fisher and Albee. Her advice: "Call him. He's in the book." Fisher tried it, and got "an extremely bright and pleasant fellow," Albee's assistant. Yes, you may send us a letter, he said, but you should know that Mr. Albee never changes his mind.

That again! Yet Fisher persevered. UPS charged $70.00 for an overnight delivery from London to New York, but a hidden surcharge was added, the letter was refused, and it came back to Fisher two days later. He was now hours from the start of rehearsals, and once more he called Albee's number. Realizing what Fisher had been put through by the kind of destiny figures that might have turned up in one of Albee's plays, the assistant suggested that Fisher photograph his letter and email it to him. "I'll see that Mr. Albee gets it," he promised.

Fisher's letter, he recalls, was "warm and open-hearted," and he got permission to play: Mr. Albee had changed his mind.

We have come to the end of our saga, and one point especially must be underlined: right from the start, with our drag queens, with Mae West's plays, with *The Captive, The Green Bay Tree, The Boys In the Band* . . . there has always been an audience for gay theatre, one large enough to prove that straights have supported it right alongside the birthright communicants.

Thus, a work as wholly gay as Matthew Lopez's *The Inheritance* (London 2018; New York 2019) not only attracts a wide audience but reduces everyone in the house to tears in a scene as memorable as any in theatre history.

It occurs at the close of the first part of this two-evening event, when the protagonist, Eric, enters a house that had once been an AIDS hospice. Suddenly the ghosts of its dead guests appear, striding onto the platformed playing area from the wings, the orchestra, even the balcony. The entire theatre becomes alive with ghosts, each one introducing himself to Eric, then joining the others around the edge of the set with a small mock-up of the house glowing with pride behind them. A requiem, the scene is as well a celebration of the memory of our dead, a time still ripe, not yet plucked up by history.

"Welcome home, Eric," says one of the ghosts. And those who saw *The Inheritance* will recall the sound of a much moved public, some openly sobbing.

Thus the parish opens up to the outsider audience, with that often difficult honesty that has enriched America's ability to stage gay life, with its queens and bull daggers, its enchanters and terrorizers, its Eva Le Gallienne proposing Ibsen for the masses to Franklin Roosevelt and Jerry Herman breaking open his closet to write the gay national anthem. They're all saying welcome, and you *mussst* come over!

For Further Reading

The Gay & Lesbian Theatrical Legacy (Michigan, 2005) is a wide-ranging anthology made of life-and-work reviews of all the major figures, along with names that seldom turn up nowadays—songwriter Nancy Hamilton; all-rounder George Birimisa; choreographer Robert Alton, a major stylist in thirties and forties musical comedy in his use of the ensemble as a blend of individuals rather than robots working in unison; Adah Isaacs Menken, one of the most famous actresses of her day, the mid-nineteenth century.

Each essay is a model of its kind, followed by little bibliographies to point scholars to arcane source material. All along the way, there are surprises for the aficionado. For instance, Carson McCullers is here—did everyone know she was gay? It emphasizes how penetratingly queer Edward Albee's adaptation of *The Ballad Of the Sad Café* is and suggests an answer to the question of why Miss Amelia so hated her husband, Marvin Macy: perhaps she is a lesbian and was offended (or just plain shocked?) by his idea of a suitable wedding night.

Another surprise is the presence of a few lesbian versions of the drag queen: the *male* impersonator. Sherry A. Darling's essay on Annie Hindle tells how she married Annie Ryan . . . in 1886! Darling quotes the parson who officiated at the wedding: "I believe they love each other and that they will be happy." So marriage equality is older than previously thought.

The book even offers an explanation for why so many gay men—Marc Blitzstein, John Latouche, Paul Bowles, et al.—married women. As we've seen, it was almost comme il faut in olden days, and Daniel-Raymond Nadon's article on Eric Bentley quotes his subject on why this kept happening: "You had every reason to be straight in those days" and, not having the wide perspective on sexuality that we command today, you "went into marriage" thinking that "because you like or love a woman, you will very likely end up totally straight." Hetero marriage was thought to be a cure.

So this book is much more than data. So, too, are the best biographies. Steven Bach's *Dazzler*, on Moss Hart (Knopf, 2001), Helen Sheehy's *Eva Le Gallienne* (Knopf, 1996), and Joel Lobenthal's *Tallulah!* (Regan, 2004) are great reads, and their respective subjects are of course essential in comprehending gay theatre history. Such actors aren't just talented: they're fascinating, and the best books tell us why. Howard Pollack's *The Ballad Of John Latouche* (Oxford, 2017) brings this almost fatally elfin creature to life, incidentally cleaning up a lot of confusion about exactly who wrote what on the musical *Candide*. Pollack quotes Dorothy Parker on why she dropped out of the collaboration early on: "Too many geniuses." The best thing about these narratives of Old Gay is how they reveal what life was like in the subculture among these high-achievement bohemians who all seemed to know one another.

John Lahr's *Tennessee Williams: Mad Pilgrimage Of the Flesh* (Norton, 2014) lives up to the rich allure of its subtitle, with six hundred pages of lavish adventures both on- and offstage. Lahr interviewed many Williams associates, so the book reads as a wild party of the acting world. Many years ago, I attended an afternoon bash at the Gotham Book

Mart (in New York, as known for its connections to Famous Authors as for its unusual inventory), and Williams was there, paired with an unappetizing young "friend" and studiously avoiding Gore Vidal, also in attendance. Williams was completely zoned away on pharmacopeia, and at one point dramatically swept his arm out and knocked over a table and everything on it. Vidal, who was behind me, murmured, "Pop goes the weasel."

Lahr missed that particular shindig, but he does get around, unveiling aspects of Williams' life that have somehow eluded the mythmakers. For instance, we find that the tale of Elia Kazan's forcing Williams to write a new third act for *Cat On a Hot Tin Roof* is incomplete as popularly recounted. Yes, Kazan needed that alternate third act, but, Lahr tells us, he offered to put the original version back in before the New York opening, and again to stage it for the national tour. "It's been four years now that this horseshit [i.e., Williams' alleged victimization] has been in the press. . . . YOU NEVER ONCE SAID A WORD [of correction]!!"

A less duplicitous Williams is on view in James Grissom's *Follies Of God* (Knopf, 2015), concerned with the playwright's relationships with actresses. A high point is the meeting of two of our leading players, Williams and . . . Eva Le Gallienne! It's like Eleanor Roosevelt dancing with Shakespeare's Puck, though the pair had one thing in common: both were out at a time when everyone else was closeted. Yet she really knew what she was while he admitted he "was not terribly educated about lesbians" and "had not a much better understanding of what we called the male homosexual."

So this was no meeting of minds. He saw her as "a stern, spinsterish Shaker woman" and kept trying to trip her up with prankish comments. "I knew he was performing for me," Le Gallienne told Grissom. And Williams confessed, "I wish I had . . . her resilience." Two tremendous talents from two distant planets.

Howard Teichmann's *Smart Aleck: The Wit, World and Life Of Alexander Woollcott* (Morrow, 1976) is, as the title suggests, more a personality study than a bio. Woollcott is remembered as fastidious, cultured, and bombastic—like his replica, Sheridan Whiteside, in *The Man Who Came To Dinner*. But he was as well one of the first household-name gays in America. Just as Katharine Cornell's assumption of Shaw's Saint Joan must have had at least some people wondering about Cornell's sexuality (if only because her husband, Guthrie McClintic, was so femme), surely audiences at *The Man Who Came To Dinner*—play and movie alike—would have noticed that the Sheridan Whitesides of the world could not possibly be straight.

Surprisingly, Teichmann actually goes into Woollcott's sexuality, and with no attempt to beard him, so the book becomes another puzzle piece in the reconstruction of gay cultural history. It's an amusing read, too, filled with anecdotes. Here's one: Teichmann recalls an all-star benefit evening in which Woollcott played opposite Madge Kennedy in a scene from Shakespeare. As his few appearances on film reveal, Woollcott was the worst actor alive, and the audience pelted him with boos. As he reached the wings, he said, "I had no idea how unpopular Madge Kennedy was."

Kaier Curtin's very fully researched *"We Can Always Call Them Bulgarians"* (Alyson, 1987) concentrates on "The Emergence Of Lesbians and Gay Men On the American Stage," ending in the early 1950s. The aim is to reveal the step-by-step of gays' beguiling society's bien pensants: first comes a cultural presence, then civil rights. But Curtin does append a last chapter of the *New York Times'* war on gay theatre.

The book offers many odd events along the way, such as how a flop could get away with gay characters simply by having closed before the enemy could muster its forces. "Nothing came of their very brief engagements except the homophobic reviews of newspaper critics," Curtin notes. Conversely, Herman Shumlin, producer and director of *The Children's Hour*, felt the play could foil the bigots on good reviews. "With raves," Shumlin told Curtin, "Nobody would dare to touch us. The critics [,] in defending themselves, would have to come to our defense."

In histories centering on men only, John A. Clum contributes *Acting Gay: Male Homosexuals In Modern Drama* (Columbia, 1992) and, on gay men and the musical, *Something For the Boys* (Palgrave, 1999). Jordan Schildkrout offers the arrestingly off-beat *Murder Most Queer* (Michigan, 2014), examining the use of gay killers in play-making. It's astonishing how many there are—not only those known to the aficionado, from Mae West to Charles Busch, but countless others. Schildkrout spends most of his time with the best-known titles, looking into not only what the playwrights are saying but how the audience might be reacting.

Thus, for *Compulsion* and other plays on the Leopold and Loeb case, Schildkrout imagines the public as a kind of jury bringing in possible "verdicts," eleven in all. For instance, there's "The 'Guilty of Love' Verdict," wherein gays are relieved that the real killer was Loeb (straight), not Leopold (gay, with a crush on Loeb), thus in effect "to separate the queer from the killer." Comparably, Schildkrout finds much to explore in *Deathtrap*, and one wishes these titles could come back so we can join the author in his fascinating investigations.

Now to Albee. Everybody's first stop should be Mel Gussow's bio (Simon & Schuster, 1998), as Gussow was one of the few critics Albee trusted and thus had unusually intimate access. Albee was still alive and working when the book came out, but it reaches well into his third period and tells a complete story. The book's cover art shows us the young Albee, always serious and wary, but *Conversations With Edward Albee* (Mississippi, 1988) presents the senior playwright, now amused at everything. He looks great here, stylish and content, because he outfoxed the censors. He said, Let there be light; it was blasphemy. Die, censors. *Conversations* collects a bit over two hundred interviews, from 1961 (in *The New Yorker*, with their ace interrogator Lillian Ross) to 1986 (with Joe Pollack, who asks whom Albee has in mind for his next play and is told, "Once you start to think about actors, you're writing roles, not characters."). As we expect, Albee is guarded in his first period but mischievous and on a spree by his third. In the academic mode is *The Cambridge Companion To Edward Albee* (2005), awfully arid, though Brenda Murphy is good on *Three Tall Women* and Stephen Bottoms, the book's editor, has a smart chat with Albee at the close.

We should take note also of Columbia's original-cast LP set of *Who's Afraid Of Virginia Woolf?* (Masterworks Broadway CD), celebrated in its day for how vividly it captured the show. There was a glitch in that the four actors, over the days of "living into" their roles, had added tiny bits here and there—an "and," an "if"—and Albee the purist insisted that everyone go back to exactly what he had written.

They couldn't—not if the discs were to preserve the vitality of the performance. Albee did allow the discs' producer, Goddard Lieberson, to add a line for Honey so the listener would know that George had just stalked in with the rifle aimed at Martha's head. But the author wanted everything else bona fide.

Impossible. It would have cut off the electricity of the production and preserved a false document. So Albee at last accepted a compromise: the actors could play what they had been playing at the Billy Rose Theatre . . . with one exception. As Uta Hagen recalled at a Dramatists Guild panel, Albee "Made Arthur [Hill] do a long speech with a lectern [i.e., reading it word for word from the script instead of playing it as he did on stage], which was *very* damaging to Arthur's performance." It's still the greatest recording ever made of spoken-word theatre.

Index